The Philosophy of
Generative Linguistics

Peter Ludlow

OXFORD

UNIVERSITY PRESS

OXFORD
UNIVERSITY PRESS

Great Clarendon Street, Oxford, OX2 6DP,
United Kingdom

Oxford University Press is a department of the University of Oxford.
It furthers the University's objective of excellence in research, scholarship,
and education by publishing worldwide. Oxford is a registered trade mark of
Oxford University Press in the UK and in certain other countries

© Peter Ludlow 2011

The moral rights of the author have been asserted

First published 2011
First published in paperback 2013

Impression: 1

British Library Cataloguing in Publication Data

Data available

Library of Congress Cataloging in Publication Data

Data available

ISBN 978-0-19-925853-6 (Hbk.)
ISBN 978-0-19-967447-3 (Pbk.)

Printed in Great Britain by
MPG Books Group, Bodmin and King's Lynn

For Sarah Jo Milbrandt

Contents

Preface

This is not a book about everything that calls itself linguistics, or even everything that calls itself *generative* linguistics. There are many enterprises that go by the name 'linguistics' in the academy today, and no doubt philosophical issues arise for all of those enterprises. There are likewise many interesting aspects of generative linguistics that I can only touch on in passing here—generative phonology being a notable case in point. My goal in this book is to explore the philosophical questions that arise in the conduct of one particular branch of inquiry, beginning with the Standard Theory of Chomsky (1965) and extending to the *Principles and Parameters* (P&P) framework of current generative linguistics, understood broadly to include both *Government-Binding Theory* as initially articulated in Chomsky (1981) and the *Minimalist Program* as initially outlined in Chomsky (1995a).

I should note that my aim in this book is not in *arguing for* the generative framework so much as explaining its motivation, describing its basic mechanisms, and then addressing some of the many interesting philosophical questions and puzzles that arise once we adopt the general theoretical approach. Of course my interest in generative linguistics is driven by my belief that it has been and continues to be successful, but very little that I say here hangs on whether the program is ultimately true. Even the best theories are overthrown or modified beyond recognition, but that doesn't mean we shouldn't be interested in understanding and interpreting those theories and making sense of the practices being engaged in by those working within the theory, nor that we shouldn't be interested in understanding when those practices were successful and when they failed.

I won't address all of the interesting foundational questions that arise—for example whether the language faculty evolved slowly due to selectional pressures or whether it is a "spandrel" in the sense of Gould and Lewontin (1979), or whether linguistic structures might serve as the language of thought, or even questions about the proper place to draw boundaries between syntax, semantics, and pragmatics. Such questions are interesting to me, and there were even chapters devoted to these questions in earlier versions of this book, but in the end I decided that other questions came first— questions about the ontology of linguistics, about the nature of data, about language/world relations, and questions about best theory criteria. The issues addressed here are thus, in my opinion, more basic.

Of course many of the philosophical concerns that arise within generative linguistics arise in other areas of linguistics and indeed arise even in other areas of philosophical investigation, ranging from epistemology (for example the role of intuitions/judgments in theorizing) to ethics (the plausibility of being normatively guided by rules that we don't have clear access to). Accordingly, those working in these areas are encouraged to join in the discussion. It is my hope that, among other things, this work will bring the philosophy of linguistics to a wider philosophical audience and show that we have many shared philosophical questions. Similarly, it is also my hope that the philosophical issues addressed here are laid out clearly enough so that linguists will feel comfortable engaging these issues as well. I appreciate the difficulties in speaking to both linguistic and philosophical audiences at the same time (or at least I do now). If I have had some success in this effort, this book will contribute to more frequent and more productive exchanges between linguists and philosophers on foundational issues.

Acknowledgments

Earlier versions of this material were presented in various talks, courses, and mini-courses that I have given over the last decade and a half, and the material has been undergoing constant revision during that time. Much of this material was initially presented in mini-courses that I taught at the Central European Summer School in Generative Linguistics, at Palacky University in the Czech Republic in the summers of 1995, 1996, and 1997, then in a course that I taught at the University of Venice when I held the Fulbright Chair in the Philosophy of Language in the Spring of 1998, and then in a course which I taught at SUNY Stony Brook in the Fall of 1998. More recently the material has been presented in the Summer School in Philosophy of Language and Linguistics at Beijing Normal University in the Summer of 2007, my graduate seminars at the University of Toronto in the Fall of 2007, at Northwestern University in the Winter Quarter of 2009, and at the University of Nova Gorica, Slovenia, in December 2007.

Smaller fragments of the material were presented in various venues. Portions of Chapter 2 were presented in a series of lectures on the Nature of Language that I gave in the Department of Linguistics at the University of Novi Sad, Yugoslavia, in the Fall of 1997 and then in the Department of English at the University of Jaen, in Jaen, Spain, to the Department of English at Complutense University in Madrid, to the Department of English and German Philology at Autonoma University in Barcelona, and to the Department of Philosophy, Kings College London (all in the Fall of 1998).

The material in Chapter 3—in particular the material on linguistic judgments—was presented at the Philosophy of Linguistics conference at the Interuniversity Center in Dubrovnik, Croatia, in 2006, at the Department of Linguistics at the University of Toronto in the Fall of 2007, at the 2007 Eastern Division Meeting of the American Philosophical Association in Baltimore, at the University of Buffalo in the Spring of 2008, and at the University of North Carolina and Northwestern University in the Fall of 2008.

The material in Chapter 4 grew out of conversations with Peter Railton and Barry Smith, was developed in a graduate course I taught at the University of Toronto in the Fall of 2007, and was subsequently presented in my talk at the University of North Carolina and at the University of Oslo, Norway, in the Fall of 2009.

The material in section 5.2 grew out of a talk given to the Society for Philosophy and Psychology at the University of Maryland in 1990, and was revised in a number of the courses and mini-courses mentioned above. The material in section 5.3 was originally presented at a conference on the epistemology of language at the University of Stirling and appeared as "Externalism, Logical Form, and Linguistic Intentions," in

A. Barber (ed.), *The Epistemology of Language*, Oxford: Oxford University Press, 2002, 132–168.

The material in Chapter 6 was presented in lectures before the Riejka Branch of the Section for Analytical Philosophy, Croatian Philosophical Society, Riejka, Croatia, 1995, at the Department of Cognitive Science, Johns Hopkins University, 1995, and at the Conference on Naturalizing Semantics, Maribor, Slovenia, 1996. Once again, a number of revisions were made in the various mini-courses and talks mentioned above. A version of the material was published in "Referential Semantics for I-Languages," in N. Hornstein and L. Antony (eds.), *Chomsky and His Critics*, Oxford: Blackwell, 2003. The sketch of the expressivist alternative to referential semantics was originally presented to the Recursion Conference at the University of Massachusetts, Amherst in May 2009.

In Chapter 7 the section on formal rigor is adapted from "Formal Rigor and Linguistic Theory," *Natural Language and Linguistic Theory* 10, 1992: 335–344, and the section on simplicity is from "Simplicity and Generative Grammar," in R. Stainton and K. Murasugi (eds.), *Philosophy and Linguistics*, Boulder: Westview Press, 1998. The material on optimal switching points was developed in my epistemology course at the University of Toronto.

As I said, this material has evolved quite a bit over the years and it has benefited from numerous comments and suggestions from audience members and students. It would be impossible for me to remember everyone who has lent a hand thus far, but certain individuals stand out for their contributions throughout most if not all of the period that I have been working on these issues. These individuals include Alex Barber, Josh Brown, Liz Camp, John Collins, Michael Devitt, Imogen Dickie, Frankie Egan, Sam Epstein, Danny Fox, Steven Gross, James Higginbotham, Benj Hellie, Dunja Jutronic, Richard Kayne, Phil Kremer, Richard Larson, Ernie Lepore, Lanko Marusic, Tatjana Marvin, Bob Mathews, Robert May, Nenad Miscevic, Stephen Neale, Paul Pietroski, Geoffrey Pullum, Gurpreet Rattan, Lori Repetti, Georges Rey, Barry Schein, Gabriel Segal, Stuart Shieber, Barry Smith, Rob Stainton, Tim Sundell, Jonathan Weisberg, Emma Wellman, and Edwin Williams. Special thanks are due to Rob Stainton and Barry Smith for helpful comments on the penultimate drafts of some of these chapters.

Further thanks are due to Tom Wasow who lit a fire under me about these issues in a class on the Philosophy of Linguistics that he taught at Stanford back in 1986, when I was a visiting scholar at the Center for the Study of Language and Information. My greatest debts are to James Higginbotham, who has influenced this work the most, and Noam Chomsky, who has carried on a correspondence with me on these issues since 1990, and who has commented on earlier versions of many portions this work.

Abbreviations

AP	adjectival phrase
C/I	conceptual/intentional
CNPC	complex noun phrase constraint
CP	complementizer phrase
CSC	coordinate structure constraint
DS	deep structure
ECP	empty category principle
EST	extended standard theory
FA	functional application
FLN	faculty of language narrowly construed
GB	government-binding theory
GPSG	generalized phrase structure grammar
IV	intransitive verb
LF	logical form
LFG	lexical functional grammar
NLP	natural language processing
NP	noun phrase
PA	predicate abstraction
P/A	perceptual/articulatory
PF	phonetic form
PM	predicate modification
P&P	principles and parameters
PP	prepositional phrase
QR	quantifies raising
S	sentence
SR	semantic representation
SS	surface structure
SSC	sentential structure constraint
TN	terminal node
TV	transitive verb
UG	universal grammar
VP	verb phrase

Oh, that's the most fascinating topic of all.

Noam Chomsky

Introduction

This work is an attempt to explore some of the many interesting philosophical issues that arise in the conduct of generative linguistics. By 'generative linguistics' I mean that branch of linguistics that attempts to explain and understand language related phenomena by constructing a theory of the underlying mechanisms that give rise to those phenomena. In this sense of 'generative', chemistry and biology are generative as well. The facts of chemistry are explained in part by the properties of and interaction of more basic elements (atoms, for example). Likewise the facts of biology are also explained in part by the properties of and organization of more basic elements (proteins, for example). In the linguistic case we can say that language related phenomena or facts are explained in part by the properties of and interaction of more basic elements. It is the task of generative linguistics to discover those more basic elements, to learn their properties, and to understand how they interact to help account for macro-level language related phenomena.

While I am going to explore a number of different issues in the chapters that follow, there are three basic themes that are woven through the work.

The first theme is that generative linguistics at its best is concerned with **understanding and explanation**, and not just with observation and data gathering. To this end, generative linguistics is interested in underlying mechanisms that give rise to language related phenomena, and this interest will often trump the goal of accumulating more data.

The second theme is what I call the **Ψ-language hypothesis**. It is the hypothesis that the underlying mechanisms (the more basic elements) posited by generative linguists are fundamentally psychological mechanisms and that generative linguistics is a branch of cognitive psychology, but that it doesn't follow that cognitive psychology must therefore be interested in psychological states individuated narrowly. It is consistent with the Ψ-language hypothesis that psychological states (and indeed syntactic states) are individuated in part by the embedding environment.

The third theme is what I call the **principle of methodological minimalism**. It is the thesis that best theory criteria like simplicity and formal rigor all really come down to one thing: seek methods that help linguists to do their jobs effectively and with the minimum of cognitive labor.

In some chapters, all three of these themes will be active. In Chapter 3, for example, where I discuss linguistic data, I will make the case that linguistic judgments are valuable because they can provide a way of targeting inquiry. They can thus be illuminating of underlying explanatory mechanisms (the first theme) and they also allow us to gather data in an efficient way (the third theme). Most chapters will feature some combination of these three themes.

The Plan

Chapter 1 of this book provides a survey of some work in generative linguistics over the past 45 years. The survey is not intended to be comprehensive, but is designed to give a flavor of some of the examples and topics that I want to address in this book. Chapter 2 introduces some of the ontological questions that arise in linguistic theory. These involve questions about the object of study, the nature of rules and representations (and principles and parameters) in linguistic theory, the ways in which these rules and representations are instantiated, and questions about whether there is some sense in which we know or cognize these rules and representations. Chapter 3 takes on the topic of the role of data within linguistic theory and in particular the controversial role of so-called linguistic intuitions or judgments. Chapter 4 explores the possibility that the rules and representations that we have play a role in individual normative rule guidance for us, even though the rules are not accessible to us in relevant senses. Chapter 5 takes on philosophical worries that have been lodged against rules and representations (e.g. by Quine) and rule following (e.g. in Kripke's reconstruction of Wittgenstein's rule following argument). Chapter 6 turns to the nature of the semantic theory and character of language/world relations, and Chapter 7 takes up methodological issues involving so-called best theory criteria like simplicity and formal rigor.

In more detail, the structure of each chapter is as follows.

Chapter 1: Linguistic Preliminaries

I provide a brief survey of some of the changes that have taken place in generative linguistics since 1965, with an effort to document the shifting nature of the arguments and theoretical machinery deployed, as well as to highlight some of the philosophical disputes and puzzles that are addressed in this book. I'll start in section 1.1 with the so-called Standard Theory of Chomsky (1965) and its evolution into the Extended Standard Theory of the 1970s. In section 1.2 I will look at the so-called Government-Binding theory of the 1980s. I'll then turn (section 1.3) to the Principles and Parameters framework, which grew out of Government-Binding Theory. I'll conclude (section 1.4) with some remarks on the Minimalist Program. Again, my goal will not be to give a complete survey, but merely to introduce enough linguistic theory so that we can engage the foundational issues in a productive way.

Chapter 2: The Ontology of Generative Linguistics

2.1 E-Language, I-Language, and Ψ-Language: Noam Chomsky has advanced the I-language thesis—in effect the idea that the object of study in linguistics is not an external social object but rather a natural psychological object and that linguistics is a chapter of cognitive psychology. I will agree that linguistics is a chapter of cognitive psychology, but will argue that cognitive psychology need not be understood as being exclusively internalist. I'll argue that linguistics can be construed as a chapter of cognitive psychology understood *anti-individualistically*—i.e. that psychological states are individuated in part by embedding environmental conditions. The *Ψ-Language Thesis* is the thesis that the object of study in linguistics should be the underlying cognitive mechanisms, but that we should divorce this project from individualism about psychology.

2.2 Having Linguistic Rules and Knowing Linguistic Facts: Do we know grammars? Do we know languages? I argue that we *have* linguistic rules (in the form of grammars), and that it is by having the linguistic rules that we do that we *know* some facts about our language. We have the individual rules and grammars that we do because the parametric states of our language faculties are set the way they are.

We know languages in some loose sense (perhaps the sense that we know them by acquaintance), but we also know (in a stricter sense) many of the facts about our language. There are also many facts about our language that we do not know about, and we are not in a position to come to know those facts even with the help of extensive introspection. Explicit knowledge of most linguistic facts is the product of intensive scientific investigation relying upon the linguistic data that are available to us.

2.3 Levels of Explanation in the Theory of Grammar: If one is studying Ψ-language one is in effect studying Universal Grammar (UG), which is the initial state of the language faculty. I will distinguish between UG, which we can think of as a natural kind, and the instantiation of UG within a particular individual, UG_i. We can also distinguish between UG_i and the grammar that the agent knows by virtue of being in the state UG_i—we can all this grammar G_i. Modifying a suggestion from George (1989), we can now distinguish between G_i (the grammar the individual *i* has), the psychogrammar (which is the psychological state by virtue of which the individual has G_i), and the physiogrammar (which is the low level biophysical state upon which the psychogrammar supervenes). I will argue that when we are investigating UG we are in effect investigating the psychogrammar and the physiogrammar (also construed as natural kinds). I will argue that the principles and parameters framework is in effect an investigation into the psychogrammar, and the so-called Minimalist Program of Chomsky (1995a) is in effect an investigation into the structure of the physiogrammar.

2.4 Abstracta and Non-isomorphic Representation: If grammars are abstract objects, then what does it take for us to have a particular grammar (G_i)? Many linguists and philosophers suppose that if we have a grammar then that means that the rules of the grammar are "hard coded" as data structures in our mind/brain. I will argue that it is a mistake to think that having a particular abstract rule R involves internally instantiating a line of code that is isomorphic to the rule R. There may be many ways by which our lower level cognitive architecture might underwrite such states.

2.5 Types and Tokens: The object of investigation may be the cognitive mechanism (UG) that gives rise to linguistic phenomena, but there are important questions about the nature of the linguistic phenomena that provide evidence for our theory of UG. It is common practice to produce and refer to objects like sentences in linguistic inquiry. Is linguistics actually concerned with these objects or are they merely triggers that we use to talk about psychological objects? If we are concerned with the external linguistic objects, what kinds of objects are these? Following work by Szabó (1999) I suggest that linguistic tokens are *representations* of more complex abstract structures.

2.6 Derivation vs. Representation: Some linguists have argued that the rule systems posited in earlier versions of generative linguistics have been superseded by nonrepresentational derivational theories. I argue that this smacks of an earlier dispute in computer science between advocates of procedural versus declarative languages. That dispute is now understood to be vacant, as is—or so I shall argue—the dispute between derivational and representational theories of grammar.

Chapter 3: Data, Intuitions, Judgments

3.1 Linguistic Phenomena, Linguistic Data, Linguistic Theory: I argue that much of linguistic practice turns on the role of what I will call *linguistic phenomena*. To a first approximation, linguistic phenomena are facts about the acceptability and interpretation of linguistic objects. I argue that these facts or phenomena are *explained by* the theory of grammar. Linguistic *data*, on the other hand, *provide evidence for* the linguistic phenomena. As we will see, there are many potential sources of data, some (especially linguistic intuitions) much more controversial than others.

3.2 Linguistic Intuitions are Linguistic Judgments: Among other sources of data, generative linguists often use so-called linguistic intuitions as evidence when constructing our theory of grammar. Many linguists and philosophers take these intuitions to be "Cartesian" in the sense that they are the inner voice of competence. Contrarily, taking a leaf from Williamson (2004) I argue that linguistic intuitions are not "the voice of competence," but are merely defeasible judgments about linguistic phenomena or facts.

3.3 Linguistic Judgments are Reliable (enough): Thinking of linguistic intuitions as judgments can help us avoid being traumatized by the possibility of error in our linguistic data gathering (error is simply something that we have to live with). It can also help us to see that some consultants may be better judges than others. I make the case that linguistic judgments are useful, economical, and on the whole reliable sources of data.

3.4 Linguistic Judgment as Scientific Experimentation: I argue that when linguists isolate particular judgments to make the case for their theories they are involved in a fairly standard form of scientific investigation. That is, they are setting up controlled, replicable experiments in which they and other experimenters are judging whether a sentence is acceptable and/or what its interpretation might be. This leads to the question of which judges are good judges and why. I point out that this is similar to the question of what makes for a good experimenter in any science and leads us as well into what is sometimes called "the experimenter's regress." I'll offer that we can break the regress by identifying good experimenters using easy cases where judgments converge.

3.5 On the Alleged Priority of the Data: In this section I take up a series of objections that have been raised to the effect that generative linguists often fail to pay attention to the available linguistic data. I'll argue that this reflects a misunderstanding about the nature of the enterprise—to wit: It assumes that all data that appear prima facie linguistically relevant must somehow be covered by a mature and acceptable theory of the faculty of language narrowly construed (FLN). In point of fact many of the data might not be relevant to the cognitive mechanism we are investigating. I'll draw an analogy to the famous cases in epidemiology, where classes of symptoms that were grouped together often did not turn out to have the same explanations. A number of conditions that were considered constitutive of polio later came to be understood to be caused by something other than polio once we developed the viral theory of polio.

I'll also argue that even once we isolate evidence that is relevant to the faculty of language, it is hardly sound scientific practice to dismiss good theories (or dismiss theory altogether) on the grounds that stray data are not explained. There is more to good theory construction than so-called data coverage. We want explanatory adequacy in addition to descriptive adequacy—and this will involve a number of factors including the embeddability of the theory into other sciences and best theory criteria.

Chapter 4: A Role for Normative Rule Governance?

Perhaps concerned that any talk of normativity flirts dangerously with prescriptivism, generative linguists tend to shy away from such talk. But I argue that the rules of grammar establish *individual* norms for us and that they provide regulative guidance for our linguistic behavior even though we may not recognize those rules under all descriptions or even acknowledge that they exist.

It's one thing to talk about individual norms but quite another to formalize the notion in a coherent way. Accordingly, I adopt and extend a proposal by Railton for a notion of normative rule governance in ethics.

Chapter 5: Worries about Rules and Representations

5.1 Quinean Indeterminacy Arguments: The idea that linguistic theory involves the investigation of rules and representations (or principles and parameters) of a cognitive computational system has led to philosophical questions about the nature of these rules and representations. For example, Quine (1970) argued that since many possible grammars may successfully describe an agent's linguistic behavior, there is no way in principle for us to determine which grammar an agent is using. In response, Chomsky (1980a) argued that if we consider the *explanatory adequacy* of a grammar in addition to its *descriptive adequacy*, then the question of which grammar is correct is answerable in principle. That is, if we consider that a grammar must be consistent with the theory of language acquisition, acquired language deficits, and more generally with cognitive psychology, then there are many constraints available to rule out competing grammatical theories.

5.2 Kripke/Wittgenstein Concerns about Rules: Another set of worries, this time about rule following, have stemmed from Kripke's (1982) reconstruction of arguments in Wittgenstein (1958, 1956). I argue that there are several components to the Kripke/Wittgenstein argument, but that the really difficult problem is the metaphysical determination problem—the worry that there can be no brute fact about what rules and representations a system is running apart from the intentions of the designer of the system. Since, when studying humans, we have no access to the intentions of the designer there can be no fact of the matter about what rules and representations underlie our linguistic abilities. The conclusion drawn by Kripke is that "it would seem that the use of the idea of rules and of competence in linguistics needs serious reconsideration, even if these notions are not rendered meaningless" (1982, 31 n. 22).

I'll then visit an argument due to Soames (1998a), that the rule following argument trades on a mistake that Kripke ought to have noticed—that the inability of an agent to know a priori what links her usage of a rule today with previous uses does not entail that there is no necessary connection between her current and previous uses, nor does it entail that there is no fact of the matter about what rule she is using. The argument may, however, force us to accept the possibility that the determining facts are facts about the environmental embedding of the agent.

5.3 Externalism about Syntax?: What follows if the constitution problem leads us to conclude that the linguistic rules and representations an agent has are constituted in part by environmental conditions (social, physical, or both). One possibility is that we could be forced into being externalists about syntax! In this section I explore the feasibility of this radical sounding doctrine.

Chapter 6: Referential Semantics for Narrow Ψ-Languages

6.1 The Compatibility of Referential Semantics and Narrow Ψ-Languages: If we reject the considerations in Chapter 5, and endorse Chomsky's idea that Ψ-language is individualistic, we immediately encounter an important question about the nature of semantics, and in particular *referential* semantics—construed as theories of the relation between linguistic forms and aspects of the external world. In short, the worry is this: Putnam (1975a) and many other philosophers have held that we need referential semantics to characterize linguistic meaning—that meanings "ain't in the head"—but if this is right, then it is hard to see how semantics can be part of the language faculty, which is supposed to be individualistic (and hence "in the head").

However, as we will see, even if syntax is individualistic, it is arguable that the tension in these views is apparent only, since the connection between individualistic Ψ-languages and referential semantics would parallel the connection between individualistic and relational sciences in other domains (for example, it would be similar to the connection that holds between the studies of primate physiology and primate ecology—facts about physiology can shed light on the primate's relation to its environment, and vice versa). As we will also see, inferences between individualistic and relational sciences are imperfect, but data from one domain can nevertheless be relevant to the other.

6.2 Chomsky's Incompatibilist Arguments: This apparent tension between I-language and referential semantics has led commentators such as Hornstein (1984), Chomsky (1993, 1995b) to be skeptical of the possibility of a referential semantics. On Chomsky's view, for example, compatibilism commits us to the existence of entities like flaws in arguments and the average American—entities that Chomsky takes to be implausible.

6.3 The "Bite the Bullet" Strategy and Chomsky's Response: In this section I take a closer look at Chomsky's incompatibilist arguments, and I develop a response that I call the "bite the bullet" strategy—i.e. I argue that there just are things like flaws and holes. Chomsky (2003a) has objected to the bite the bullet strategy on he grounds that it amounts to ducking the interesting questions about how we come to assign the complex meanings to words that we do.

6.4 The Compatibilist Bites Back: I argue that opting for entities like flaws and supposing that substances like water have amorphous properties does not foreclose the investigation into questions about the underlying mechanisms by which linguistic elements come to have the referential semantics that they do.

6.5 The Prospects for a Non-referential Semantics: If we were to reject referential semantics what would the alternative be? It is easy to offer hand-waving solutions such as that the alternative will be a use theory or an expressivist theory, but working out the details of these proposals is easier said than done. In this section I attempt to work out the details of an axiomatized expressivist semantics of natural language, highlight some of its positive features, and also note some outstanding difficulties.

Chapter 7: Best Theory Criteria and Methodological Minimalism

7.1 Simplicity Criteria: The first methodological issue relates to the use of simplicity in the choice between linguistic theories. While tight definitions of simplicity within a linguistic theory seem to be possible (see Halle 1961, Chomsky and Halle 1968, Chomsky 1975a), finding a notion of simplicity that allows us to choose between two competing theoretical frameworks is another matter. Some writers (e.g. Postal 1972, Hornstein 1995) have argued that generative semantics and the Minimalist Program respectively are simpler than their immediate competitors because they admit fewer levels of representation. Alternatively, I argue that there is no objective criterion for evaluating the relative amount of theoretical machinery across linguistic theories. The only plausible definition of simplicity would be one that appealed to "simplicity of use"; in other words, simplicity in linguistics may not be a feature of the object of study itself, but rather our ability to easily grasp and utilize certain kinds of theories.

7.2 Formal Rigor: If the language faculty is an internal computational/representational system, a number of questions arise about how to best go about investigating and describing it. For example, there has been considerable attention paid to the role of formal rigor in linguistic theory. On this score, a number of theorists (e.g. Gazdar, Klein, Pullum, and Sag 1985, Bresnan and Kaplan 1982, Pullum 1989) have argued that the formal rigor of their approaches—in particular their use of well-defined recursive procedures—counts in their favor. However, as we will see, it may be that this sort of approach to rigorization would be out of synch with the development of other sciences (and indeed, branches of mathematics) where formalization follows in the wake of the advancing theory. I argue that the relevant notion of formal rigor in linguistics (and perhaps for any science) should be *sufficient* rigor for us to make progress in the task at hand.

7.3 Minimal Effort and Optimal Switching Points: On my proposal, the methodological issues involving formal rigor and simplicity all answer to the demand that we construct our theories in such a way as to make the most progress with the minimal expenditure of cognitive labor (simple enough and rigorous enough for us as investigators to make optimal progress). This opens the door to interesting questions about the cost of adopting more rigorous methods and strategies for simplification of theory. Consider the case of new rigorous methods. In early stages of theory development the costs may not be worth it, but as results become harder to come by more rigorous methods may be justified in spite of their cost. We thus need to look at optimal switching points—the conditions that signal it is time to adopt more rigorous methods (or seek further theoretical simplification).

1

Linguistic Preliminaries

1.1 Transformational Grammar from ST to EST

To a first approximation, linguistics is concerned with how humans pair sounds (or other perceivable forms) with meanings.[1] The theory of grammar is the theory of the mechanisms by which this is accomplished. We can think of there being three components to the grammar—a phonological component, a syntactic component, and a semantic component. The phonological component has to do with the representations that are relevant to the production and perception of speech (e.g. the combination of features by which vowels are formed, the metrical (rhythmic) patterns of the language, etc.). The syntax has to do with the form or structure of sentences (for example, that a sentence might consist of a subject and predicate or a noun phrase and a verb phrase). The semantic component has to do with the assignment of meanings to linguistic forms. For the most part in this book I will be concerned with the enterprise of generative *syntax* (although the relation to semantics will be explored in Chapter 5). Much could be written about the philosophy of generative phonology, but that will not be covered here. Furthermore, discussion of generative syntax that follows is not intended to be complete, nor even balanced to highlight the most important empirical results and discoveries. My mission in this chapter is simply to introduce those aspects of empirical research that raise the most interesting philosophical questions and those aspects that can inform our discussion in subsequent chapters.

Generative linguistics can best be appreciated if we examine it against the backdrop of American structuralism, in particular as articulated by Bloomfield (1933, 1939). American structuralism adopted a number of key assumptions from logical positivism, including the following.

(i) All useful generalizations are inductive generalizations.
(ii) Meanings are to be eschewed because they are occult entities—that is, because they are not directly empirically observable.

---

[1] Special thanks are due to Rob Stainton for comments on this chapter.

(iii) Discovery procedures like those advocated in logical positivism should be developed for the proper conduct of linguistic inquiry.

(iv) There should be no unobserved processes.

All of these assumptions were rejected at the inception of generative linguistics (see Chomsky 1975a: introduction, for a detailed discussion). As regards discovery procedures, for example, Chomsky rejected them while still a matriculating graduate student, then holding a position in the Harvard Society of Fellows:

By 1953, I came to the same conclusion [as Morris Halle]: if the discovery procedures did not work, it was not because I had failed to formulate them correctly, but because the entire approach was wrong... [S]everal years of intense effort devoted to improving discovery procedures had come to naught, while work I had been doing during the same period on generative grammars and explanatory theory, in almost complete isolation, seemed to be consistently yielding interesting results. (1975a, 131)

More generally, Chomsky rejected methodological first principles, arguing that one ought to adopt whatever resources are at hand that work, expressing this idea as follows in the 1958 Texas Conference on Problems of Linguistic Analysis in English, in an exchange with James Sledd of UC Berkeley.

CHOMSKY: The process that I use for investigating language is the one that I was taught. It is described in Harris' *Methods*. I use it for want of a better, though I know that it does not give me all the results that I want. When I can go beyond the method, fine, I go beyond it. Suppose I suddenly get a bright idea that such and such a reformulation will work better, I try it. I don't sit down and see how I could have gotten to the same result by defining the methods in a more and more rigorous way. If you don't have any bright ideas, then you simply experiment with the data, using the methods you have been taught. . . .

. . .

SLEDD: You are doing a kind of restatement linguistics, and so feel that you can make use of whatever others of us do, whenever it helps you to more knowledge of the language. You take what is useful, and put it into your machine. Isn't that so?

CHOMSKY: Exactly. And I don't care how I get from data that someone has presented to me, to a useful formulation. Questions of that sort don't interest me, though they might be important for some other field, say the psychology of invention.

Generative grammarians also rejected the assumption that all processes should be "observable" processes—early theories of transformational grammar offering key examples of unobservable processes. For example, in the "Standard Theory" of generative grammar as developed in Chomsky (1965), the grammar is divided into two different "levels of representation"—initially called *Deep Structure* (hereafter DS) and *Surface Structure* (hereafter SS). Transformational rules map from DS representations onto SS representations, so that the picture of the grammar is something like the following.

$$DS \text{ --- }_{\text{transformations}} \to SS$$

The names 'Deep Structure' and 'Surface Structure' were probably unfortunate in that they led to the imputation of properties to these levels of representation that were not intended.

To put it simply, DS representations are merely representations that are generated by what is known as a *Context-Free Phrase Structure Grammar*. Here is an example of a toy (emphasis on *toy*) context-free phrase structure grammar:

(i) S → NP VP
(ii) VP → tense V′
(iii) V′ → V (NP)
(iv) NP → *John*
(v) NP → *Bill*
(vi) NP → det N′
(vii) N′ → (adj) N
(viii) V → *see*
(ix) V → *like*
(x) tense → *PAST, PRES, FUT*

These phrase structure rules are in effect instructions for building (generating) tree representations for linguistic structures. For example, the following tree is derived from successive applications of rules (i–v) above.

(1)

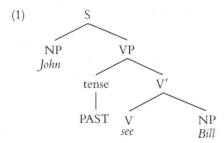

From time to time we will find it useful to "linearize" trees like this for expository purposes, but the resulting structural descriptions will encode the same information. We thus take structures like (a) and (b) to be notational variants of each other.

(a)

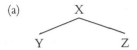

(b) [x Y Z]

The linearized version of (1) above would thus be (1′).

(1′) [s [NP John][VP [tense PAST] [V′ [V see][NP Bill]]]]

As a notational shortcut, I will sometimes omit structure within brackets. So, in cases where fine structure is unimportant, I might represent (1′) as in (1″), or something with an intermediate amount of structure. The general principle is to show as much structure as necessary to make the point; omitting structure in a representation like (1″) is not to say the structure isn't there in the linguistic object being represented.

(1″)   [$_S$ John saw Bill]

Crucially, for generative linguists the objects of analysis in linguistic theory were not the so-called *terminal strings* of words, but rather *phrase markers*—structured objects like (1) or (1′). As we will see, structures like (1) carry significantly more information than an unstructured string of words. For example, the adverb 'reluctantly' can be inserted between 'John' and 'saw', but not between 'saw' and 'Bill' (unless comma intonation is added suggesting that 'reluctantly' is a parenthetical aside). One possible explanation is that the VP forms a *constituent*, which cannot be split by the adverb.

Grammars that generate the same set of unstructured strings of words are said to have the same *weak generative capacity*. If two grammars generate the same structures (including tree structure) we say they have the same *strong generative capacity*. Generative linguistics has, since the beginning, been concerned with *strong* generative capacity.

As I said above, the simple toy grammar above is a context-free phrase structure grammar. This is a kind of grammar that is familiar to computer scientists, and the properties of such formal languages are fairly well understood. From the beginning, Chomsky has argued that such grammars are *not* sufficient to describe the structure of natural languages.[2] We could also add that such grammars do not provide us the resources to describe important relations holding between linguistic forms in natural language. For example, we might think that there is a kind of natural relationship between sentences like 'John saw Bill' and 'Bill was seen by John' and that we would like to capture this relationship. The nature of such relations can be formalized using *transformations*.

In the Standard Theory transformational rules operated on these DS representations (in effect, on the products of context-free phrase structure rules) to yield SS representations. Here are some examples of transformational rules.

Passivization: NP1 V NP2 → NP2 be-en V by NP1

Affix Hopping: Aff V → V-Aff

Passivization converts a DS in active form to an SS representation that we would recognize as being in passive form. Affixes are elements like tense and aspectual markers, which (on Chomsky's early theory) are generated in a preverbal position at DS. Affix hopping moves them into a post-verbal position as suffixes. In this case, affix

---

[2] As with most claims in linguistic theory, this one has been challenged. Context-free phrase structure grammars can be generalized to account for phenomena like wh-movement and displaced constituents (see Gazdar et al. 1985), although there are arguably limits as to whether such grammars can account for all natural language constructions (see for example a worry about Swiss German raised in Shieber (1985)). I set this question aside here, as the debate does not impinge on the kinds of issues I'm addressing in this book.

hopping will move the affix '-en' from a preverbal position to one in which it is attached to the verb 'see', yielding 'seen'. So, for example, the successive operations of Passivization and Affix Hopping would take a deep structure representation like (1) and (abstracting from complications with tense) yield the surface structure representation in (2).

(2)

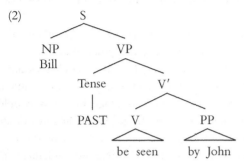

The standard written sentence in (3) below therefore designates a complex object consisting of (at a minimum) the ordered pair of the DS and SS representations corresponding to (1) and (2).

(3) Bill was seen by John

We could think of (3) as being our written shorthand convention for representing the ordered pair consisting of the DS representation given in (1) and the SS representation given in (2).

Other examples of transformations included the following (I'm indicating the location where the noun phrase is moved from for heuristic purposes; the idea that this location should have a syntactically significant element is a later development that will be discussed shortly).

Topicalization: [. . . NP . . .] → [NP[. . . _ . . .]]

For example from the DS [John likes Bill] we get [Bill[John likes _]]

Wh-movement: [. . . WH . . .] → WH did [. . . _ . . .]

For example from the DS [John saw who] we get [Who did [John see _]]

It is natural to think that the goal here was to formalize an intuitive connection between a passive and a non-passive form of a sentence (they certainly seem to be importantly related). However, a case can be made that this was not Chomsky's principal motivation—that the motivation was actually one of theoretical simplicity. Speaking of Chomsky's earlier (1957) book *Syntactic Structures* and the introduction of transformations there, Newmeyer (1986) argues as follows:

Chomsky's arguments for transformation rules in Syntactic Structures were all simplicity arguments . . . They all involved showing that a grammar with phrase structure rules alone required great complexity, a complexity that could be avoided only by the position of a transformational rule. (24)

We will return to the question of simplicity in Chapter 7. For now I want to draw attention to the fact that early generative linguists were committed not only to "unobserved" processes in the guise of transformations, but also to unobserved levels of representation.

No less significant than the introduction of unseen processes and levels of representation was the nature of some of the data that generative linguistics admitted—it was not limited to corpora of utterances or written strings, but also included speakers' judgments of acceptability and meaning. Thus, example (3) is not a datum because it has been written or spoken, but rather because speakers judge that it is (would correspond to) an acceptable linguistic form. Here again, generative linguists broke with prevailing methodology in structuralist linguistics and, indeed, behaviorist psychology, by allowing individual judgments as data (more on linguistic judgments in Chapter 3).

Having broken out of the behaviorist mindset of then prevalent linguistic theorizing, generative grammar subsequently evolved in response to a number of discoveries and explanatory pressures. Some of the most remarkable advances came in the form of Ross's 1967 Ph.D. dissertation, which catalogued numerous transformations, but crucially, Ross also observed (building on a proposal in Chomsky 1962) that certain syntactic environments seemed to block the transformations.

For example, while we can extract 'the book' from 'Bill illustrated the book' to yield 'that's the book that Bill illustrated', consider what happens when we attempt a similar extraction from the following:

(4)   [$_S$ Bill married the woman who illustrated the book]

The resulting (5) is clearly bad.

(5)   *[$_S$ That's the book that [$_S$ Bill married the woman who illustrated __]]

Ross observed a number of these effects (which he called "islands"—as in stranded on an island) and stated conditions on movement that would explain and predict these island effects.

For example, he accounted for the above island (the discovery of which he attributed to Ed Klima) by positing the *Complex Noun Phrase Constraint*, which he formalized as follows:

(CNPC): No element contained in an S dominated by an NP with a lexical head noun may be moved out of that NP by a transformation. (Ross (1974, 178). Page numbers are from the excerpt of his dissertation in Harman (1974))

To explain, one node X dominates another node Y if and only if there is a direct downward path from X to Y in the tree. The CNPC says that if there is an S inside an

NP (for example a relative clause inside an NP) and the NP has a lexical head noun (in this case 'woman'), you cannot extract something from inside that S. Illustrating with (4'), we see that this is precisely what has happened. Forming a structure like (5) involves extracting 'the book' from inside an S (the relative clause 'who illustrated the book' which is contained inside an NP ('the woman who illustrated the book').

(4')

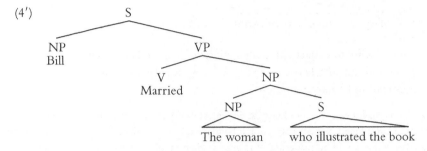

Another such constraint was the *Coordinate Structure Constraint*:

(CSC): In a coordinate structure, no conjunct may be moved, nor may any element contained in a conjunct be moved out of that conjunct.

An example of a coordinate structure is a conjunction. To illustrate this constraint, consider the D-structure (6), and the resulting S-structure (7), where we have attempted to extract 'what sofa' via wh-movement.

(6) [s He will put the chair between [NP [NP some table] and [NP what sofa]]]

(7) *[s What sofa will he put the chair between [NP [NP some table] and [NP ___]]]

Ross took the constraints stated thus far to be universal—to hold across all human languages. But he also identified constraints for which this did not hold. One such constraint was the *Sentential Subject Constraint* (SSC):

(SSC): No element dominated by an S may be moved out of that S if that node S is dominated by an NP which itself is immediately dominated by S. (1974, 194)

This was designed to block movement that would result in forming (9) from the DS representation (8):

(8) [s [NP that [S Mary was going out with who]] bothered you]

(9) *[s Who did [s [NP that Mary was going out with ___]] bother you]]

The idea is the following: Ross is thinking of the that-clause—'that Mary was going out with who' as an NP. This NP is in turn dominated by an S, as illustrated in the following tree.

(10)

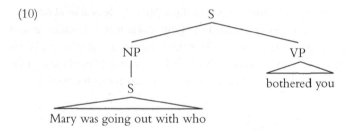

Getting the 'who' to extract requires jumping out of an S that is dominated by an NP that is in turn immediately dominated by an S. As noted above, Ross did not consider this constraint to be universal.

That the languages whose rules I know to be subject to [SSC] far outnumber those whose rules are not so constrained suggests that a search be made for other formal properties of these latter languages which could be made use of to predict their atypical behavior with respect to this constraint. At present, however, whether or not [SSC] is operative within any particular language can only be treated as an idiosyncratic fact which must be stated in the conditions box of the language in question. (1974, 194)

Ross was noting cross-linguistic variation with respect to this constraint but he was also indicating a belief that variation across languages with respect to such properties ought to have some explanation (a theme we will return to when we discuss the Principles and Parameters framework in section 1.3).

Generative Semantics

Starting in the 1960s some generative linguists hypothesized that DS representations might be generated via *projection rules* from a level of representation which we might call Semantic Representation (or SR), that encoded meanings, or more accurately, meaning representations. According to this idea, the model of the grammar would be something like the following:

(11)   SR — ₚ₍₀ⱼₑ𝒸ₜᵢₒₙ₋ᵣᵤₗₑₛ → DS — ₜᵣₐₙₛ𝒻ₒᵣₘₐₜᵢₒₙₛ → SS

One central idea that crystallized with the Katz-Postal hypothesis (after Katz and Postal 1964) was the idea that the DS representations might be generated from word and sentence meanings. Thus, if two sentences had the same meaning they must have the same DS representation. If there is an ambiguity, it would correspond to there being distinct DS representations. Here is the statement from Katz and Postal (1964, 157).

Given a sentence for which a syntactic derivation is needed; look for simple paraphrases of the sentence which are not paraphrases by virtue of synonymous expressions; on finding them, construct grammatical rules that relate the original sentence and its paraphrases in such a way that each of these sentences has the same sequence of underlying P-markers [DS representations]. Of course, having constructed such rules, it is still necessary to find *independent syntactic justification* for them. [emphasis theirs]

Probably in the background of this proposal was work on the computational theory of mind and the language of thought hypothesis which Jerry Fodor was developing at the time and which is fully articulated in Fodor (1975).

Subsequently, a number of linguists, including Ross, George Lakoff, Paul Postal, and others, developed a research program that extended this idea in fairly radical ways. The research program came to be known as *generative semantics*, and the resulting battle with Chomsky and other generative linguists has come to be known as the "Generative Semantics Wars." Although the conflicts led to some interesting reading (see Newmeyer 1986 and Harris 1993) only a couple of elements of that dispute are relevant to us.

One element concerns the range of the phenomena to be explained by the theory of grammar (we could also call this the range of the *explananda* of the theory of grammar[3]). Even if we are interested in a broad class of language related phenomena, it need not be the case that the principal object of investigation (the theory of grammar) should explain everything in this pre-theoretical domain of investigation. That is, even if we agreed that there was a broad range of language related phenomena to be explained, it does not follow that there is a single mechanism (the theory of grammar) serving as the sole *explanans* for all of them.

This point became salient in the generative semantics era because of a tendency of generative semanticists to attempt to sweep up more and more language related phenomena and take them to be targets of explanation (explananda) for the theory of grammar. Up until that point, the kinds of facts that were the targets of explanation in generative linguistics were fairly constrained, but particularly under Lakoff's influence the supposed domain of linguistics became broader and broader, and the theory of grammar was pressed into service as the potential explanans for more and more phenomena. In part, the generative semantics wars can be seen as a dispute over precisely how broad the target of theory of grammar should be.

In the end, any phenomenon remotely related to language was taken to be an explanandum of the theory. Synonymous expressions were derived from a common underlying structure (famously, 'kill' from 'cause to die'). Selectional restrictions were also argued to have syntactic explanations. Thus the oddness of 'the hot dog ate John' was not because of real world knowledge, but had an underlying syntactic/semantic explanation (McCawley 1968, Lakoff 1968, Lakoff and Ross 1976). Pronouns were derived from noun phrases by the operation of pronominalization. Soon generative semantics would be extended to account for logic, and then fuzzy logic was incorporated into the theory to account for graded judgments (Lakoff 1973). Lakoff, in Parrett (1974, 151) showed just how broadly the net was to be cast. The theory was going to accommodate

---

[3] My use of the term 'explananda' and 'explanans' diverges from that of, for example, Hempel, since he took the explananda and explanans to be the linguistic descriptions of the thing explained and the explanation. I'm using them to speak of the phenomena themselves.

not just syntax-semantic, phonetics-phonology, historical linguistics, anthropological linguistics, etc., which form the core of most academic programs in this country, but also the role of language in social interaction, in literature, in ritual, and in propaganda, and as well the study of the relationship between language and thought, speech production and perception, linguistic disorders, etc.

Or to put it another way, when you have a really good hammer, everything begins to look like a nail. I think it is one thing to suppose that generative linguistics intersects with these areas, but the idea that it will subsume them is an entirely different matter. In my view, matters were taken to their limit when Ross (1970) and Sadock (1969, 1970) proposed that pragmatic phenomena (and speech act phenomena) could be treated as syntactic phenomena. Thus, speech acts like assertion were analyzed as involving a syntactic operator 'I assert that'. Anyone familiar with the story of Achilles and the Tortoise will see how this strategy is bound to fail; one would need a speech act theory for the new syntactic form, which presumably would receive a syntactic account, and a regress has begun.

It is interesting to reflect on the basic assumptions about the nature of inquiry driving the generative semanticists. Of course, once one takes it to be the job of generative linguistics to subsume all of these phenomena, one quickly sees the task as hopeless. At that point, one either becomes less ambitious about the goals of generative linguistics, or settles into a kind of pessimism about generative linguistics as did Postal (1976, 203):

This is the first in a random, possibly nonfinite series of communications designed to show beyond any doubt that there exists no linguistic theory whatever. There are apparently endless numbers of fact types not incorporable within any known or imaginable framework. In particular, what has been called the theory of transformational grammar, seems to have only the most partial relation to linguistic reality.

In the same essay Postal continues on this theme, arguing that science requires an *a priori* statement of the facts that are to be the target of the theory:

Many people today are engaged in the attempt to construct linguistic theories. My view is that an important difficulty with all such attempts is that there is not a good a priori statement of the full range of known facts which a theory must handle. To the extent that theories are formulated in the absence of explicit awareness of this range of facts, they are dreamlike. (205)

I plan on returning to this point in my discussion of data-first approaches to linguistics in Chapter 3, but I don't mind giving away the punchline now: This attitude is deeply confused. Science begins with some pre-theoretical domain of interest, but the phenomena of interest in this domain are certainly not complete or set in stone (certainly not a priori!) and the phenomena of interest can change radically as the theory progresses. Furthermore, many phenomena which we initially take to be the target of our theory turn out not to be explananda of the theory after all. Consider, for example, the case of polio, which I will discuss in Chapter 3; many of the phenomena that we initially called "polio" turned out to be caused by something other than the polio virus.

The generative semantics research program collapsed rapidly (it was probably out of steam by 1972), and how could it not collapse given the kind of sweeping set of phenomena that they tried to bring under the theory of grammar. It is not my intention to get into the sociology of science, but there is a very interesting question about the pros and cons of their effort. On the one hand some of the most brilliant linguists of the last 50 years sank with the program, and not all of them contributed to generative linguistics again after the demise of the program. On the other hand, they did push the envelope and while not everything they explored could be incorporated under the umbrella of generative linguistics, a surprising amount of it subsequently has been.[4] The point being that perhaps we want some members of the research community to try and expand the target of investigation, even if the effort is philosophically misguided and on balance a failure.

I don't mean to make it sound like generative semantics failed simply because its advocates bit off more than they could chew or that their theory was unconstrained or that the Katz-Postal hypothesis was anchored in some very suspect philosophy of mind (all or which are probably true). There were finely targeted empirical objections as well. For example, in 1967 Chomsky presented a talk, which was later published in 1970 as "Remarks on Nominalization," which sat like a time bomb set to go off as soon as people began to read the work and follow its line of reasoning.

We can set up the "Remarks" argument like this: It is the claim of generative semanticists that sentences having similar meanings are derived from a common structure. For example, generative semanticists took structures having nouns like 'refusal' and 'belief' to be transformationally derived from structures having the verbs 'refuse' and 'believe'. This is certainly a natural thing for a generative semanticist to think—the words have closely related meanings, and if similar meanings imply a common source (at DS or some level of semantic representation) then what could be more natural than to think than the nouns are transformationally derived from the verbs?

---

[4] Personally, I've been deeply influenced by their work in natural logic (see Ludlow 1995, 2002b), and have collaborated with Richard Larson and Marcel den Dikken (1997) on a proposal due to Ross and McCawley that there is an implicit clause (and verb 'have') in a sentence like 'John wants a unicorn'—that is that at some level of representation it has a structure like [s John wants [s John has a unicorn]]. The difference is that while Ross and McCawley took the superficially simpler structure to be derived from the more complex one (which they took to be its D-structure), we took it to be a positive thesis about its SS representation.

The difference between the newer proposals and the older ones tracks the difference between the generative semanticists and the so-called "interpretivists" of that period. The former took syntactic forms to be generated from, in effect, the language of thought (in the sense of Fodor 1975). The interpretivists argued for a kind of autonomy of syntax and argued that interpretation would take place on SS representations—or perhaps a level of representation that was downstream from SS. And of course, the most important element to all of this is that the mapping from DS to SS must be tightly constrained.

In "Remarks," Chomsky makes the case that some nouns come from verbs, but that not all of them do. So, Chomsky was happy to argue that gerundive constructions like 'John's believing in God' is derived, but 'John's belief in God' is not. Similarly 'John's refusing the offer' is derived, while 'John's refusal of the offer' is not.

Here is the argument.

First, gerundive nominals occur with aspectual verbs while so-called derived nominals cannot. Thus consider the contrast between (12) and (13).

(12)   John's having criticized the book
       John's having been refusing the offer just when Trump arrived.

(13)   *John's having criticism of the book
       *John's having been refusal of the offer

Second, gerundive nominals take adverbs before the gerund while so-called derived nominals take adjectives.

(14)   John's sarcastically criticizing the book
       John's emphatically refusing the offer

(15)   John's sarcastic criticism of the book
       John's emphatic refusal of the offer

Third, the gerundive nominals occur in subject raising and dative shift, but the same is not true of the so-called derived nominals.

(16)   its being certain that John will win (subject raising) →
       John's being certain to win

       John's giving the book to Bill (dative shift) →
       John's giving Bill a book

(17)   the certainty that John will win ↛
       *John's certainty to win

       John's gift of a book to Bill ↛
       *John's gift of Bill a book

If 'certainty' and 'gift' are transformationally derived, why don't they behave like the gerundives do?

On top of all that, the relation between so-called derived nominals and their corresponding verbs is highly irregular. Not every verb has a corresponding noun. Why should this be if this is supposed to be a productive process? Furthermore, when we do have verb–noun correspondences the meaning relation is often obscure (consider 'do'/'deed' and 'ignore'/'ignorance').

Other linguists weighed in with additional arguments. For example Bach (1970) took aim at the pronominalization transformation in his paper "Problominalization" pointing out that it would lead to an infinite regress with so-called Bach-Peters sentences like (18).

(18)   Every pilot who shot at it hit some MiG that chased him

It seems that the DS for this would have to be (18′).

(18′)   Every pilot who shot at *some MiG that chased him* hit some MiG that chased *every pilot who shot at it.*

But these can't be the base representations, because they too have pronouns (which by hypothesis were derived) and so we are off on a regress of exponentially larger base forms.

Jerry Fodor (1970) also got into the mix with his paper arguing against "kill" being derived from "cause to die". One simple version of his argument is this: If you attach a temporal adverb to the biclausal structure you get an ambiguity, but you do not get such an ambiguity if you attach it to the single clause structure, as the following contrast shows.

(19)   Uma caused Bill to die yesterday

(20)   Uma killed Bill yesterday

Sentence (19) could be true even if Bill died today and not yesterday (perhaps Uma administered a slow acting poison yesterday).

Returning to "Remarks on Nominalization," probably the most significant contribution in Chomsky's paper was the introduction of so-called *X-bar theory*—a proposal that at once gave an account of the apparent similarity between verb phrases and noun phrases, offered a natural way of stating rules and generalization that were cross-categorial, and ultimately led to a way of simplifying the phrase structure component of the grammar.

Recall that in the Standard Theory the DS representations are generated from a series of phrase structure rules like the following.

$VP \rightarrow tense\ V'$
$NP \rightarrow det\ N'$

The insight of X-bar theory was that you could state these kinds of relations in a more general way if you thought in terms of phrases, heads, specifiers, and complements.

For example, obviously enough, VP, NP, AP, and PP indicate *phrases* (verb phrase, noun phrase, adjectival phrase, and prepositional phrase respectively). The categories V, N, P, and A are heads. The complement of the phrase is another phrase. So, for example, consider the structure in (21).

(21)

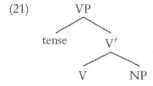

In this structure, V is the head, NP is the complement, and tense is the specifier.

Chomsky argued that we can generalize these structures in the following way, where X is any head (V, N, A, or P):

$S \rightarrow N'' V''$
$X'' \rightarrow \text{Spec-}X' X'$
$X' \rightarrow X \ldots$ ('...' indicating possibly another X^n phrase, for example an NP or PP)

Now here comes a very interesting insight. We can state important constraints on phrase structure and movement rules by having them apply to X' level taxonomy—that is, we can state general constraints that only make reference to heads or specifiers or complements. For example, one generalization that we will return to when we look at the Principles and Parameters framework is the idea that languages tend (with obvious exceptions like German) to be either head-initial (head to the left) or head final (head to the right).

Additionally, Chomsky suggested that the traditional categories of V, N, A, and P might be analyzed as being bundles of features—to a first approximation $\pm$N and $\pm$V. The resulting paradigm is the following:

	+N	−N
+V	A	V
−V	N	P[5]

The use of N and V to describe the features is probably confusing—Chomsky could just as easily have used 'foo' and 'bar' as labels for these features. Indeed, subsequent authors such as Jackendoff (1977) explored the idea that the features were $\pm$*subject*, $\pm$*object*, and $\pm$*det*. The point of interest for us is that Chomsky was effectively proposing a kind of sub-atomic approach to syntactic categories (this wasn't new in generative *phonology*—phonemes had long been thought of as bundles of features). On the one hand this took the description of the property of language ever further away from the kinds of properties that were in some sense directly perceivable, but on the other hand it allowed linguists more easily to state generalizations that cut across traditional grammatical categories—some linguistic properties might apply to elements that are −N, for example (we will see an example of this in a bit).

It is interesting to reflect on the fact that Chomsky's work was moving in this "lexicalist" direction at a time when generative semanticists continued to expand the

---

[5] This cell is blank in Chomsky's original proposal, but subsequent work filled out the paradigm.

expressive power of their transformations (or projection rules) to incorporate larger and larger classes of data. Chomsky was clearly moving in the opposite direction; far from extending the transformational component to phenomena like synonymy and selectional restrictions, he was putting the brakes on its application even to nominals like 'refusal' and 'criticism'—nominals that were *considered* to be so obviously the result of transformational processes that it was packed into their labels: "derived nominals"!

While generative semanticists were taking the tool of transformations and extending it in less and less restricted ways to broader classes of phenomena, Chomsky was looking for probes to test the limits of that tool. "Remarks on Nominalization" was an effort to show some of those limits. As it turns out, "Remarks" was only the beginning.

The Extended Standard Theory

Ross's (1967) work on island constraints ushered in a gold rush of researchers looking to discover new transformations and island effects. But the gold rush, while productive, had a down side.

The number of transformations had begun to proliferate in a way that generative linguists found troubling. Why troubling? Early on in the development of generative grammar, Chomsky had made a distinction between the *descriptive adequacy* and the *explanatory adequacy* of an empirical linguistic theory (see Chomsky 1965, 1981, 1986). In particular, if a linguist theory is to be explanatorily adequate it must not merely describe the facts, but must do so in a way that *explains* how humans are able to learn languages; linguistics was supposed to be embeddable into cognitive science more broadly. But if this is the case then there is a concern about the unchecked proliferation of rules—such rule systems might be descriptively adequate, but they would fail to account for how we acquire a language-specific grammar (perhaps due to the burden of having to learn all those language-specific rules).

A broad range of researchers in the field thought that the Ross constraints were simply too random a collection to be plausible, and they sought ways to unify them under some simpler explanation. Not surprisingly, Chomsky was in the middle of this effort, casting it as a way of finding more general conditions on transformations (i.e. general constraints on movement) with the goal of reducing the complexity of the grammar. One ingenious hypothesis advanced in Chomsky (1973) was that we might be able to cover a large number of the facts by replacing *all* the specific transformations with a single movement rule (initially it was *move-NP* but this would soon be generalized to "move anything anywhere") and replacing all (or at least most of) the island constraints with a handful of abstract general constraints—to a first approximation, the following three constraints on movement:

Subjacency: Very roughly, an element cannot cross both an S and an NP node in a single movement. This is effectively a generalization of the Complex Noun Phrase Constraint discussed above. Consider (5′) which is (5) represented at a finer level of detail. Notice that both an NP and an S node have been jumped in the extraction from the complex noun phrase 'the woman who illustrated the book':

(5′)   ⋆That's the book . . . [$_{NP}$ the woman who [$_S$ illustrated ___]]

Specified Subject Condition:

No rule can involve X, Y in the structure
$$\ldots X \ldots [_a \ldots Z \ldots -WYV \ldots]$$
where Z is the specified subject of WYV in a.

This can be thought of as a generalization of the Sentential Subject Condition, which accounted for the contrast between (8) and (9), and extends also to the contrast between (22) and (23), where (23) has a specified subject and (22) only a null subject. Hence in (23) 'the candidates' cannot be linked with 'each other'.

(22)   The candidates expected [PRO to defeat each other].

(23)   ⋆The candidates expected [the soldier to defeat each other].

The Specified Subject Condition also accounts for the contrast between (24) and (25), on the hypothesis that 'John' is behaving as a kind of intervening subject in (24), but not in (25):

(24)   The men saw [$_{NP}$ the pictures of each other]

(25)   ⋆The men saw [$_{NP}$ John's pictures of each other]

Tensed-S Condition:

No rule can involve X, Y in the structure
$$\ldots X \ldots [_a \ldots Y \ldots]$$
where a is a tensed sentence.

The tensed-S Condition accounted for the contrast between (26) and (27) by blocking the possibility of a binding relation between 'the candidates' and 'each other'. It does this because the lower clause "that each other would win" is tensed.

(26)   The candidates expected each other to win.

(27)   ⋆The candidates expected that each other would win.

This version of the theory became known as the *Extended Standard Theory* (EST). Of particular interest to the philosophy of linguistics, I think, is the fact that these constraints were becoming much more distant from the routine descriptions of language that we learn in grammar school (involving words and word order and theoretical notions like subject and predicate), so that while there were fewer constraints, it seemed ever less plausible that language learners *consciously* learned them. It became clear that the kinds of rules deployed by language users were not learned at mother's knee, but more plausibly prewired in us, or were perhaps artifacts of other prewired aspects of our cognitive architecture.

Two subsequent additions to the EST led to the criticism that, with those additions, EST was effectively recapitulating generative semantics efforts to link syntactic forms with meanings. These developments were the introduction of trace theory and the introduction and development of a level of representation called LF (to suggest logical form).

Earlier we represented the site where a moved constituent had been with an underscore "_", and as I indicated at the time this was just for heuristic purposes. A number of linguists (e.g. Postal 1970, Ross 1969, Emonds 1970) had suggested that there might be some benefit to leaving something behind—an empty node (Emonds) or a "doom marker" (Postal and Ross).

Chomsky (1973) proposed treating the extraction site as being a "trace" that would be bound either by the moved WH word or the quantified noun phrase that moved out of the position. This idea was developed in Wasow (1972) and Chomsky (1975b).

Philosophers of course immediately like this idea, since it makes SS representations look plausibly like tree-shaped versions of formulae of first order logic. In fact, Reinhart (1976) argued that one could define a notion of syntactic scope off of these tree structures using the notion of c-command as follows.

Let's say that a node α in a tree dominates a node β just in case there is a direct downward path from α to β. Then a node α in a tree *c-commands* a node β just in case the first branching node dominating α dominates β. Or to put it in simple terms, if you want to know what a node α c-commands, you go to α's mother node; everything below that mother node is c-commanded by α. The next step is to hypothesize that the c-command relation effectively plays the same role as scope in formal logic. In other words, perhaps c-command just is scope.

You can see why some linguists thought that this might be a jazzier form of generative semantics. It looks like the new trace-laden structures are being introduced in order to account for meanings. Of course, the problem with generative semantics was never that it attempted to account for meanings. From the beginning, generative linguists had been explicit about wanting to account for form-meaning pairs. This was one of the key points on which they had broken away from American structuralism after all. The problem with generative semantics was not the interest in meanings, but rather that the mechanisms were wildly unconstrained, the class of phenomena targeted by the theory was too large, and the Katz-Postal hypothesis just wasn't working.

Still, if trace was to be introduced, it would have to be empirically fruitful—that is, it would have to integrate with the explanatory structure of the syntactic theory and yield some theoretical discoveries in the bargain. As it turns out, the introduction of trace met both of the desiderata. Examples of this integration included *weak crossover* and *movement asymmetry*.

Crossover facts had been initially noticed in Postal (1971): In example (28) 'who' and 'him' can be understood as coreferential while in (29) this is not possible.

(28)   Who said Mary kissed him?

(29)   Who did he say Mary kissed?

Wasow's contribution was to note that these facts could be explained by the introduction of trace theory. When we look at these structures with trace introduced, we get the following distribution of facts.

(30)   Who$_i$ [e$_i$ said Mary kissed him]

(31)   *Who$_i$ [he$_i$ say Mary kissed e$_i$]

We can then hypothesize that the coreferential reading in (31) is blocked for the same reason it is blocked in a sentence like (32).

(32)   *He$_i$ said Mary kissed John$_i$

One early way of characterizing this is as the "leftness condition" (Chomsky 1976): A variable cannot be the antecedent of a pronoun to its left (as it would have to generate the missing binding relations in (31) and (32)).

   Meanwhile, Fiengo (1977) argued that a large class of movement asymmetries could be accounted for if we thought of traces as behaving like bound anaphors. For example, contrast (33) and (34).

(33)   John likes himself

(34)   *Himself like John

The general account for the behavior of reflexives is that they must be c-commanded by their antecedents (within a particular local domain). Well, if traces must also be c-commanded, then any movement that involved moving an element lower in a clause would result in a structure that violates this principle, because if an operator went lower it would no longer c-command its trace.

   Chomsky had gone out on a limb by proposing that all the transformations could be swept away in favor of a rule that one can move anything anywhere. Fiengo's observation helped vindicate this proposal by showing that with the introduction of trace and independently motivated principles governing reflexives, one can immediately rule out an entire class of movements—i.e., downward movement.

   Quite apart from whether the introduction of trace theory was leading the field back to generative semantics, some linguists worried about the introduction of so-called "phonetically unrealized syntax." Of course, strictly speaking, *no* syntax is phonetically realized. (We don't pronounce S or NP or VP and even the phonetic realization of word and sentence boundaries is dubious—words are often resyllabified, as when Long Islanders put the g in 'Long' with 'Islanders' as though saying 'Lawn Guylanders'). But some linguists did (and still do) have issues with the idea that there could actually be inaudible syntactic objects like traces. Linguists continue to offer approaches that attempt to avoid traces. These range from Cooper (1982)—titled "Binding in

Wholewheat★ Syntax (★Unenriched with Inaudibilia)" to recent work by Jacobson (1999). Now of course traces *can* be eliminated (just as Quine (1960b) showed that variables could be eliminated in first order logic). The question is whether there is good reason to eschew so-called inaudibilia in the syntax.

Concerns like this raise an issue that we will return to in Chapter 2, which is the question of whether there really is a deep and important difference between linguistic structures that have inaudibilia like trace and those that do not. As I will try to make clear in the next chapter, I think these worries about inaudibilia are largely misplaced, since they rest on a confusion about the nature of representations in cognitive science. As I will argue, the case for representations is not secured by whether they are conservatively faithful to what we imagine the articulated form of utterances must be, but rather by whether they play a helpful role in theory construction. In particle physics we don't posit quarks, spin, charm, and superstrings because they are faithful to what we see, but because they play valuable roles in our theories.

Similar considerations arise with respect to the distinction between theories that rely heavily on constraints on representations and those that rely heavily on constraints on movement. As I will argue in Chapter 2, it is an error to think that one of these approaches is conceptually more sound within cognitive science; we ought to adopt whatever approach makes our theorizing the easiest (this is the principle of methodological minimalism that I alluded to in the introduction). This becomes salient when we consider the way in which Chomsky and other generative linguists have shifted between constraints on representation and constraints on movement with relative ease.

For example, Chomsky (1976) ("Conditions on Rules of Grammar") argued that the presence of trace would allow linguists to radically rethink the constraints on movement that they had been proposing (e.g. Chomsky himself in 1973). In effect, most of the constraints on movement could be eliminated and replaced with constraints on representations. Indeed, as Chomsky saw it, the only real constraint on movement needed was subjacency. The rest of the work could be done by the specified subject condition, applying it now to traces.

This approach to constraints on representation was expanded in Chomsky's (1980b) paper "On Binding", which reformulated the constraints as follows.

The Opacity Condition (formerly the SSC): An anaphor cannot be free in the domain of the subject of NP or S′.

The Tensed-S Condition (renamed the Propositional Island Condition).

The Nominative Island Constraint: A nominative anaphor cannot be free in S′.

Here Chomsky also observed that given these constraints you could make the movement rule even more general—calling it *move-α* instead of *move-NP*. In effect, you can move anything anywhere and the constraints on representation (and the subjacency constraint on movement) would do the necessary work.

One of the interesting features of the Extended Standard Theory was the introduction of the level of representation LF (suggesting a similarity to the philosopher's notion of logical form).

DS → SS → LF

↓

Phonetic Form

The level LF involved a rule mapping from SS to LF. Called QR, the rule simply said "adjoin quantified NP to S." (May 1977)

For example, consider sentence (35) and its SS representation (35-SS).

(35)   John loves everyone

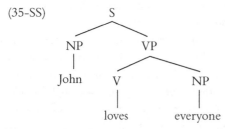

(35-SS)

To generate the LF representations we adjoin the NP to the topmost S node (creating a new S node) and leaving behind a co-indexed trace—in effect a bound variable.

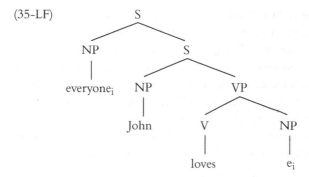

(35-LF)

Over the next decade or so a number of arguments were offered in support of QR and LF. Quite naturally, it was seen as a way of providing structural representations that could account for quantifier scope ambiguities. For example, consider sentence (36) and its SS representation.

(36)   Every man loves some woman

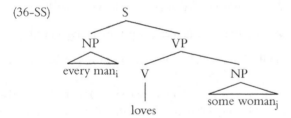

(36-SS)

Given that either NP could raise first, this predicted two possible LF structures for the sentence, as indicated in LF1 and LF2.

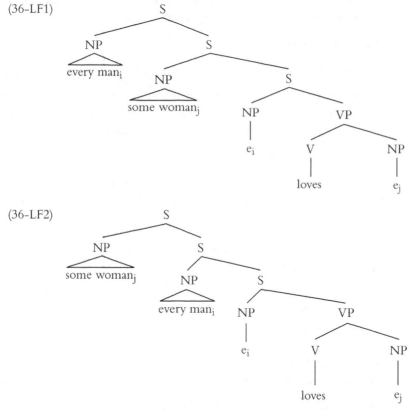

(36-LF1)

(36-LF2)

Another argument for QR was that it could account for de re/de dicto ambiguity. To see this, consider (37) and the two resulting scope LF representations (37-LF1) and (37-LF2). In the case of (37-LF1) the quantifier takes scope outside of the attitude verb and generates the de re reading. In (37-LF2) it retains scope inside the attitude verb (by adjoining to the lower S) yielding the de dicto reading.

(37)   John believes that a man is following him

(37-LF1)   de re: [$_S$ (a man)$_i$ [$_S$ John believes that [$_S$ e$_i$ is following him]]]

(37-LF2)   de dicto: [$_S$ John believes that [$_S$ (a man)$_i$ [$_S$ e$_i$ is following him]]]

Other arguments were more subtle. For example, consider the crossover facts adduced by Higginbotham (1980).

Higginbotham argued that there was a contrast between (38) and (39), in that (interpreting the sentence with binding relations as specified by the indices) we judge the interpretation corresponding to (38) to be awful, but the interpretation corresponding to (39) significantly better (actually, the judgments about (39) have been disputed, an issue that we will return to in Chapter 3; for now just let me say that if you are having trouble getting the reading it helps to stress 'saw').

(38)   *Who$_i$ did his$_i$ sister see e$_i$

(39)   His$_i$ sister saw John$_i$

Higginbotham suggested that the relevant generalization here was the again leftness condition of Chomsky (1976), which, recall, was that "a trace cannot be the antecedent of a pronoun to its left". Given this generalization, consider (40).

(40)   His sister saw everyone

This sentence cannot mean that everyone is such that his sister saw him. The explanation is that if we propose QR, the leftness condition will automatically rule out (41).

(41)   *[everyone$_i$ [his$_i$ sister saw e$_i$]]

Cross-linguistic evidence for LF was introduced by Huang (1982). Suppose that in Chinese, as in English, the following facts hold:

(42)   'believe' takes only [−WH] complements (that is, complement clauses without WH words)
I believe [Bill left]
*I believe [who left]
Who do you believe [e left]?
*Do you believe [who left]?

(43)   'wonder' takes only [+WH] complements
*I wonder [Bill left]
I wonder [who left]
* Who do you wonder [e left]?
Do you wonder [who left]?

(44) 'know' takes both kinds of complements
      I know [Bill left]
      I know [who left]
      Who do you know [e left]?
      Do you know [who left]?

Now consider the following facts from Chinese.

(45) Zhangsan xiang-zhidao [ta muqin kanjian shei]
      Zhangsan wonder   his mother see   who

This must be interpreted as an indirect question as in (45').

(45') 'Zhangsan wondered [who his mother saw e]'

(46) Zhangsan xiangxin [ta muqin kanjian shei]
      Zhangsan believe   his mother see   who

This must be interpreted as a direct question as in (46').

(46') 'Who did Zhangsan believe [his mother saw e]'

(47) Zhangsan zhidao [ta muqin kanjian shei]
      Zhangsan knows his mother see who

This may be interpreted as either an indirect or a direct question, as in (47'–47'').

(47') 'Zhangsan knows [who his mother saw e]'

(47'') Who does Zhangsan know [his mother saw e]'

Huang's insight was that these are precisely the results we would expect if we supposed that the WH elements were moving between SS and LF. The WH elements are in the lower clause at SS, but if the verb demands a −WH complement, the WH element is forced to move at LF, yielding a direct question interpretation. If the verb demands a +WH complement, the WH word must stay in place yielding an indirect question interpretation, and if it allows both complements then both readings are possible. I won't go into details here, but Huan noted other interesting effects of this invisible operator movement, including the weak crossover effects we noted above.

Perhaps the most compelling argument for LF came from the phenomenon of "antecedent contained deletion," initially noted in Ross (1969), Bouton (1970), and Sag (1976). Consider (48).

(48) John suspected everyone that Mary did

If the deleted VP is simply reconstructed, we get the following.

(49) John suspected everyone that Mary <u>suspected everyone that Mary did</u>

But now we have begun an infinite regress. An ellipsed VP must be inserted for 'did' again (presumably the VP 'suspected everyone that Mary suspected everyone that Mary did), leaving yet another ellipsed VP to be reconstructed.

Adapting a proposal from Sag (1976), May (1985) proposed the following. Suppose that QR takes place before the VP is reconstructed, so that the application of QR to (49) is (49'):

(49')   (everyone$_j$ that Mary did)$_i$ John suspected e$_i$

After reconstruction of the VP we now get (49'') which has just the right interpretation (everyone who is such that Mary suspected them, is such that John suspected them):

(49'')   (everyone$_j$ that Mary suspected e$_j$)$_i$ John suspected e$_i$

As Larson (1987) showed, this can be extended to free relatives with missing prepositional phrases. Consider the following contrast:

(50)   I'll live in whatever town you live

(51)   *I'll live in that town you live

Larson's explanation was that 'whatever town you live' is a QP with a deleted PP and undergoes QR:

(50')   (whatever$_j$ town you live [PP])$_i$ I'll live in e$_i$

and after reconstruction of the PP the result was the structure in (50''):

(50'')   (whatever$_j$ town you live in e$_j$)$_i$ I'll live in e$_i$

Finally, there are the Orson Welles sentences, noted in Ludlow (1985), which were inspired by watching Orson Welles hawking Paul Masson wine on television.

(51)   We will sell (no wine)$_i$ before its$_i$ time

Notice that the NP does not c-command the variable at S-structure

(52)

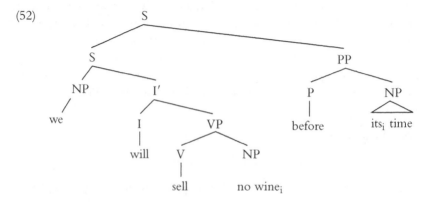

QR would account for the possibility of the very natural reading in which Orson Welles is saying no wine is such that we will sell it before it (that wine) is ready. Without QR one only predicts the reading in which one does not sell any wine before the appropriate time for some unspecified referent of 'it'.

Another interesting class of facts involves the inverse linking cases discussed in May (1977).

(53)   Someone from every city despises it

May noted that this is ambiguous between a reading in which every city is such that someone from it despises it, and one in which a well travelled person despises something. Notice that binding is not possible in the latter case, presumably because the quantifier does not c-command the pronoun.

(54-a)   (every city)$_i$[[Someone from e$_i$] despises it$_i$]

(54-b)   *[[Someone from (every city)$_i$] despises it$_i$]

In Chapter 7 we will look very briefly at alternatives to QR, principally to consider the claim that if you can avoid another level of representation (LF) and rules like QR the result is a simpler or more elegant theory. As we will see, I have my doubts about whether this is in fact the case.

Semantics

Looking back to the generative semantics era it is easy to forget just how in the dark we were about semantics. While Grice's theory of pragmatics was out there, it had not been fully absorbed by most philosophers and linguists. But just as significantly, it took work such as Lewis (1972) and the work collected in Montague (1974) to show how you might construct a compositional semantic theory that began by assigning semantic values to the lexical items and then show that (directed by the syntactic tree structures) the semantics could compute the semantic values of the larger constituents from the meanings of the lexical items.

To be sure there were disagreements about the character of the semantic theory. Montague and Lewis (and Partee and her students in linguistics) had advocated a kind of model-theoretic semantics in which meanings were set-theoretic objects that helped to account for the entailment relations between sentences.

Others such as Higginbotham (1985), following a suggestion of Davidson (1967), proposed an "absolute" truth-conditional semantics that dispensed with the notion of truth in a model (and for the most part kept the resources first order and otherwise minimal). Barwise and Perry (1983) advocated a form of *situation semantics*—the semantic values would be constructed from components of the actual world.

There was also wide variation about whether more work was to be done by the semantics or the syntax. That is, some semanticists argued that one should avoid "invisible" syntactic structure and that one could do this by introducing the appropriate model-theoretic resources into the semantics.

Despite all of this apparent variation, a widespread consensus emerged. All of these approaches are interpretivist. All of them took the semantics to be something that could "read" the meaning of the linguistic structure by computing it from the assignments of semantic values to the lexical items and computing the rest from the syntax. Thus, a clear consensus emerged around a basic thesis: that a compositional semantics assigns meanings to some level of linguistic representation (probably LF, perhaps SS). This is not to minimize the significance of the points of disagreement, and we will take up some of those in Chapter 6.

1.2 Government and Binding Theory

Work in the late 1970s was progressing in a number of disconnected albeit fruitful directions. For example, beginning with Jackendoff (1974) a great deal of work was done on X-bar theory. Philosophers and linguists like Fiengo, Higginbotham, and May worked on the development of LF and binding theory. Others continued to work on ways of accounting for the Ross Constraints. Work by Vergnaud introduced case theory into the mix.

In 1979, Chomsky gave a series of lectures in Pisa, Italy, in which he tied all of these threads together in an intricately interconnected package. The lectures were published as *Lectures on Government and Binding* in 1981 and the framework came to be known as Government-Binding Theory (or GB for short).

The theory consisted of several "modules"—called modules because their descriptions were related to narrow classes of specific linguistic phenomena. In a certain sense, however, 'module' was a funny name for them, since 'module' connotes a narrow bandwidth of communication between modules. As we will see, the interaction between modules was dense and complex, although the results were often breathtaking.

In Chomsky (1981) the components of the grammar were the following.

(i) **Bounding Theory**. This had to do with constraints on movement such as subjacency (S and NP together might be thought of as a bounding node).

(ii) **Government Theory**. This defines the relation between the head of a construction and the categories that depend on it. I will give an example in a bit, but among other things government theory interacted with trace theory in that a trace had to be "properly governed." Another example might be the notion of abstract case, which is assigned under government.

(iii) **Theta-Theory**. This dealt with the assignment and functioning of thematic roles, such as agent, patient, instrument, etc. This module interacted with government theory in that theta-assignment took place under government.

(iv) **Binding Theory**. This treated the properties that explain the relationship between grammatical elements such a pronouns, anaphors, names, and variables with their antecedents.

(v) **Case Theory**. This had to do with the assignment of abstract case—for example, nominative case might be assigned to an NP.

(vi) **Control Theory**. This determined the potential references of 'PRO'. So, for example, contrast 'John promised Bill PRO to leave' and 'John persuaded Bill PRO to leave.' In the first case 'PRO' is controlled by 'John' and in the second case it is controlled by 'Bill'.

(vii) **X-Bar Theory**. As discussed before, this was now doing the work previously done by the phrase structure component, in effect constraining the class of DS representations.

We saw that after the development of trace theory linguists searched for appropriate ways of stating structural constraints. GB provided a way of accounting for these effects, but also at the same time accounted for some puzzles in the binding theory. One interesting element of GB was the *Empty Category Principle (ECP)*, which accounted for subtle contrasts in the acceptability of a range of structures involving phonetically unrealized elements like trace and PRO. Formally, the ECP was stated as follows.

ECP: A trace must be properly governed

Proper Government: α properly governs β, if and only if α governs β, and
(i) α is N, V, or A or
(ii) α is co-indexed with β

Government was a phrase structure relation, closely related to c-command, but more local. To illustrate how the ECP worked, consider the contrast between (55) and (56).

(55)   [Who$_i$ do you think [e$_i$ arrived]]

(56)   *[Who$_i$ do you think [that [e$_i$ arrived]]]

In (56), the 'that' prevents the verb 'think' from properly governing the trace of movement. That is to say, the trace of movement is an empty category that in this case is not close enough to the upper V to be governed by it because of the intervening complementizer 'that'. The lower V does not c-command it (does not have scope over it) and hence also does not govern it. The wh-element 'who' is co-indexed with the trace, but is also too far away to govern it. From a semantic point of view the trace is sitting there perfectly interpretable, but a syntactic constraint has been violated. Traces (like other empty categories) for some reason like to be blanketed by nearby lexical predicates (V, N, A).

The ECP accounted for a very broad range of phenomena, including those involving LF quantifier movement. So, for example, consider the following contrast.

(57)   Someone believes that everyone is a spy

(58)   Someone believes everyone to be a spy

There seems to be a contrast here in that it is much easier to hear the 'everyone' as taking scope over 'someone' in (58) than it is in (57). If we think of the ECP as being an LF constraint, there is a natural explanation parallel to the explanations for the contrast between (55) and (56); in (57) the intervening 'that' prevents the trace of LF movement from being properly governed:[6]

(57′)   *[everyone$_i$ [Someone believes that [e$_i$ is a spy]]]

Binding theory obviously played an important role in GB, and it interacted with other components of the grammar in very interesting ways. Chomsky formalized the binding theory according to three principles: A, B, and C.

A. A bound anaphor must be bound in its governing category
B. A pronoun must be free in its governing category
C. A lexical NP must be free

One of the interesting subsequent discoveries is that we can sharpen these principles a bit if we avail ourselves of the following taxonomy.

+anaphoric −pronominal	bound anaphors, NP-trace
−anaphoric +pronominal	pronouns
−anaphoric −pronominal	lexical NPs, logical variables
+anaphoric +pronominal	PRO

Using this taxonomy, we can revise the binding theory in terms of its basic features:

A. A [+anaphoric] NP must be bound in its governing category
B. A [+pronominal] NP must be free in its governing category
C. A [−anaphoric −pronominal] NP must be free

One of the interesting consequences of this was the question of what happens to PRO in the binding theory. Since it is both [+anaphoric] and [+pronominal] it looks like it must be both free and bound in its governing category. But notice that there is a way out. PRO *could* occur, but it would have to occur in places where it has no governing

---

[6] This obviously can't be the whole story, given that in 'John believes that someone is a spy' it appears this could be a de re belief about some individual. One could argue that this means that 'someone' has at least escaped the scope of 'believes' and this should leave the trace ungoverned. Alternatively one could argue that this reading is not generated scopally in this case.

category (otherwise it would violate either principle A or principle B). Are there places where PRO could have no governing category? Well yes, if it is ungoverned, and the only place it can be ungoverned is in the subject of an infinitival clause (tense would govern it, so it cannot appear in a tensed clause—hence we can't say things like [John wants PRO gone]). This became known as *the PRO theorem*, and it does a nice job of illustrating the rich deductive structure of GB. Of course given that the PRO theorem has been abandoned (Chomsky himself dropped it in Chomsky 1995a) there is an interesting question about how such a sweet result could simply disappear (and therefore whether it was a result at all). This goes to the question of explanatory loss that happens as a theory advances (sometimes called Kuhn loss). We won't address that topic head-on, but it will come up from time to time in this book.

For linguists that were used to a theory that contained a stock set of explanatory tools (for example phrase structure rules and transformations) the new framework was shocking. Even the generative semanticists, although theoretically unconstrained, had placed all the explanatory work on the transformational component (or on clearly specified projection rules). Now that component had dissolved to virtually nothing ("move anything anywhere") and the constraints on movement did not come from a single set of explicit rules, but seemed to be the result of a cacophony of various unrelated factors.

Consider, for example, the account of passive in Chomsky (1981).[7] In this new account, passive was not the result of a single transformation (or two transformations if we count affix hopping). Rather passive was the product of a number of linguistic properties interacting in subtle ways.

Take a classic example of a sentence and its passive form.

(59)   Sam kissed Lilo

(60)   Lilo was kissed (by Sam)

'kiss', obviously, is a transitive verb. In this way it contrasts with the following intransitive verbs (verbs that don't take subjects but no objects).

(61)   *Lilo danced Sam

(62)   *Lilo seemed Sam

(63)   *Lilo arrived Mary

Accordingly, we can say that passivization converts a transitive verb into an intransitive verb. But it does more than that. It also converts the object of the transitive into the subject of the intransitive verb. Consider (59) and (60) again. 'Lilo' is the object in (59) but is converted into the subject in (60).

Another property of passives is that active and passive instances of the same verb differ in their form. To a first approximation, this difference is something like the

---

[7] My exposition of this case borrows from Roberts (1985).

addition of morpheme like '-ed' (as in 'kiss' → 'kissed'). In some cases, of course, there is a change in the stem verb ('sink' → 'sunk', 'sang' → 'sung').

As we saw earlier 'en' is the preferred affix for a broad class of cases (as in (64)), and linguists sometimes take /en/ to be the underlying form of the passive affix—it might be pronounced as '-ed' in some cases. Consider (64)

(64)   Sam was given a DVD by Lilo

Example (64) shows us that ditranstive verbs—verbs like 'give' that can take an indirect object—can passivize. But now consider the following interesting cases.

(65)   Sam was believed to be a musical genius

(66)   Sam was considered smart

(67)   Sam was spoken about

(65) and (66) tell us that so-called exceptional case-marking verbs can passivize. That is, verbs like 'believe' and 'consider' can case-mark an NP in a lower clause (as in 'I consider Lilo a singer'—tense isn't case-marking 'Lilo', the verb 'consider' is). (67) shows us that objects of PPs can passivize. We can generalize these observations as follows: the first NP case-marked by an active V cannot appear following V+en.

Pulling together all the observations made thus far, we have the following.

(i) Passives are case-intransitive
(ii) The subject of the passive is the object of the corresponding active
(iii) Passives are formed from actives by the affixation of /en/.

All of these properties can be accounted for by the interaction of case theory and theta-theory. So, for example, Chomsky (1981, 124–127) correlates the properties of passive with the following claims about case and theta-assignment in passive:

(68)   NP/S is not a theta position in passives

(69)   NP/VP is not assigned case in passives

DS is supposed to be a pure representation of argument structure, so the DS for our passive must be as in (70) (Lilo is the patient of kiss, and so must be governed by 'kiss' at DS).

(70)   [e (was) kiss+en Lilo]

Since passive doesn't assign case inside the VP, 'Lilo' must move into subject position, otherwise the case filter will be violated.

(70′)   [Lilo$_i$ was kissed e$_i$]

Of course this raises the question of where the properties in (68) and (69) come from. Rouveret and Vergnaud (1980) had proposed that /en/ was of category [+V]—in effect neutral between Verb and Adjective (recall our discussion of X-bar syntax earlier). Following standard assumptions in morphology (Lieber 1980, Williams 1981), the affix in effect becomes the head of the word and determines its categorial status. So, for example, if you affix /en/ to something that is [+V −N], the result is something that is [+V]—the categorial status of the affix trumps that of the stem.

Here we get a nice payoff from the introduction of the "subatomic" features like [+V] that Chomsky introduced in "Remarks on Nominalization." Deploying this technology a decade later, Chomsky proposed that case assigners are [−N]. Because main verbs are [+V −N] they can assign case. Passive morphology converts the verb into a non-case assigner by converting it into something that is [+V].

In effect, everything in the analysis of passive falls out from the assumption that the passive morpheme is [+V]. The account is complicated in one sense, but breathtakingly simple in another sense. You don't need a passive *transformation*, you just need the passive morpheme to have the feature [+V]. The rest is driven by independently motivated properties of the grammar—the case filter, theta-theory, standard assumptions about feature projection in morphology, proper governance, etc.

Just as the earlier generation of linguists broke from Chomsky during the "generative semantics wars," a similar break took place during the advent of GB theory. It isn't written about in quite such epic terms because the debates were relatively more civil, but they were contentious for all that. One concern expressed by a number of generative linguists was that in the move to GB too much formal rigor had been sacrificed. One can see where this impression came from. Things were very tightly defined in linguistics up until GB, but Chomsky certainly hadn't laid out a stock of rules like he had in *Aspects*.

On the other hand, just because it hadn't been done doesn't mean it *should* be done (more on this in Chapter 7). It also doesn't mean that it *couldn't* be done. Johnson (1991) and Stabler (1992) both showed that it was possible to formalize GB syntax and use the formalization to construct natural language parsers. In fact, there was nothing particularly difficult about the formalization part. We will return to the formalization question (especially with respect to GB) in section 7.2.

1.3 The Principles and Parameters Framework

As we noted earlier, from the very beginning generative linguists supposed that they were investigating the mechanisms that explained macro-level phenomena. Even through Government and Binding Theory, however, there was little insight into the character of the mechanism itself. Generative linguistics had been able to identify a compelling stock of very interesting (indeed quirky) rules, but the field had no real handle on the underlying mechanism giving rise to those rules, and hence little insight into the structure of the object of investigation itself. This changed with the emergence of the Principles and Parameters framework. Indeed, Chomsky (2000a, 8) claimed that the P&P framework "gives at least an outline of a genuine theory of language, really for the first time." Commentators such as Smith (2000) went so far as to say that it is "the first really novel approach to language of the last two and a half thousand years."

The core idea of the P&P framework is this: Each human is born with a language acquisition device that is largely prewired, but which leaves open a handful of parameters—we can think of these parameters as toggle switches. When a child is exposed to linguistic data the parameters/switches are set, and the language the child learns is determined by the combination of parameters that have been set. Baker (2001) argues that the parametric theory provides us with a kind of periodic table that maps out the space of human languages and the relations holding between them. For example, Baker suggests that many of the apparently radical differences between English and Mohawk (an indigenous American language spoken in an area that now comprises parts of Quebec, Ontario, and New York) are determined by a single parameter setting (Baker's "polysynthetic parameter"). Baker also claims that thanks to the P&P framework the current historical position in linguistics is comparable to that of chemistry during the development of the first periodic table by Mendeleyev.

To illustrate the difference in perspective using an analogy from biology, traditional grammarians have been impressed by superficial similarities between languages, much like we might want to put whales and fish in the same taxonomy because they have the same shape and inhabit the same locations. But of course this would be an error; there are deeper differences that lead us to classify whales as mammals. On Baker's version of the principles and parameters model, the parametric settings of English and Indonesian are nearly identical, with Edo and Khmer being closer relatives to English than French is. A systematic attempt to integrate the Principles and Parameters framework into the theory of language acquisition has subsequently emerged and an industry studying the role of parameters in language acquisition has likewise emerged in psycholinguistics (see Lightfoot 1993 and Hyams 1986 for surveys).

A good example of a parameter, originally due to Rizzi (1982), is one that involves subjacency. Recall that Chomsky's initial account of subjacency effects was that an NP could not simultaneously extract from both an NP and an S node. Rizzi noticed that the variation between extraction facts in Italian and English could be accounted for if we hypothesized that the relevant bounding node in Italian was NP and so-called S' (recall that S' is the node that has for its daughters the complementizer 'that' and the S that it introduces for its daughters). Thus the core principle of subjacency would be stable across languages, but there would be a "subjacency parameter" as to what the bounding nodes would be in different languages.

The interesting thing about the principles and parameters model is that it seeks to find deeper level parameters that can account for a broad range of macro-level phenomena. Consider the following illustration from Baker (2001), citing early work by Richie Kayne and Luigi Rizzi.

The simplest Italian sentences look very much like the simplest English and French sentences. So, for example, we have the following paradigm.

(71) Jean arrivera (French)
Jean will-arrive

(72) Gianni verrà (Italian)
Gianni will-come

Italian falls outside of the English/French paradigm in that the subject can follow the verb. Thus we have the following contrast:

(73) Verrà Gianni
will-come Gianni

(74) *Arrivera Jean
will-arrive Jean

A second difference between English/French and Italian is that the latter is what linguists call a "pro-drop" language; in cases where we might use a pronoun to refer to someone who is already salient in the discourse, Italian allows (favors) that the pronominal element drops out altogether. Thus we have the following contrast.

(75) Verrà (Italian)

(76) *Arrivera (French)

So far the differences under discussion would be obvious to anyone what had both French 101 and Italian 101, but as Rizzi and Baker stress, the languages differ in more subtle ways too.

For example, a third difference between English/French and Italian is exemplified by the following paradigm. Consider how we might form a question from a sentence like (77)

(77) Chris will see someone in the park

In English, we replace 'someone' with the WH-word 'who' (or 'whom' if you prefer) and front it as in (78).

(78) Who will Chris see ____in the park?

French and Italian work like this in simple cases too. But now consider a more complex sentence like (79) and the French example (80).

(79) Who did you say that Chris saw ____in the park?

(80) Qui veux-tu que Marie épouse ____?
Who want-you that Marie marries ____?

In both of these examples the position being questioned is the object position—the person seen or the person married. But now notice what happens when we question the subject position.

(81)   *Who did you say that ____saw Chris in the park?

(82)   *Qui veux-tu que ____épouse Jean?

This is in contrast with the Italian case, where we can question the subject position with no problem.

(83)   Chi credi che ____verrà?
       Who you-think that ____will come?

The French and Italian versions can be repaired by avoiding the complementizers 'that' and 'que'. In English we simply drop the complementizer and in French we can convert it to 'qui' as in (81′) and (82′).

(81′)   Who did you say ____saw Chris in the park?

(82′)   Qui veux-tu qui ____épouse Jean?

A fourth difference between languages like French and English on the one hand and languages like Italian and Spanish on the other hand is that the former require that every tensed clause must have a subject of some kind. So, for example, in English and French we introduce a "pleonastic it" in cases like the following:

(84)   It is raining (English)
       Il pleut (French)

(85)   Piove (Italian)
       Lleuve (Spanish)

And indeed, it turns out that every language we know of goes one way or the other on this point. Some languages (like French, English, Edo) require that tensed clauses have subjects. Other languages (like Italian, Spanish, Romanian, Japanese, Navajo) don't have this requirement.

As Baker notes, the contribution of Chomsky, Kayne, and Rizzi was to show that all of these macro-level effects fall out from a single parameter—the Null Subject Parameter. The first and fourth cases we discussed fall out straightforwardly from this parameter: Because Italian and Spanish are null-subject languages they needn't bother with introducing subjects (hence 'verrà' is fine by itself) and pleonastic subjects need not be introduced in weather sentences (hence stand-alone 'piove').

What about the second paradigm? We said that English and French don't allow the subject to follow the verb, but this isn't exactly correct. The Null Subject Parameter doesn't prohibit the subject from moving to the end of the sentence; it merely requires that we introduce a replacement subject of some form, and of course we can do this in both French and English. Hence the following are fine:

(86)   There appeared a boat on the horizon

(87)   Il est arrivé trois hommes.
         It is (has) arrived three men.

The explanation for the third paradigm is simply that if a language does not allow null subjects then any tensed clause must have a subject. Hence examples like (81) and (82) are unacceptable in English and French. Notice that this only applies to subjects. French and English don't require that sentences have objects. Hence we feel no compulsion to say 'It rained it'.

Chomsky (1981) suggested that these and two additional paradigms all fell out from a single parameter and suggested that this greatly simplified the language acquisition process for children. Simply by being exposed to a sentence like 'It is raining' or alternatively 'piove' is evidence for setting the null subject parameter. The resulting cascading effects were what Chomsky called a "parametric cluster."

As Chomsky observed, viewed from the macro level there are a number of possible variations. There is no reason why a language couldn't be pro-drop but prohibit the questioning of object positions. Strictly speaking, just based on the six facts related to this parameter, there could be $2 \times 2 \times 2 \times 2 \times 2 \times 2 = 64$ different Romance languages. But in reality there are only two—the French-like languages and the Italian-like languages.

Interestingly, the parametric model seems to undermine the idea that the function of the language faculty is to be a mechanism for maximizing the communicative function of language. Recall that just a minor flip of a switch (caused, for example, by language contact) can have a cascading effect with the consequence that the resulting language is very different. Baker (2003) makes the case that, far from being a high fidelity copying system, the language faculty is functionally much closer to an encrypting system. He draws on analogies to real world encryption to make his case for the Babelizing nature of the language faculty:

Claims that a biological system has a particular function are often reinforced by comparing it to products of human engineering that have that function. When the two have detailed structural similarities, the claim that they have similar functions gains support, a classic example being the comparison between the vertebrate eye and a camera. The way human languages differ can be compared to cryptographic techniques of the 16th century. Sixteenth century cryptographers used a variety of techniques: they both replaced and rearranged symbols in systematic ways, and they performed these transformations both at the level of letters and at the level of words and phrases. This layered complexity evolved over time with the explicit purpose of defeating particular code-breaking strategies (such as frequency analysis). Natural languages also differ from one another in ways that show layered complexity, using substitutions and arrangement at multiple levels. Many of the specific tricks of the early cryptographers have striking analogies in natural language. This gives credence to the notion that natural languages have the same concealing function as man-made ciphers.

Baker's point here is that it does not appear that the function of language is to aid or enable communication. Indeed, there are other less extreme proposals for the function of the language faculty. Chomsky has argued that the purpose—or at least the primary use—of the language faculty is for inner thought. Alternatively the selectional advantage might be something as simple as having a system that can generate certain metrical patterns—in effect for creating poetry.

An alternative, of course, is simply to say that UG is a kind of "spandrel" in the sense of Gould and Lewontin (1979)—that is not really *for* anything. It might be the by-product of the evolution of other cognitive faculties that did have some selectional value.

Discussions of this nature tend to get highly charged but this much is clear: Most of the interesting properties of the language faculty that we discussed in sections 1.1–1.3 don't appear to have anything to do with communication. The properties are weird, and quirky, and if anything they seem to inhibit communication in some respects.

This is what generative linguists do. They study these quirky features of natural language and attempt to deduce the mechanisms by virtue of which the language faculty gives rise to these phenomena. It does not appear that fidelity of copying or aiding communication could play any sort of role in the explanation of these properties, hence syntacticians look elsewhere for the answers.

1.4 The Minimalist Program

Still working within the general principles and parameters framework, Chomsky (1995a, 2000b) articulated a research program that came to be known as *the Minimalist Program*. The headline idea behind the Minimalist Program has been the working hypothesis that the language faculty is not the product of messy evolutionary tinkering—e.g. there is no redundancy, and the only resources at work are those that are driven by "conceptual necessity." Chomsky (2001b) has been drawn to D'Arcy Thompson's (1966) proposal that the core of evolutionary theory consists of physical/mathematical/chemical principles that sharply constrain the possible range of organisms. As Chomsky (2000a, 163) puts it, "physical law provides narrow channels within which complex organisms may vary" and natural selection is only one factor that determines how creatures may vary within these constraints. Other factors (as Darwin himself noted) would include non-adaptive modifications and unselected functions that are determined from structure. In this case, the idea would be that those principles not only constrain low level biological processes (like sphere packing in cell division) but also that such factors might be involved across the board—even including the human brain and its language faculty.

Here is a way to illustrate the project. We can think of linguistics as a theory of the system that human agents have by virtue of which the appropriate representations interfacing with the human perceptual/articulatory (P/A) system are paired with the appropriate representations interfacing with the human conceptual/intentional (C/I) system. The system linking these interfaces is the *minimal* system that satisfies "legibility" constraints or conditions imposed by both the P/A system and the C/I system. Following Hauser, Chomsky, and Fitch (2002) we can call this minimal system the *faculty of language narrowly construed* (FLN). Let's call the level of representation that interfaces with the P/A system *PF* (for phonetic form) and let's call the level of representation that interfaces with the C/I system *LF* (for logical form). We thus have the following picture:

P/A ↔ PF ↔ LF ↔ C/I

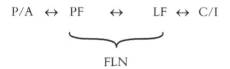

FLN

So the FLN is an optimally efficient wiring solution to the problem of linking these interfaces. One plausible story about the FLN is that it uses very simple operations like *merging* two elements (for example the words 'red' and 'ball') and moving elements as necessary (and only as necessary) to meet the interface legibility requirements. The hallmark of the resulting wiring solution is recursion, meaning that the process of merging elements in this way yields recursive structures.

What do I mean by recursion here? Consider the following toy phrase structure grammar.

(1) XP → XP ConjP (where X is I, D, V, or P)
(2) ConjP → Conj XP (where Conj is 'and', 'or')
(3) S (IP) → DP I′
(4) I′ → I VP
(5) DP → det NP
(6) NP → N′ (PP)
(7) N′ → (adj) N′
(8) N′ → N
(9) NP → NP CP
(10) CP → wh C′
(11) C′ → C S
(12) VP → V XP

As I am using the term 'recursion', rules 1, 7, 9 would be recursive rules because the rules "call themselves," and *combinations* of rules like 3–5–9–10–11 would be recursive, because the topmost rule in the derivation is called again lower in the derivation. I am calling the output of such rules (the trees generated by such rules) recursive *structures* because the structures have "descendent" nodes that are the same type as their ancestors. For example, I take the following to be recursive structures because a category S occurs within S in the first structure and N′ occurs within N′ in the second.

(88)

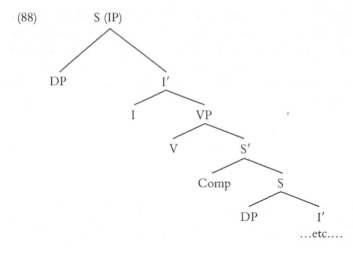

(89)

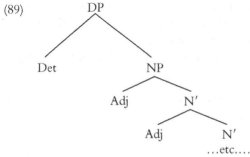

As we saw in sections 1.1–1.3, linguistic structures are more complex than this and in current grammatical theory they would not be the product of rules like those I specified in the toy grammar above.

Of course, a simple merge operation and the resulting recursive structures do not, by themselves, put strong constraints on linguistic theory—nature is full of various kinds of simple processes generating recursive patterns after all (for example spiral patterns in shells and galaxies)—and some of the most interesting properties of natural language (subjacency, for example, or the basic principles of binding theory) don't seem to have anything interesting to do with recursion by itself. So the interesting properties of language appear to fall out from the fact that the system yielding these recursive structures must also meet some rather strict interface conditions. If there are no constraints imposed by the interfaces, then nothing forces the interesting properties of language into relief—we just get vanilla recursive structures, and not the quirky structures we find in natural language.

This raises interesting questions about the nature of the interface. Here, the linguistics literature is thin on detail, but I think a plausible story can be told about how the need to be legible to the semantics puts constraints on the possible kinds of recursive structures.

To be as concrete as possible in our discussion of semantics let's assume a standard approach to interpretivist natural language semantics (in the sense of section 1.2), adopting the notation and basic theoretical background articulated in Heim and Kratzer (1998).

For our purposes we assume the basic elements of a semantic theory are elements of type e and t, where we can think of elements of type e as being entities or referents and elements of type t as being truth values. Predicates of the language can be thought of as functions that map from elements of type e to elements of type t. So, for example, the predicate 'food' can be thought of as a function that maps from individual entities onto true or false. More complex elements like adjectives can be thought of as mapping from function to function etc. To a first approximation, (and borrowing some online course notes from Barbara Partee) the picture is something like this.

Syntactic category	Semantic type (extensionalized)	Expressions
ProperN	$<e>$	names (*John*)
S	$<t>$	sentences
CN(P)	$<e, t>$	common noun phrases (*cat*)
NP	$<e>$	"referential" NPs (*John, the king, he$_i$*)
	$<<e, t>, t>$	noun phrases as generalized quantifiers(*every man, the king, a man, John*)
	$<e, t>$	NPs as predicates (*a man, the king*)
ADJ(P)	$<e, t>$	predicative adjectives (*carnivorous, happy*)
	$<<e, t>, <e, t>>$	adjectives as predicate modifiers (*skillful*)
REL	$<e, t>$	relative clauses (*who(m) Mary loves*)
VP, IV	$<e, t>$	verb phrases, intransitive verbs (*loves Mary, walks*)
TV	$<e, <e, t>>$	transitive verb (*loves*)
is	$<<e, t>, <e, t>>$	*is*
DET	$<<e, t>, <<e, t>, t>>$	*a, some, the, every, no*

Semantic rules for the lexical items specify the particular functions. To illustrate, let's use the notation [[α]] to indicate the semantic value of α, and consider a couple of examples of lexical rules by which the semantics specifies the meaning of an expression.

(90) [['Schleiermacher']] = Schleiermacher

(91) [['ponders']] = $\lambda x \in D_e$. true, iff x ponders

We can read (90) as saying that the semantic value of the name 'Schleiermacher' just is Schleiermacher, and (91) as saying that the semantic value of 'ponders' is a function from any object x in the domain of things of type e (individuals) onto truth or falsehood. It maps onto truth if and only if x ponders. Of interest to us a bit later will be the rules for the connectives, which we can give as follows:

(92) [['and']] = $\lambda p \in D_t$. [$\lambda q \in D_t$. true, iff p = q = true]

(93) $[[\text{'or'}]] = \lambda p \in D_t. \, [\lambda q \in D_t. \, \text{true, iff } p = \text{true or } q = \text{true}]$

(94) $[[\text{'not'}]] = \lambda p \in D_t. \, \text{true, iff it is not the case that } p = \text{true}$

To illustrate, (92) says that the semantic value of 'and' is a function that inputs a truth value, and yields a new function that maps from truth values onto truth values. In particular, it inputs a truth value p, yielding a new function which inputs a truth value q and outputs true just in case both p and q are true.

Now, for my money, the most interesting feature of formal semantics is discovering how much one can accomplish with such limited resources. You might think that given the infinite number of syntactic constructions you might encounter there must be an infinite number of semantic rules to interpret them, or at least an awful lot of rules. But once the lexical rules are in place we get by with interpreting all those structures just using a handful of very simple semantic rules. Following Heim and Kratzer (1998), let's characterize them as follows.

Terminal Nodes (TN): If α is a terminal node, then $[[\alpha]]$ is specified in the lexicon.

Non-Branching Nodes (NN): If α is a non-branching node, and β is its daughter node, then $[[\alpha]] = [[\beta]]$.

Functional Application (FA): If α is a branching node, $\{\beta, \gamma\}$ is the set of α's daughters, and $[[\beta]]$ is a *function* whose domain contains $[[\gamma]]$, then $[[\alpha]] = [[\beta]] \, ([[\gamma]])$.

Predicate Modification (PM): If α is a branching node, $\{\beta, \gamma\}$ is the set of α's daughters, and $[[\beta]]$ and $[[\gamma]]$ are both in $D_{<e, t>}$, then $[[\beta]] = \lambda x \in D_e.$ true iff $[[\beta]] \, (x) = 1$ and $[[\gamma]] \, (x) = 1$.

Predicate Abstraction (PA): If α is a branching node whose daughters are a relative pronoun and β, then $[[\beta]] = \lambda x \in D_e. \, [[\beta]]^x$

Now clearly this is just a first pass and I'm leaving out detail, but it won't matter for the discussion that follows. The point is that this semantics is rich enough to interpret all the structures that can be generated by the toy grammar I gave above. And then some. And this, to me, is impressive.

But now if we think of the semantics (or the semantics module) as being the locus of contact with the C/I interface, then these semantic rules determine the conditions for structures being legible. That is to say, if a structure is to be legible, then it must be a structure that can serve as an input for these rules. It must be visible to the rules.

For example, only binary branching and non-branching structures are visible to these rules—ternary branching structures are thus not legible. Furthermore, while these rules can "read" binary structures in which both daughters are nouns (as in 'foil ball') they cannot read structures in which there are pairs of referential expressions (expressions of type e). So these rules cannot read 'that that' or 'she she'.

But notice also that if some of these rules were missing then certain recursive structures would not be legible. For example:

If **Predicate Modification** was missing then recursive structures that involved noun–noun recursion would be out, as would structures involving NPs with recursively iterated PP modifiers, like 'dog in a city in a county in Texas...'

If **Predicate Abstraction** was missing, then recursive structures involving relative clauses would not be legible (at least on the Heim and Kratzer analysis of relative clause structures), since predicate abstraction is a device that takes a CP and converts it into an expression of type $<e, t>$. Without PA the structure corresponding to 'this is the cat that ate the rat that ate the cheese that...' would not be legible.

Of course, some recursive structures are made possible not by these basic semantic rules but by the lexical rules. Canonical examples of recursion involve the logical connectives.

So for example consider a lexical rule like the following, which is the 'and' used to conjoin predicates as in (sang and danced):

(95) $[[\text{and}]] = \lambda f \in D_{<e,t>}. [\lambda g \in D_{<e,t>}. [\lambda x \in D_e. \text{ true, iff } f(x) = g(x) = 1]]$

Without a lexical rule like this, then barring the introduction of conjunction reduction there would be no way to interpret the structures with conjoined predicates—for example a construction like 'She sings and dances and acts and...'.

We can put the point this way. Certain kinds of lexical rules are preconditions for a large class of recursive structures—for example, those involving logical connectives. To a first approximation, these are lexical rules that involve mapping from a function of a particular type onto a function of the same type. That is, the lexical rules must specify functions that are (i) higher order and (ii) type reflexive.

First order functions—for example those that are $<e, t>$—are not sufficient by themselves for recursive structures like those generated by our toy grammar to be legible. Higher order functions that are not reflexive are also not sufficient (by themselves) for recursive functions to be legible. For example determiners are higher order, but not reflexive in the sense I have indicated.

You can get recursion without type reflexivity, but only if you have a semantic derivation that forms a type reflexive theorem. So for example, sentential complements appear to be of this form: [John believes that Mary believes that...]. Successive application of rules can generate the type reflexive theorem. On the semantic end, what is permitting these recursive syntactic structures (like 'John believes that Mary believes that...') to be legible is what we could call a **derived type reflexive theorem**. In this case, what is allowing the recursive structure is that once axioms are combined in a derivation, the resulting step or theorem is type reflexive.

Summing up, we can chart out the preconditions for the legibility of recursive structures as follows.

PM: required for noun–noun compounds, and NP–PP recursion
PA: required for relative clause recursion

Type reflexive lexical rules: required for [adj [adj [. . . [N]]] recursion, logical connective recursion, etc.

Derived type reflexive theorems: required for sentential complement recursion

I don't mean to suggest that this approach to the interface is canonical. Rather, I'm trying to give a plausible story about how the interface might place constraints on the grammar and give rise to some of the linguistic phenomena (e.g. the kinds of recursive structures) that we observe. Are these kinds of interface constraints plus minimal operations like merge sufficient to account for the core phenomena that we canvassed in sections 1.1–1.3? Here work is preliminary—certainly too preliminary to evaluate—but suggestive. Kayne (2002) and Zwart (2002) have offered stories about deriving basic principles of binding theory within the minimalist framework, Collins (2002) has offered an account of phrase structure that supersedes X-bar theory, Hornstein and Uriagereka (2002) have explored minimalist explanations for facts that we would ordinarily take to be LF phenomena.

Not surprisingly, a number of philosophical themes have already emerged from the Minimalist Program. One topic has to do with the interface and the question of whether a naturalistic account of semantics can be given, as seems to be required by the theory. (I take this up in Chapter 6.) Another theme—one that was also central in the days of Generative Semantics—is the suggestion that it is better to explain fewer facts if one is interested in gaining deeper explanations. That is, the price of deeper understanding may be that some things we thought were the target of linguistics turn out not to be. (I take up this topic in Chapter 3.) Yet another theme that has emerged is the idea that the Minimalist Program has the advantage of being conceptually *simpler*. (I take up this topic in Chapter 7.)

Finally, one of the themes that has emerged from the Minimalist Program, is the suggestion due to Epstein and Seely (2006), that within the research program linguistic explanation is *derivational* rather than representational. By this they mean that it is the basic operations themselves that account for linguistic phenomena, and not constraints that we might state over linguistic representations. For example, in the work on binding theory by Kayne and Zwart cited above, the idea is that binding relations are not stated as relations between objects on a phrase structure tree but rather are determined by merging operations (the antecedent and trace are related by virtue of being merged before the antecedent moves).

At least for Epstein and Seely the pendulum has swung away from Chomsky's (1976) suggestion that most of the work could be done by constraints on representations (for example on relations between traces and their antecedents). We will take up this topic in the next chapter, but I don't mind providing a spoiler here. The dispute between derivational and constraint based representational theories in linguistics tends to have the hallmarks of an earlier dispute in computer science between those who advocated declarative languages (like Prolog) and those who advocated procedural languages (like C and its dialects). In computer science the consensus emerged that the dispute came to nothing, for the simple reason that at the lower levels the machines were doing pretty much the same thing whether the higher level language was procedural or declarative. The different kinds of programming languages provide us with different ways of reasoning about and programming the action of the machines—the best one is the one that is the easiest for us to use given the problem at hand.

I think a similar situation holds when we look at the difference between constraint based (representational) and derivational approaches to the theory of grammar. The different approaches do not reflect a deep difference in the structure of the mind/brain, but rather reflect different ways we can interpret what is happening. The choice may well depend upon the state of the theory at a particular moment (Chomsky's work, for example, seems to shift from being derivational to being constraint based and back depending upon the needs of the theory he is constructing at the moment). It is important that we not mistake aspects of the theory that are designed to help us theorize better for aspects that reflect basic properties of the mind/brain. It is especially important that we not deploy these aspects of the theory as first principles from which to theorize.

Of course, this issue is philosophically subtle, and before we can tackle it we need to sort out some questions about the ontology of linguistics. We turn to that work next.

2

The Ontology of Generative Linguistics

2.1 E-Language, I-Language, Ψ-Language

E-Language

Most generative linguists take the standard view of language as being orthogonal to their interests if not fundamentally incoherent. The standard view (a view routinely adopted by philosophers) takes languages as being independent abstract objects ("the English language" or "the French language") that we learn to some degree or other and which we then use for purposes of communication. Indeed, these abstract objects are typically considered to be "inventions" that humans developed specifically to enable communication.

For generative linguists, the problem with this view enters at the very beginning—when we think about what "speaking the same language" comes to. Typically, the question of who counts as speaking a particular language like German is determined more by political boundaries than facts about linguistic properties like those described in Chapter 1. For example, there are "dialects of German" that, from a linguistic point of view, are closer to Dutch than to "standard" German. A similar point holds for some standard assumptions about the supposed difference between official languages and dialects; the distinction doesn't cut much ice from the point of view of the structure of language. For example, in the Italian linguistic situation there are a number of so-called dialects only some of which are recognized as "official" languages by the Italian government. Are the "official" languages intrinsically different from the "mere" dialects? Not in any interesting linguistic sense. The decision to recognize them as separate languages is entirely a political decision. (As Max Weinreich is supposed to have said, "a language is a dialect with an army and a navy.") In this case, an "official language" is a dialect with substantial political clout and maybe a threat of separatism.

Nowhere is this more clear than in the linguistic situation in former Yugoslavia, a case also discussed in Devitt (2006). Before the dissolution of Yugoslavia, we often spoke of the language Serbo-Croatian. Now we speak of two distinct languages—Serbian and Croatian. Did something change? Did we finally recognize that there were two distinct languages all along? Well, American English and British English are at least as dissimilar as Serbian and Croatian so why don't we distinguish *those* languages as well? Obviously we might if we found it politically expedient to do so. Now of course it may be sensible to talk about languages individuated in this way (politically); the point is that this notion of language is not the target of generative linguistics.

Chomsky (1986) drew a distinction between two distinct conceptions of the nature of language, calling them I-language and E-language respectively. *I-language* is understood as referring to the language faculty, construed as a chapter in cognitive psychology and ultimately human biology. *E-language*, on the other hand, is a covering term for a loose collection of theories that take language to be a shared social object, established by convention, and developed for purposes of communication.

The notion of language we have been regarding with some suspicion here is in effect the E-language conception of language. Since much of the trouble comes in with the political dimension of language individuation, one might think that it will help to give up the talk of languages construed as E-languages, and retreat to talk about E-*dialects*. This doesn't solve the problem. To illustrate, Chomsky (2000a, 27) reports that in his idiolect the word 'ladder' rhymes with 'matter' but not with 'madder'. For many other speakers of English, the facts do not cut in this way. Do those people speak the same dialect as Chomsky or not? There is no empirical fact of the matter here either; it all depends on individuals' desires to linguistically identify with each other. Even appeals to mutual intelligibility will not do, since what we count as intelligible will depend much more on our patience, our ambition, and our familiarity with the practices of our interlocutors than it will on brute linguistic facts.

Even when our individuation of languages is keyed to apparent linguistic similarities rather than political borders it is not really clear that languages so individuated carry any explanatory interest—which is not to say that such notions of language are without utility. Chomsky (1994b; 2000a, ch. 2) has compared talk of languages in this sense to saying that two cities are "near" each other; whether two cities are near depends on our interests and our mode of transportation and very little on brute facts of geography. The notion of "same language" is no more respectable a notion in the study of language in linguistics than "nearness" is in geography. Informally we might group together ways of speaking that seem to be similar (relative to our interests), but such groupings have no real explanatory role in generative linguistics. This is not to say that generative linguists don't engage in talk about "English" and "English speakers." They certainly do, just as geologists use terms like 'near' when planning where they might conduct some research. Such talk is extremely useful (indeed, I am using it throughout this book) but it has to be understood as a rough gloss over a class of more or less similar linguistic phenomena—perhaps a population from which trained linguistic consultants more or less conform on some underspecified class of judgments of linguistic acceptability or form-meaning pairings, or better, a population of individuals whose language faculties are more or less in the same parametric states (in the sense of section 1.3).

If E-languages and E-dialects are not the targets of explanation in generative linguistics, is it possible to construct a notion of E-*idiolect*?—that is, can the target be idiolects individuated by external criteria like an individual's spoken or written language? (This seems to be a notion under consideration in Devitt (2006).) Apparently this will not work either. In the first place, you speak in different ways with different groups of individuals (for example, you use a different vocabulary among philosophers than among family members, or at least I do) and indeed at different stages of life (contrast your use of language at age 3 and age 30). Do all of these ways of speaking count as being part of the same idiolect? What unifies them other than that they are ways in which one happens to have spoken? Still worse, we certainly can't identify one's E-idiolect with some corpora of utterances and inscriptions, for these intuitively include speech errors and typos. On the basis of what can you say that a given hiccup is an error and not part of the spoken corpus of your E-idiolect? If we try and identify errors by appealing to your language community that lands us back in the problem of individuating E-languages and E-dialects; there is simply no fact of the matter that can help us to identify language communities in any meaningful way.

I-Language

On the I-language approach, however, the problem of individuating I-idiolects takes the form of a coherent empirical research project. Your idiolect (I-idiolect) is determined by the parametric state of a computational faculty; this faculty determines your linguistic *competence*. Speech production that diverges from this competence can be attributed to *performance* errors. Thus, the competence/performance distinction is another way of talking about the distinction between linguistic forms that are part of your grammar and those that are simply mistakes.

The case for the I-language/E-language distinction does not rest wholly on troubles with individuating E-languages, however. There are also features of our linguistic competence that seem to have no explanation in the social realm; for example, the I-language conception seems to be necessary to secure any account of the *productivity* of our linguistic competence—the fact that we are capable of producing and comprehending novel speech forms of unbounded length up to limits of memory and attention span. It also seems to be necessary to underwrite the *systematicity* of our linguistic competence—the fact that if we can comprehend the sentence 'Fido loves Fifi', we are pretty much guaranteed to comprehend a sentence of the form 'Fifi loves Fido'. Not only does our linguistic competence suggest *productivity* and *systematicity*, but it seems reasonable to think that our competence is underwritten by a *recursive* process of some form (as we saw in section 1.4). Thus, we happily produce and comprehend linguistic forms with patterns that seem to be the result of recursive processes: "This is the cat that ate the rat that ate the cheese that . . .".

Chomsky's choice of the term 'I-language' is playing off of several interesting features of the language faculty—what we might call the *three i*'s of I-language.[1]

---

[1] Thanks to Paul Pietroski for bringing this to my attention.

First, he is addressing the fact that we are interested in language faculty as a function in *intension*—we aren't interested in the set of expressions that are determined by the language faculty (an infinite set we could never grasp), but the specific function (in effect, grammar) that determines that set of expressions. Second, the theory is more interested in *idiolects*—parametric states of the language faculty can vary from individual to individual (indeed, time slices of each individual). Thirdly, Chomsky thinks of the language faculty as being *individualistic*—that is, as having to do with properties of human beings that do not depend upon relations to other objects, but rather properties that supervene on events that are circumscribed by what transpires within the head of a human agent (or at least within the skin).

I think that this last *i* can be separated out from the mix.

Ψ-*Language*

The distinction between individualistic and relational properties can be illustrated by the distinction between one's rest mass and one's weight. My rest mass is what it is simply because of my physical constitution. My weight depends on the mass of the planet or moon I am standing on.

It is natural to think that psychological states are like the former example, but as Burge (1986) argued, this is far from clear. A good case can be made that our psychological states are determined in part by our environmental embedding conditions. Let's call such a view about psychological states *externalism*. We can now distinguish two versions of externalism, which I will call *robust externalism* and *modest externalism*.[2] According to robust externalism, mental states actually have external objects as their constituents. For example, a desire for water might supervene on a relation between me and that substance in the external world that we call 'water'.

Modest externalism holds that psychological states supervene on intracranial states, but that those states are *individuated* widely. Donald Davidson (1987) has given a good example of this. If I am sunburned then my sunburn supervenes on a state of my skin; it doesn't supervene on a relation between my skin and the sun. However, being sunburned is different than having my skin damaged in precisely the same way by a chemical. One is a sunburn and the other is a chemical burn. In this case whether it is a sunburn or a chemical burn is determined by the *cause* of the burn.

Just to be extra careful, we need to distinguish two kinds of wide individuation here—*methodological wide individuation* and *constitutive wide individuation*. Methodological wide individuation concedes that we need to look outside in order to figure out the internal states of the system, but that those states really are just narrow states. On this approach, the external facts provide *evidence for* the internal facts but they play no role in the metaphysical grounding or determination of those facts. By modest externalism, I intend to be speaking of constitutive wide individuation—if those external states did

---

[2] Thanks to Jim Higginbotham for discussion here.

not hold then the internal states could not exist. My sunburn is a property of my skin, but without the sun, it simply could not be sunburned—no matter what kinds of chemical burns we manage to induce.

It is arguable, that many of our psychological states, ranging from perceptual states to our propositional attitude states, are individuated by reference to the external world. As I'll argue, even computational states might be individuated widely (what a machine computes is a function of its embedding environment and not the physics of the machine in isolation—more on this in sections 5.2 and 5.3).

For now though, I intend the term 'Ψ-language' to be neutral as to whether psychological states are individuated widely or narrowly (or both). When appropriate, I will distinguish between *wide Ψ-language* and *narrow Ψ-language*.

Of course, while psychological states may include external objects as part of their individuating conditions, almost all of the interesting questions involve the issue of *how we represent* those external objects and the cognitive mechanisms involved in how we come to represent them as we do. It is not so very interesting to say that a frog perceives a fly and therefore stands in a relational psychological state involving both it and the fly. We want to know the mechanisms at work and these will involve complex data structures and computations that may or may not be sensitive to whether the frog is perceiving a fly or a bit of rock.

I consider it plausible that generative linguistics should be concerned with the linguistic rules that we have, and that this in turn should be understood in terms of a computational system in our cognitive psychology, but I don't see that such a view entails that we have to understand human psychology individualistically. Certainly, the case for I-language outlined in this section placed a great deal of emphasis on the language faculty as a chapter in our psychology, but nowhere did it seem to require that psychology must be individualistic. We can happily talk about computing over rules without sliding into individualism. As we will see in section 6.1, this is saliently the case when we consider semantics.

To crystallize the opposing views here, it will be useful to rely on my distinction between I-language and Ψ-language, where the latter is a thesis about the language faculty that is part of our cognitive psychology, but which we do not suppose to supervene exclusively on intracranial facts. Like I-language, we can take Ψ-language to be a computational system that is part of our biological endowment; we simply remain neutral on the assumption that the relevant computational states supervene exclusively on individualistic properties.

2.2 Having Linguistic Rules and Knowing Linguistic Facts

The first time I saw Chomsky give a talk, it was on the topic of knowledge of grammar. At the time (around 1980) I could not understand why he was using the term 'knowledge' in describing our relation to linguistic rules. Like most philosophers, I assumed that, to a first approximation, knowledge was justified true belief. The linguistic rules that Chomsky was talking about were not the sorts of things that people *believed* even upon reflection (e.g. the rule *subjacency* that we discussed in section 1.1), nor was it clear that linguistic rules were the sorts of things that were true or correct, since there wasn't a question of having the wrong linguistic rules. You just have the rules that you do. Finally, talk of justification didn't make sense for grammatical rules; there is no issue of my getting the right rule in the wrong way (say from an unreliable teacher or peer). So linguistic rules weren't believed, they weren't true in any sense, and even if they were true and we did believe them there is no reason to think those beliefs would be justified. That is 0 for 3.

Things are different for a prescriptive grammarian, for in that case there *is* a question of knowing the prescriptive rules of your language. Maybe some sort of official academy of language or someone in a power relation with respect to you determines what those rules are. In that case I might come to believe a rule like 'never split an infinitive', and (according to the prescriptivist) there could be a question of whether it is a "correct" rule for English, and there is even a question about whether I am justified in believing the rule (did I get it from a reliable source?). But for a generative linguist this picture is deeply confused. As we saw in Chapter 1, generative linguists are engaged in an enterprise that is both descriptive and explanatory. It is descriptive in that they are interested in the linguistic rules that individual people actually have, and it is explanatory in that they are interested in why those people have the rules that they do. The explanation typically involves an innate language acquisition device that admits of parametric variation (recall the discussion in section 1.3). Whatever we choose to call our relation to the resulting body of linguistic rules, 'knowledge' is not a happy term.

There are of course exceptional cases where the idea of knowledge of rules makes perfectly good sense. There are "surfacey" rules like lexical rules (e.g. that 'snow' refers to snow) which are accessible to us and which are the kinds of things that could be got right or wrong since I might be prepared to defer to my community on what the correct rule is, but these are not the kinds of rules that linguists typically concern themselves with.

Of course we can talk about trained linguists knowing rules like subjacency, but this isn't the kind of knowledge that typical language users have; it is a kind of theoretical knowledge that is only available to those acquainted with professional linguistics. It is scientific knowledge.

About the time Chomsky gave the talk I heard, he also (Chomsky 1980a, 69–70) introduced the term 'cognize'—suggesting that it was a kind of technical precisification of the term 'knowledge' and he offered that we might also say that we "cognize grammars." While 'cognize' may have started out as a sharpening of 'knowledge' its use has drifted in the linguistics literature to the point where it simply means we mentally represent grammars. This weakening seems to retire the worries about using 'knowledge' (i.e. that rules of grammar aren't true and we don't believe them), but it raises questions of its own. Suitably watered down, 'cognize' suggests that linguistic rules are merely structures in the computational system that is the language faculty. (For example, we could think of the rules as being like lines of code that are accessed by a natural language processing system.)

This makes sense for an account of linguistics that takes linguistics to be a *performance* theory, but it seems inadequate if we take linguistics to be (as Chomsky does) a *competence* theory. The problem with the term 'cognize' is that once it is watered down to mean what 'encodes' does, the meaning seems too thin. A competence theory suggests that linguistic rules are more than just data structures or lines of code involved in our computations.

We have the makings of a dilemma here. On the one hand, 'knowledge' just doesn't correctly describe our relation to linguistic rules. It is too thick a notion. On the other hand, 'cognize', without further elaboration, is too thin a notion, which is to say that it is too thin to play a role in a competence theory. One advantage of the term 'knowledge'—and presumably Chomsky's original motivation for using it—is that knowledge would play the right kind of role in a competence theory: Our competence would consist in a body of knowledge which we have and which we may or may not act upon—our performance need not conform to the linguistic rules that we know.

Is there a way out of the dilemma? I'm going to make the case that the best way to talk about grammatical rules is simply to say that we *have* them. That doesn't sound very deep, I know, but saying that we have individual rules leaves room for individual norm guidance in a way that 'cognize' does not. I'll say a bit more about the details of this (like what it means to have a linguistic rule), but for now I just want to be clear on how this avoids our dilemma. The problem with 'knows' was that it was too thick, and introduced features that are simply not appropriate for the rules that generative linguists are concerned with. We don't *believe* that we have rules like subjacency, nor is there some sense in which subjacency is a true rule for us. But it is certainly appropriate to say that we *have* subjacency (or that my idiolect has the subjacency rule or some parametric variation of it).

Saying we have a rule like subjacency is also thicker than merely saying we cognize it (or at least it can be made thicker). Saying I have such a rule invites the interpretation that it is a rule *for me*—that I am normatively guided by it (we will explore this in detail in Chapter 4). The competence theory thus becomes a theory of the rules that we have. Whether we follow those rules is another matter entirely.

I've rejected talk of knowledge for linguistic rules, but I haven't rejected it for all aspects of linguistics; I think that there are kinds of linguistic knowledge that we have (even if tacit). That is, there are certain kinds of linguistic facts or phenomena that we can have knowledge of, although the nature of this knowledge is going to be somewhat partial.

Let's say that Universal Grammar (UG) is the system that accounts for the different individual grammars that humans have. UG is thus not to be confused with the theory of grammar itself; rather UG is an object of study in the theory of grammar.

For example, if we think of UG as being the initial state of the parametric system discussed in section 1.3, then individual grammars are the result of parameters being set. I have the grammar that I do—call it G_{PL}—because of the way the parameters were set in response to the linguistic data I was exposed to. Let's also not confuse the grammar that I have with the resulting state of the parameter setting of UG in me. Let's call the resulting state of my parameters being set as UG_{PL}. We can say that I have the grammar G_{PL} because I am in parametric state UG_{PL}.

As a further preliminary, let's say that a grammar *generates* a language (or *language narrowly construed* in the sense of Hauser, Chomsky and Fitch (2002)). We can now make a distinction between the language narrowly construed that is generated by my grammar G_{PL}—we can call this language L_{GPL}—and other phenomena that we might pre-theoretically take to be linguistic, or part of my "language" understood loosely speaking. Let's call this pre-theoretical collection of phenomena that involve my language L_{PL}. To illustrate the distinction, consider the contrast between the following two sentences involving center embedding.

(1)   The cat the dog bit ran away

(2)   The mouse the cat the dog bit chased ran away

We might hypothesize that although I judge (2) to be unacceptable, it is still well formed or legible in L_{GPL}; perhaps I merely judge it to be unacceptable because of processing difficulties. So (2) is well formed according to L_{GPL} but not acceptable in L_{PL}.

Accordingly, L_{GPL} should not be expected to line up with all of the phenomena that we pre-theoretically take to be linguistic or part of my language. The range of phenomena in L_{GPL} are determined by theoretical investigation and they at best overlap with the range of phenomena in L_{PL}. Clearly there can be disagreement about the range of phenomena that fall under L_{GPL}. In section 1.1 we saw that a number of the generative semanticists pressed for a very broad understanding of what the theory of grammar might be expected to account for, so in effect they were arguing that we expand the range of phenomena explained by G_{PL} to include most if not all of L_{PL}. I think it is fair to say that most generative linguists today take the range of phenomena explained by the theory of grammar in isolation to be limited. However, it also seems fair to say that the interaction of the theory of grammar with other considerations can contribute to the explanation of a broad range of phenomena—perhaps even most of the phenomena falling under L_{PL}. More generally, let's say then that L_{PL} is a function of L_{GPL} + processing considerations + pragmatic considerations + socio-cultural factors, etc.

I've already given a case (center embedding) where processing limitations interact with the grammar to explain a phenomenon that fell under L_{PL}. Other phenomena might be explained by the fact that I have been inculcated with prescriptive rules. For example, I might find a sentence like 'I ain't got no money' unacceptable. Is the explanation for this that it violates G_{PL} or is it because I was drilled by grammar school teachers not to use 'ain't' and "double negatives" (actually, this is not really a double negative, but the use of a negation as a negative polarity item). In advance of inquiry there is no way to know, because phenomena do not wear their explanations on their sleeves.

I have been using the terms 'phenomena' and 'facts' interchangeably. For the moment let's stick with the term 'facts' and make a distinction between two kinds of facts (or at least two ways of individuating facts). Let's say that there are surfacey facts (S-facts) and explanatory facts (X-facts) about L_{PL}. S-facts are facts like this: 'Who did you hear the story that Bill hit' is not acceptable. X-facts incorporate information about the explanations for these surfacey linguistic facts—for example this: 'Who did you hear the story that Bill hit' is unacceptable because it violates subjacency. I will also be making the case that the source of our knowledge about S-facts includes our judgments (what are sometimes called linguistic intuitions—this is a topic that I will explore in detail in Chapter 3).

Of course, our knowledge attribution reports are often forgiving of what we don't know, so that sometimes we might say that an agent recognizes a subjacency violation in a sentence, when the agent would merely report that the sentence is not right and have no idea what subjacency is. I don't have an issue with this sort of knowledge report, but to be clear we should call this a *charitable attribution* of knowledge of an X-fact.

To understand the role of linguistic judgments in this picture it will be useful if we can get clear on the difference between linguistic *theory*, linguistic *phenomena* or *facts*, and linguistic *data*. Following more general work in the philosophy of science by Bogen and Woodward (1988) we can illustrate the relation between theory, phenomena, and data as follows.

Theory → explains/predicts → **phenomena** ← are evidence for ← **data**
      ← are evidence for ←

Theory is the theory of grammar in this case. Following Bogen and Woodward, I will take *phenomena* to be stable and replicable effects or processes that are potential objects of explanation and prediction for scientific theories. In this case the phenomena will include the pre-theoretical domain of language-related facts. While pre-theoretically we can't say which facts *provide evidence* for the theory of grammar (the theory of UG), some facts will provide such evidence (more or less directly). We will also say that the theory *contributes to* the explanation and prediction of these facts. We can also say that I have knowledge of some of the linguistic phenomena.

I will take *data* to be observational evidence for claims about phenomena. The data come from token events of observation and experimentation. For example, an act of measuring the freezing temperature of a liquid might yield the datum that the fluid froze at n degrees (this is not to be confused with a written record of the measurement—we can call this a *record of the datum*). This datum is a piece of evidence for the more general phenomenon (fact) that the fluid freezes at n degrees. The data are token-based, and the phenomena are type-based.[3] We can, of course, aggregate data. So, for example, we might aggregate the results of several observations to show that the average freezing temperature in our experiments is n degrees. It still counts as data on my view because we are aggregating over token experiments/observations.

This distinction between data, records of data, and sources of data applies also to linguistic methods that appeal to corpora of written sentences. In this case an occurrence of a sentence in a written corpus is not the datum. Rather the datum is *that* the sentence was found in the corpus on a particular search. This datum provides evidence for several kinds of phenomena. In the first place it provides evidence for the phenomenon *that* the sentence occurs in the corpus. We can aggregate these data (either by counting occurrences or statistically generalizing over data) to show, for example, that it occurs 1000 times or a certain percentage of the time. Again, this is still a datum in my usage because it is an aggregation over token observations. It may also, via inference, provide evidence for the phenomenon that the sentence is acceptable to a number of language users.

As with all data, linguistic data come from observation and experimentation (for example, they may be found in a corpora or they may be the result of acts of judging that tokenings of linguistic forms are unacceptable; as we will see there are many other potential sources of data). Such data provide *evidence for* phenomena (both surfacey and explanatory linguistic facts) that are in turn *explained by* the theory of grammar.

Let's make this a bit more concrete with some specific examples from linguistics.

Consider subjacency, and the case where an act of judgment by me is the source of a datum. As noted earlier, we do not have judgments about rules like subjacency, nor do we have judgments that a particular linguistic form violates subjacency. Rather, our judgments of acceptability provide evidence for the existence of these phenomena. We can illustrate the idea as follows:

Grammatical Rule for G_{PL}
Subjacency: Moved elements can't jump an NP and an S node without an intervening landing site

Explanatory fact about L_{GPL} (potential object of theoretical knowledge for PL)
'[$_S$ who$_i$ did you hear the story that Bill hit e$_i$]' is ungrammatical because it violates subjacency

Explanatory fact about L_{PL} (potential object of theoretical knowledge for PL)
'who did you hear the story that Bill hit' is unacceptable in L_{PL} because it violates subjacency

Surfacey fact about L_{PL} (potential object of knowledge for PL)
'who did you hear the story that Bill hit' is unacceptable for PL

---

[3] Thanks to Herman Capellan for discussion here.

Datum (content judged by PL)

That a particular tokening of 'who did you hear the story that Bill hit?' is unacceptable to PL

Source of datum (act of judgment by PL)

PL's act of judging that 'who did you hear the story that Bill hit?' is unacceptable

The next illustration involves the case of reflexives. We again distinguish between the linguistic phenomenon, which involves complex notions from binding theory and the data (in this case linguistic judgment), which are much more "surfacey."

Grammatical Rule for G_{PL}

Reflexives must be bound in their governing category

Explanatory fact about L_{GPL} (potential object of theoretical knowledge for PL)

'[$_{NP}$ himself]' can be bound by '[$_{NP}$ John]' in '[$_S$ Bill said that John likes himself]' because it is in the same governing category, and '[$_{NP}$ Bill]' cannot bind '[$_{NP}$ himself]' because it is not in the same governing category

Explanatory fact about L_{PL} (potential object of theoretical knowledge for PL)

'himself' can be bound by 'John' in 'Bill said that John likes himself' because it is in the same governing category, and 'Bill' cannot bind 'himself' because it is not in the same governing category

Surfacey fact about L_{PL} (potential object of knowledge for PL)

'himself' can be associated with 'John' but not 'Bill' in 'Bill said that John likes himself'

Datum (content judged by PL)

Judgment that 'himself' can be associated with 'John' but not 'Bill' in a given tokening of 'Bill said that John likes himself'

Source of datum (act of judgment by PL)

PL's act of judging that 'himself' can be associated with 'John' but not 'Bill' in a given tokening of 'Bill said that John likes himself'

Summarizing thus far, grammatical rules generate linguistic facts—facts about our language. We have knowledge about some of those facts (mostly the surfacey facts), and often our knowledge is underwritten by the judgments that we make about those surfacey facts. We can get things wrong, of course, but as we will see in Chapter 3, this doesn't undermine our knowledge. Indeed, you could make the case that the possibility of getting it wrong is a prerequisite for something being a candidate object of knowledge.[4]

But this leaves open the question of what role this knowledge plays for us and how it interacts with the individual grammatical rules that each of us has (e.g., in my case the rules specified by G_{PL}). I'm suggesting that it is our knowledge of these facts that helps us follow the rules of our individual grammars. This is a complex issue that will be taken up in

---

[4] This Wittgensteinian point was first brought to my attention by Sidney Morgenbesser, but buried somewhere in long term memory until Barry C. Smith reminded me of the point recently.

Chapter 4. Before we get there, however, we have more preliminaries to knock down—not least of which is the question of what sorts of things UG, UG_{PL}, G_{PL}, L_{GPL}, and L_{PL} are.

2.3 Levels of Explanation in the Theory of Grammar

Whether we are thinking of the grammar in terms of a wide Ψ-language or narrow Ψ-language, there are many levels of explanation on which we can talk about and investigate Ψ-language.

In the previous section I said that Universal Grammar (UG) is the system that accounts for the different individual grammars that humans have. Again, it is important that UG not be confused with the theory of grammar itself; UG is an object of study in the theory of grammar.

For example, we could think of the theory of UG as the parametric system discussed in section 1.3. To go back to the metaphor introduced there, UG is the prewired box with switches that can be flipped in different combinations. Individual grammars result from parameters being set. I have the grammar that I do—call it G_{PL}—because of the way the parameters were set in response to the linguistic data I was exposed to.

What sort of thing is G_{PL}? I'm going to argue that it, like the language L_{GPL} that it generates, is an abstract object. This is not to reject the idea that UG is a feature of our cognitive psychology. Let's follow George (1989) and distinguish between an agent's grammar (for example the grammar G_{PL} that I have), the agent's psychogrammar (which is the psychological state in virtue of which I have that grammar), and the agent's physiogrammar (which is the low level biophysical state that underlies my psychogrammar).

The way I am thinking about UG, it would be a covering term for both the psychogrammar and the physiogrammar. That is, UG is a natural system that can be investigated at several levels of explanation, including both the biophysical level and the psychological level. I assume further that when we construct theories of the parameter settings of the grammar, we are in effect constructing a theory of UG at the level of psychogrammar—we are doing psychology. When we begin to explore minimalist mechanisms we are doing speculative theorizing about the physiogrammar. This isn't to say we are speculating about what neurons are up to; that is yet another level of abstraction down.

The low level principles of minimalism (and the interface conditions) explain the principles and parameters of the psychogrammar. Both are investigations of UG at different levels of explanation. The different parametric settings of UG in turn account for the different grammars that individuals have by showing how each grammar correlates to a particular parametric setting.

2.4 Abstracta and Non-isomorphic Representation

I've said that a parametric state of UG (for example UG_{PL}) determines an individual grammar (for example G_{PL}) and that this individual grammar in turn determines an individual language narrowly construed (L_{GPL}). In the previous section I suggested that G_{PL} and L_{GPL} (and L_{PL}) are abstract objects, but what does this suggestion come to?

First, we need to be clear that this talk of abstracta is not really different from talk of abstracta that one finds in other sciences. Somehow in linguistics it has led to confusion. Despite the fact that we take grammars themselves to be abstracta, it does not follow that linguistics is the study of abstracta (as suggested by Katz (1981)). Higginbotham (1983) correctly observed that we are not interested in the abstracta simpliciter; in the linguistic case we are interested in determining which of these abstract objects a particular language user *has*—which is to say that we are interested in the grammar determined by the psychogrammar realized by the agent. That is, while G_{PL} is an abstract object, that does not mean the question of which grammar is mine is not empirical. Nor does it mean that the grounding theory that explains *why* my grammar is G_{PL} and not some other grammar is not an empirical science.

But how does UG_{PL} determine G_{PL}? If we think of a psychogrammar along the lines of a computer program, there is a natural temptation to think of the rules or principles of the grammar as being "hard coded" in the machine or system. For example, imagine that we built a dedicated parser for written natural language input that applied basic phrase structure rules of the form S→NP VP, NP→Det (adj) N, etc. in a strict bottom-up fashion. Each of these rules could be encoded as a line of code and stored in the permanent memory of the parser. The parser operates by recursively working its way bottom-up from lexical items looking for rules that it can apply to the segments of the string. This is one way to think of what it is for us to know a linguistic rule: it must be explicitly encoded (and consulted or "called" as part of our linguistic processing). We could then think of each such linguistic rule as corresponding to some sort of analogous relatively stable state of the machine's architecture, which in turn supervenes on a semi-stable physical state of the machine. While this is one way to think about our having linguistic rules, it is at best a very narrow way to think about what is necessary to have such rules.

For example, suppose that we compile the simple parser just described, yielding an efficient if (to us) impenetrable algorithm in the machine language of our dedicated parser, effectively destroying the data structures corresponding to the individual phrase structure rules. I for one am not prepared to say that such a machine no longer has a psychogrammar that constitutes a cognitive state by virtue of which I have those rules.

This gets into the really complicated issue of what internal physical conditions must hold for us to have abstract linguistic rules. On the extremes, the dispositionalist will say that there are no internal requirements, while the hard core "literal computationalist" will say that there must be a one-to-one mapping from rules represented to physically isolatable and stable regions of the internal system.

Our only real constraint is that we have a set of rules, and nothing really tells us what the low level physiogrammar must look like in order for this to be possible. Must there be semi-stable locatable physical states corresponding to each rule that we supposedly have? I know of no argument to the effect that there must be.

To illustrate an alternative possibility, consider the work of Marcus (1986). Marcus proposes that the rule of subjacency (which we discussed in section 1.2) might be an artifact of the way natural language is parsed. In particular, Marcus proposed a parser that had a "look ahead" function (that is, a function that allowed it to look ahead, past the constituents it was trying to parse), but limited look ahead so that the parser would "garden path." (That is, it would not look ahead so far that it would think that 'raced' is an adjective in cases like 'The horse raced past the barn stumbled'. The parser would take it for a past tense verb.) The Marcus parser would thus explain both garden pathing and subjacency.

One might object here that Marcus is proposing a performance theory, since parsers are typically used in the context of natural language processing, but we can also imagine them being deployed as part of the system that determines the linguistic rules that we have (i.e. as part of the competence theory).

My purpose here is not to defend the Marcus proposal, which is now dated, but rather to point out that this is a possible way in which we could come to have the rule of subjacency— we could think of our linguistic rules as being grounded not just in the straight representation of linguistic rules via data structures that are isomorphic to those rules, but rather than by an underlying computational mechanism in which no isomorphic structures directly appear.

The problem is that when we talk about having abstract rules in terms of computational states of a system we know very little about what the physical properties of the system must be. Of course what makes the problem particularly deep is that we are talking about knowledge of abstracta and this is an area where our grasp of the problem is speculative at best.

One person who has addressed this problem in the area of mathematics is Charles Parsons (1983), who has suggested that our epistemic access to abstract mathematical structures is mediated by quasi-linguistic structures—a system of mathematical notation for example. In a certain sense we are pushing the problem back even further, since we are now addressing the question of our epistemic access to *linguistic* abstracta.[5]

Strictly speaking we don't know much more than that our epistemic access to these abstracta is mysterious, but of course we can also admit that there is some attractiveness to the idea that it involves a kind of isomorphism between a physically instantiated data structure and the abstract object in question. This might drive the idea that linguistic rules must be "hard coded" in the system. But the problem is that there is no real argument in support of this idea. Furthermore, as we will see in sections 5.2 and 5.3, there may not even be a brute fact about the data structure realized by the system in isolation; whether there is a data structure and what it is may well depend upon the environmental embedding of the system.

---

[5] This is not to say that Parsons didn't see there was a problem with linguistic abstracta too, and he explored various strategies for developing nominalist accounts of linguistic abstracta—for example in terms of tokens that could be brought into spatial correspondence with one another. In Ludlow (1982) I observed some difficulties with this strategy.

2.5 Types and Tokens[6]

The appeal to abstract objects in linguistics is peculiar in a number of respects, since we naturally slide between talk of types (which are abstract) and tokens (which presumably are not). This is particularly clear in the case of L_{GPL}, which illustrates this puzzling feature of the role of abstracta in linguistics quite nicely. On the one hand it is an abstract object, but on the other hand it appears that we can actually talk about perceptual tokens of, for example, sentences of L_{GPL}.

Of course the objects in L_{GPL}—the linguistic structures discussed in Chapter 1—are extremely complex, and they contain features that no one without linguistic training would be aware of (for example traces and the fact that in certain cases traces are properly governed) as well as components that are not voiced, ranging from traces of movement to PRO to various phonologically unrealized functional elements (tense, for example) and low level features like [+N] that are relevant to case marking. So, it is natural to think that we cannot possibly be talking about the utterances and inscriptions that are typically called 'sentences' and are often construed by philosophers to be the objects of linguistic inquiry. It is even difficult to imagine that the properties we are describing could in any sense *involve* these objects, given that the linguistic forms and the physical tokens are so far removed from each other in their constitution and structure—ink markings and sound waves do not evince this abstract structure in any obvious sense. For this reason, many generative linguists reject the idea that inscriptions and utterances are part of what they are studying. But if we aren't talking about such things, why does it appear that we are? What is going on?

It is part and parcel of linguistic *practice* to produce utterances and inscriptions and talk about them as though they were part of the object of inquiry. So, for example, in the previous section I spoke of the sentence 'Who did you hear the story that Bill hit' and the fact that it is not acceptable in my idiolect. But what is the thing I am talking about when I use the pronoun 'it' here?

One answer is that I am referring to the abstract inscription-type corresponding to the ink markings on the page, but this doesn't seem adequate. I might go on to say that the sentence is bad because the WH element jumped over both an NP and an S node, but none of that information is found in the expression type directly corresponding to the inscription. Apart from whether the expression type is sufficiently rich, I'm also not sure there is a clear answer to whether I am referring to the expression type or token or both.

What are the options here?

One option would be to take a leaf from Szabó (1999) and argue that the inscriptions and utterances "represent" their corresponding abstract objects in the way that a picture or a location on a map might represent a location in the real world.

There are certainly attractive elements to Szabó's view. In the first place, it handles the problem of simple expression types being too austere. No one expects a physical

---

[6] Thanks to Zoltán Szabó for discussion of issues in this section.

representation to encode all of the information of the thing represented (clearly so in the case of maps).

Furthermore, we routinely shift between talking about the representation and the thing it represents. For example, in planning a trip I might point to a map and say "we are going there, right where you spilled the coffee." This suggests that in our discussions of examples we are shifting between talking about the representations and the abstract structures they represent (perhaps we refer to the abstract structures by pointing at the representation in an act of "deferred ostension").

While attractive, the worry for this view is that we typically take such representations to be established by convention. So, for example, we understand the convention that the color blue on a map is to represent water. But who or what established the convention that the inscription 'Bill said that John likes himself' is to represent the complex structure proposed by linguists (complete with tree structure, category labels, and indices)? One possible answer is that we did not establish the convention that the token should represent all the linguistic structure that it does, but that we determined that the token was to represent the abstract object *whatever structure it turns out to have.* For example, we can agree that a region on a map will represent an unexplored territory even if we know nothing about the territory. When we come to know details of the territory, well, that is what the region on the map was representing.

It might come as a surprise to some people that the new territory, once explored, was full of mountains and forests and seas, but it's not like the representation of the territory was therefore wrong—it was simply a very coarse-grained representation of the thing it represented. Necessarily so, since prior to exploration we had no idea what it might look like. Once we know what the new territory is like we can choose to represent it at whatever grain we wish. Similarly in the linguistic case, we choose or learn that 'John said that Bill likes himself' represents an abstract object, not knowing what the structure of that object ultimately is. As we learn more about the object we may choose to represent it with more detailed tokens (linguistic trees, for example). We would only err if we projected the simplicity of the representation on the map onto reality (or if we mistook the region of the map for the territory itself).[7]

---

[7] Of course for this idea to work we need to be on board with the notion of non-isomorphic representation, as articulated in the previous section. If one wasn't on board with this then it cuts down on the options, but there are nevertheless still options. For example, Rey (2007) suggested that the uttered and written tokens serve as "triggers" for their corresponding (token) mental representations. These token mental representations might then be complex enough to have a kind of isomorphism with the abstracta (cf. the discussion of Parsons in the previous section). I suppose we could then think that when we refer to a physical token, we are really just trying to trigger a mental representation, and *that* is what we are ultimately talking about.

Another option would be to hold that the tokens are actually parts of the objects we are investigating—that sentences are very complex objects consisting of both structured abstract objects and many (accidental) perceptual manifestations. Here the metaphor is to think of linguistic objects as akin to icebergs. We can point to the part of the iceberg that is above the surface, even though 90% of it is beneath the surface, but it isn't like we aren't pointing to the entire iceberg for all that. Linguistic objects like those we discussed in Chapter 1 are very complicated and most of their structure is not on the "surface," but we can still refer to those objects by referring to the perceivable aspects of their tokens—the acoustical signals and the physical graphical

This book is not the place to solve the ancient problem of the relation between types and tokens (or more generally the relation between forms and particulars), but it is important that we recognize that the tokens we speak of here are going to be impoverished relative to the abstracta. Sometimes the talk of perceptual tokens can delude us into thinking that these are all we are talking about (as if one was deluded into thinking that in talking about icebergs one is only talking about the portion that is above the surface). Or we might be deluded into thinking that when we posit linguistic properties and elements (PRO etc.), we are, as it were, positing properties that are the reflex of external physical or social facts. As I suggested earlier, it seems implausible to suppose that the structures and forms being posited for linguistic objects (including PRO and trace, or, for that matter, word boundaries) can be found in the intrinsic physical properties of either written or spoken tokens alone; there is no interesting sense in which the relevant properties are found in physical properties of the acoustical signals or ink markings on the page. It seems equally implausible to think that these properties inhere in linguistic social relations—no tacit convention is going to yield the principles of binding theory, for example.

This position is nuanced, but for all that I think it is faithful to actual practice in generative linguistics. Although some linguists claim that externalia like inscriptions, utterances, utterance types, grammars and languages construed as abstracta play no role in generative linguistics, I think they do play a role in linguistic practice at a minimum.[8] They play a role in the identification and individuation of the specific abstract structures that we are interested in. Confusion enters into the picture when we think that these perceptual tokens are *all* we are talking about.

2.6 Derivation vs. Representation

In section 1.4 I noted that Epstein and Seely (2006) have argued for a derivational approach as opposed to a representational or constraint based approach to linguistics. There could be many motivations for such an approach, some of them reasonable, and some of them not so reasonable. For example, as I will argue in Chapter 7, it would be a mistake to think that avoiding the construction of representations is in any objective sense theoretically simpler. We just don't have sensible ways of measuring simplicity across theoretical frameworks. Alternatively, we might think that a derivational approach makes the reduction to more basic sciences easier—a prima facie reasonable

---

representations written in chalk and ink. This position is nuanced, but I see no reason it could not be developed into a defensible position.

[8] For what it's worth, it seems pretty clear that Chomsky is not one of the linguists who think that inscriptions and sounds play no role in linguistic theorizing, as his remarks in Chomsky (1993, 288) make clear:

> Some have used the term "E-language" to refer to actual utterances or texts. People are free to invent terminology as they like, but that was not the meaning I gave to the term when I introduced it; I-language approaches do not differ from others in their concern with such materials.

motivation, and one that seems to be motivating Epstein and Seely, but one that I think ultimately collapses.

My concern here is that the choice between derivational and procedural approaches has much more to do with us as theorists and little to nothing to do with the lower level architecture of the mind/brain—in particular, with what we earlier called the physio-grammar—and hence very little to do with the reductive project.

There are parallel issues in computer science. Some languages are declarative and others are procedural. As a canonical example of a declarative language we might take Prolog, and as a canonical example of a procedural language we might take C or Pascal.

Biermann (1997) describes the difference this way:

Most programs are of the form

    Do this.
    Do that.
    Do something else.
    Etc.

Thus the programmer uses the program to tell the machine what to do. Prolog programs, however, are of the form

    This is a fact.
    That is a fact.
    Something else is a fact.
    Etc.

Using Prolog, the programmer does not tell the machine how to do a calculation. The program merely states facts, and the machine automatically finds the facts needed to answer a question. (306–307)

Now, the difference between declarative and procedural languages may seem like a big deal, but the question is whether there is really something different going on down at the level of the circuits of the machine's hardware. There are clearly differences in the translation of the higher level language into assembly language and then machine language, but apart from the translation, is there a real difference?

Let's consider the difference between Prolog and Pascal on the addition of a list or array of numbers. In a procedural language like Pascal, the program might look like this, for an array of numbers A.

```
SUM:= 0;
I := 1;
while I <= N do
      begin
      SUM:= A[I] + SUM;
      I := +1;
      end;
```

In this case the location SUM stores the sum of the numbers being added, and I indexes through the array (for example, the elements of the array might be assigned the integers from 1 to N). Let's assume the array is a simple list of numbers.

In a declarative language like Prolog, on the other hand, things initially look somewhat different. First, we write a program to add a list of numbers.

f(0, [ ]).
f(S, [X|Y]):- f(Z,Y), S is X+Z.

What the first line is saying is that the function f associates 0 with the null list. The second line says that the function f associates S with a list that begins with X and ends with a list of other entries Y just in case f associates Z with Y and S is X+Z. The sum S is found by adding up everything Y but the first entry X in the list [X|Y] to obtain Z. Then X is added to Z to obtain the result. Having defined this function, if we want to add a list of numbers (say, 7, 5, and 11) we type the following.

f(X, [7, 5, 11]).

As we noted earlier, at this level of abstraction the programs appear to be doing very different things. The Pascal program is specifying operations and the Prolog program is stating "facts," but what is going on at the lower level? Consider again the Pascal instruction for a simple addition operation—for example a line of code like Z:= (X+Y).

The line of code Z:= (X+Y) is telling the computer to add X and Y, and assign the resulting value to Z, but how is it doing this? Well, first the statement is translated into assembly language, so that the result is something like the following (I'm following Biermann's very helpful exposition here).

```
COPY AX,X
ADD AX,Y
COPY CN1,AX
COPY AX,CN1
COPY Z,AX
```

These assembly language instructions are then translated into the binary codes of machine language, so the result might be something like the following.

```
00101101
01001010
00100111
00101111
00100001
```

These instructions are loaded into the computer's memory and are called and used when the instruction pointer of the computer gives their location. So if 01001010 is called, a particular circuit is activated—in this case it is a circuit that adds.

The question here is whether there is an interesting difference between the Pascal and Prolog programs at the level of circuitry, and at least as far as the addition operation goes, if the programs run on the same machine they very well could be calling 01001010 and activating the same circuit.

Higher level computer programs are fundamentally translations of complex physical actions into languages that we can understand and use to manipulate the actions of the machine. Some of these languages make it easy to manipulate the machine to carry out mathematical operations (Pascal being a canonical example) and others make it easy to manipulate the machine to serve as an intelligent data base (Prolog being a canonical example). But apart from the computational resources that are dedicated to the translation of the higher level language into assembly language and machine language, the basic operations of the machines are going to be the same.

What is the moral in the linguistics case? There are limits to what we can extrapolate from the example of digital computers, but the following does seem to be true. The higher level principles, rules, and derivations that are proposed in linguistic theory will supervene on lower level physical processes, and derivational and representation-based grammars could easily supervene on the very same lower level physical processes.

This does not mean that one approach cannot be superior to another, but it means that it would be fruitless to argue from first principles or even assumptions about our low level biophysical architecture that one approach or the other is superior. The approach we take should depend upon whichever approach makes our theorizing easier at the moment. As the theory changes and our interests change we may well shift approaches, just as we shift between computer languages depending upon the problems we are addressing. This is a theme I will return to in the discussions of formal rigor and simplicity in Chapter 7, where I argue that the simplicity comes to ease of use, and theories are rigorous enough if they are rigorous enough for current purposes.

3

Data, Intuitions, Judgments

My goal in this chapter will be to try and get clear on the nature of data in linguistic theorizing and closely consider one of the more controversial sources of data—so-called "linguistic intuitions." I'll make the case that linguistic intuitions are best described as linguistic judgments and I'll also make the case that on the whole they are reliable sources of data and that they have the advantage of also being economical sources of data.

3.1 Linguistic Phenomena, Linguistic Data, Linguistic Theory

It will be useful for us to review the distinction I made in the previous chapter between linguistic *data* on the one hand and linguistic *phenomena* on the other. Following Bogen and Woodward (1988) I illustrated the relation between theory, phenomena, and data as follows.

Theory → explains/predicts → **phenomena** ← are evidence for ← **data**
  ← are evidence for ←

Let's again take *phenomena* to be stable and replicable effects or processes that are potential objects of explanation and prediction for scientific theories. As before, the phenomena will be pre-theoretically linguistic/language-related facts. Some of these facts will be predicted to hold given the rules and representations (principles and parameters) of the grammar. Such facts will *provide evidence* for the theory of grammar (in particular, the theory positing UG), and the theory of grammar will play a role in the explanation and prediction of at least some of these facts.

As before, we take *data* to be observational evidence for claims about phenomena. The data come from observation and experimentation. In the linguistic case, linguistic data provide *evidence for* phenomena (like binding facts or "island effects") that are in turn *explained by* the theory of grammar. For example, when we addressed the specific case of reflexives and the data were linguistic judgments, we had the following paradigm.

Grammatical Rule for G$_{PL}$
Reflexives must be bound in their governing category

Explanatory fact about L$_{GPL}$ (potential object of theoretical knowledge for PL)
'[$_{NP}$ himself]' can be bound by '[$_{NP}$ John]' in '[$_S$ Bill said that John likes himself]' because it is in the same governing category, and '[$_{NP}$ Bill]' cannot bind '[$_{NP}$ himself]' because it is not in the same governing category

Explanatory fact about L$_{PL}$ (potential object of theoretical knowledge for PL)
'himself' can be bound by 'John' in 'Bill said that John likes himself' because it is the same governing category, and 'Bill' cannot bind 'himself' because it is not in the same governing category

Surfacey fact about L$_{PL}$ (potential object of knowledge for PL)
'himself' can be associated with 'John' but not 'Bill' in 'Bill said that John likes himself'

Datum (content judged by PL)
Judgment that 'himself' can be associated with 'John' but not 'Bill' in 'Bill said that John likes himself'

Source of datum (act of judgment by PL)
PL's act of judging that 'himself' can be associated with 'John' but not 'Bill' in 'Bill said that John likes himself'

As I'll argue below, data are never theory free, and accordingly the example of data discussed here is not theory free. The notion of an interpretation is certainly a theoretical notion, as are very simple notions like 'himself' and 'John' being distinct words—the notion of a word being a theoretical construct, after all. Even the notion of "acceptability" is theory-laden in important ways. For example, there is at least one sense in which 'Colorless green ideas sleep furiously' is unacceptable—it doesn't make much sense. But there is also a clear sense in which the sentence is perfectly acceptable—its form seems acceptable to us.

While no data are *theory-free*, we can make them *theory-neutral* with respect to the questions we are investigating. For example, in the case of 'John went to the bank' we want the data to be neutral with respect to whether we have a genuine example of ambiguity or whether it is a case of meaning underdetermination (for example it has been argued that the sentence might have an open meaning that gets sharpened differently on different occasions of use—sharpened to mean financial institution in some cases and fluvial embankment in others; see van Deemter and Peters 1996). The data we enlist must be neutral (or at least neutrally described) on this question, although of course they cannot be entirely theory-free. The key point is that if the linguistic phenomena we are investigating involve the question of whether there are ambiguities, binding relations, etc., the data themselves need to be theory-neutral on whether there are such phenomena as ambiguity, binding relations, etc.

The approach I'm advocating here thus appears to contrast with a standardly held view in the philosophy of linguistics, which is that the data (typically linguistic "intuitions") directly involve notions like grammaticality, binding, and other theoretical notions. Devitt, who believes the view is widely held in linguistics but goes on to reject the view, describes it as follows:

We should start by clarifying what we mean by "linguistic intuitions". We mean fairly immediate unreflective judgments about the syntactic and semantic properties of linguistic expressions, metalinguistic judgments about acceptability, grammaticality, ambiguity, coreference/binding, and the like. (2006, 95)

I do not believe this description is faithful either to linguistic practice or to the way linguists understand their practice. Linguists typically do not claim to have judgments of grammaticality and certainly not of binding facts. Rather, they claim that we have judgments of acceptability and (in some cases) possible interpretations of linguistic forms. These judgments provide evidence for linguistic phenomena (like binding) and the theory of grammar in turn explains these phenomena. In other words, we don't have judgments about linguistic rules. Those rules are discovered by sophisticated higher level theorizing. There are, however, some exceptions to this.

Linguists do sometimes employ judgments involving theoretical notions in blackboard discussions and in pursuing some questions, but they tend not to be the sort of data that emerge in papers and talks. They are more like hunches that experienced theoreticians come to rely on. For example, I've heard a leading linguist say something to the effect of "this construction feels like a subjacency violation." In another instance, in a classroom lecture I once heard Chomsky utter the following: "You need to filter out the effects of the parser here, it is clear how to do this." These are different kinds of judgments and they aren't the sort that will make it into a paper by either linguist. These were just judgments in the sense of "hunches" they had about what the cause of the judgment was, given the current state of the theory. I take it that these are the sorts of judgments that Devitt approvingly classifies as being the product of higher level processing. Whether such judgments are the product of higher level processing or not, they do not seem to me to play a role in the data of linguistics, although they may play a role in aspects of theory construction.

Returning to the matter of linguistic data, notice that I have distinguished between the source of linguistic data—acts of judgment—from the data, which are the contents or targets of those judgments. (Bill Lycan (forthcoming) has characterized this as the distinction between *intuitings* and the *intuiteds*.) That is, the linguistic judgments and the linguistic facts are *not* the same thing. Some theorists have confused the two notions.

For example, Stich (1971, 1972) argues that linguistic theory is fundamentally an attempt to account for our faculty of linguistic judgments/intuitions by systematizing or axiomatizing our intuitions. There might be some interest in such a project, but it does not seem to me to be the project that linguists are engaged in. For linguists, acts of judging yield data that support linguistic facts; acts of judging are not the primary object of study in generative linguistics (which is not to say that this capacity to judge is not worthy of study, nor that understanding the nature and limits of it is not useful to a linguist). Chomsky (1982b), for example, is pretty explicit about this, noting that some textbooks are misleading on the point.

To say that linguistics is the study of introspective judgments would be like saying that physics is the study of meter readings, photographs, and so on, but nobody says that. . . .

It just seems absurd to restrict linguistics to the study of introspective judgments, as is very commonly done. Some philosophers who have worked on language have defined the field that way. Many textbooks that concentrate on linguistic argumentation for example are more or less guided by that view. (33–34)

If this picture is right, then judgments are not the sole source of data or even necessarily the main source of data. For example, we might rely on corpus data too, and we shouldn't think that a corpus is interesting only insofar as we can infer linguistic judgments from it. On Stich's (1971, 1972) view that would seem to be the only interest of corpus data—as a kind of resource from which we can deduce linguistic judgments. Given the picture of linguistic practice that I am sketching here, it is reasonable to think that one can find direct evidence for linguistic phenomena from a corpus and many other sources.

I've just mentioned a couple sources of data but clearly the possible sources of data are vast. Here is a partial enumeration.

1. Psycholinguistic Data
2. Corpus Studies
3. Etymological Data
4. Written "Grammars"
5. Phonetic Data
6. Field Research
7. Brain Imaging
8. Linguistic Intuitions/judgments

In *principle*—which is not to say in practice—many other sources of data could be relevant here, down to religious oracles, provided they are shown to be reliable. Given the breadth of possible sources of data, my discussion here will be preliminary and I'll focus in on the more contentious topic of "acceptability intuitions/judgments" and "judgments/intuitions of possible meanings," recognizing that current practice in linguistics also relies heavily on sources of data other than linguistic judgments.

While linguistic intuitions/judgments are contentious, as Grandy (1981) and Schütze (1996) have observed, there are also good reasons why they have been valuable tools in linguistic theory. Linguistic judgments have the virtue of allowing us to study linguistic forms that occur only rarely (or perhaps previously not at all), they allow us to introduce "negative information" (for example that a certain form is not possible in a language—a kind of data that is harder to extract from a corpus). Additionally, linguistic judgments potentially provide a tool for distinguishing performance errors caused by hiccups and memory limitations from facts about the language itself, and allow us to bracket off certain pragmatic and communicative features of language (on this score see work by Larson et al. 2008).

One way of thinking about the value of linguistic judgments is by contrasting them with data that might be gleaned from a corpus. Data mining has become an extremely useful tool in other sciences (see, for example, Venter et al.'s (2004) work in biology), and linguistics is a natural target for such research since, obviously, massive amounts of data are available in digitized electronic corpora. Statistical natural language processing applies powerful statistical (and other) tools to electronic corpora (potentially all digitized written works) and it has been highly successful at mining interesting regularities and facts that might otherwise have escaped our attention.

I will return to the topic of corpora data in section 3.5. For now I just want to focus on the role that corpora might play within generative linguistics. From that internal perspective corpora data are valuable, but there is a sense in which they constitute "low hanging fruit"—easily acquired (especially with statistical natural language processing) but not necessarily the most valuable fruit given the explanatory concerns and interests that we have. Corpora may have gaps on the questions that we are concerned with. And while corpora data are valuable, they are not free of error, and can even be deceptive about the linguistic phenomena that we are interested in. Linguistic judgments can play a role in helping us to locate cases where corpora deceive us about the nature of linguistic phenomena (just as corpora data can do the same for linguistic judgments).

Finally, it is worth noting that linguistic judgments are relatively "efficient" in a sense that I will explore in section 7.3. The basic idea is that theorists want to pursue research methods that provide them the *relevant* data at the least cost. High energy physicists would love to be able to get the needed data without building super colliders, but their field of study has advanced to the point where certain crucial questions cannot be investigated without great cost. One case for linguistic judgments is that even when they are targeted on crucial questions, they are relatively cost free, and they are sufficient for answering many of the key questions of interest to linguists. This is a point made in Chomsky (1965).

The critical problem for grammatical theory today is not a paucity of evidence but rather the inadequacy of present theories of language to account for masses of evidence that are hardly open to serious question. . . . It seems to me that sharpening of the data by more objective tests is a matter of small importance for the problems at hand . . . Perhaps the day will come when the kinds of data that we now can obtain in abundance will be insufficient to resolve deeper questions concerning the structure of language. (20–21)

In his expansive and helpful work on linguistic intuitions, Conrad Schütze (2006) makes the case that this may have been true in earlier days of linguistic theorizing, but that it is no longer so, and he thus argues that now it is time to critically examine linguistic judgments. Schütze is quite correct to assert that this is an open empirical question. In section 3.3 we will examine some of his concerns (and the more drastic concerns of others). First, however, it will be useful for us to get clear on the nature of linguistic intuitions/judgments.

3.2 Linguistic Intuitions are Linguistic Judgments

A number of philosophers and linguists interpret the practice of using linguistic intuitions as involving some inner "voice of competence." Devitt (2006), for example, is very explicit about this: "I need a word for such special access to facts. I shall call it 'Cartesian'." (96)

Whether linguists actually hold to such a view is a matter I will take up shortly. For now, I want to stress (in partial agreement with Devitt) that such a view of linguistic intuition is mistaken. I am going to take a leaf from Williamson (2004), talking about so-called intuitions in other areas, and endorse his view that we ought to scrap this talk of 'introspection' and 'intuition' altogether:

> What are called 'intuitions' . . . are just applications of our ordinary capacities for judgement. We think of them as intuitions when a special kind of scepticism about those capacities is salient. Like scepticism about perception, scepticism about judgement pressures us into conceiving our evidence as facts about our internal psychological states: here, facts about our conscious inclinations to make judgements about some topic rather than facts about the topic itself. But the pressure should be resisted, for it rests on bad epistemology: specifically, on an impossible ideal of unproblematically identifiable evidence. (109)

Part of the controversy about linguistic intuitions, I think, is simply due to a pair of misunderstandings. The first misunderstanding is the idea that linguistic intuitions are objects in the Cartesian theater of the mind—quales of acceptability as it were. Others might dispense with the qualia but still fall into the second misunderstanding, which is that linguistic judgments can give us direct access to the linguistic rules that we have.

I would argue that linguistic judgments are not judgments about rules, or even rule compliance (understood in the sense that we judge that we are in compliance with a particular rule or set of rules that is transparent to us). They are simply judgments about linguistic facts, and these facts are determined by the linguistic rules.

Such judgments may or may not be accompanied by conscious phenomenal states, but whether they do need not be relevant to us. Furthermore, such judgments need not directly involve the linguistic rule system at all.

Do linguists really suppose that judgments of acceptability involve special Cartesian access to an inner theater where we hear the voice of competence? Or, for that matter, do they even suppose that we have judgments about linguistic rules? Apparently some do and some do not, although Devitt (2006) argues that the position is quite widespread. In support of his claim he offers a string of quotes (some from non-linguists) (96):

it seems reasonably clear, both in principle and in many specific cases, how unconscious knowledge issues in conscious knowledge ... it follows by computations similar to straight deduction. (Chomsky 1986: 270)

we cognize the system of mentally represented rules from which [linguistic] facts follow. (Chomsky 1980a: 9)

We can use intuitions to confirm grammars because grammars are internally represented and actually contribute to the etiology of the speaker/hearer's intuitive judgments. (Fodor 1981: 200–1)

[A speaker's judgments about the grammatical properties of sentences are the result of] a tacit deduction from tacitly known principles. (Graves et al. 1973: 325)

Our ability to make linguistic judgments clearly follows from our knowing the languages that we know. (Larson and Segal 1995: 10).

Note that none of these quotes specifically talk about special access or Cartesianism or "the voice of competence." Consider the quote from Larson and Segal, for example. Far from talking about an inner voice of competence they even eschew the term 'intuition' for the less loaded 'linguistic judgments'. Moreover, is there anyone who could possibly disagree with this quote? Surely the linguistic judgments that I make follow from my knowing the language that I know. If, for example, I knew Japanese I would have different judgments. If I didn't know any languages it seems hard to believe I could have any interesting linguistic judgments at all beyond "sounds nice" or "sounds ugly."

The second quote from Chomsky doesn't even speak to linguistic judgments, but rather to linguistic facts (which I take to be linguistic phenomena in the sense outlined above). There is a difference. As I argued above, linguistic data (intuitions or judgments) provide *evidence for* phenomena (like binding facts or "island effects") that are *explained by* the theory of grammar. When Chomsky is saying that we cognize a system of mentally represented linguistic rules from which linguistic facts follow he is talking about the relation between the parametric state of UG and linguistic phenomena. Data (and judgments) are not even under discussion in that quote.

The first Chomsky quote goes to the question of conscious knowledge, but I would take this to be knowledge of linguistic facts or phenomena (what I earlier called "S-facts")—not knowledge of the rules which give rise to the linguistic phenomena. This is entirely consistent with the picture I am advocating.

Likewise, when Fodor says that grammars contribute to the etiology of the judgments, I take this to mean that they contribute in this way: they give rise to the facts, and those facts are the objects of our linguistic judgments. To illustrate, Chomsky's writing on linguistics contributes to the etiology of what Devitt judges Chomsky's position to be, but it does not follow from this that Devitt thereby has special Cartesian access to Chomsky's thoughts about the nature of linguistics, nor even that Devitt gets it right.

The passage from Graves et al. is completely misrepresented by Devitt's editorial addition. Graves et al. are not discussing linguistic *judgments*, but rather tacit knowledge of linguistic phenomena—of what I have called explanatory facts.

I don't doubt that Devitt can find quotes suggesting another story—he even found several in earlier drafts of this book—but I chalk this up to careless exposition in my case, and perhaps also in some of the others. Indeed, you can also find misstatements in Chomsky. So, for example, in the transcripts of the 1959 Texas conference (Hill 1958) Chomsky at one point (p. 167) says "I believe that native-speaker intuitions are what everybody studies," but a few pages later in the transcript says the following: "I think we start with nothing better than intuition, and then we try to refine it by testing. I dislike reliance on intuitions much as anyone, but if we are in such a bad state that it is only intuition that we are using, then I feel we should admit it." It is my view that the second quote more accurately reflects the way generative linguists manage the relation between linguistic judgments and the linguistic theory. In the first quote Chomsky did not mean to say that intuitions are the *object* of study. He meant they are the tools we use to probe the object of study. Cherry picking quotes is not a reliable way to make progress on this issue.

With this understanding of the nature of linguistic judgments, we can supplement our earlier picture of the organization of the grammar. Building on that earlier picture, the theory of grammar posits that for an individual i, there is a grammar G_i (an abstract object) that the agent has, the psychogrammar (the psychological mechanism by virtue of which the agent has the grammar) and the physiogrammar (the physical state underlying the psychogrammar). The grammar G_i in turn determines the language L_{Gi} and is part of the explanation of the linguistic phenomena L_i that the agent i (perhaps tacitly) knows. Linguistic data provide evidence for these linguistic phenomena, and among the data are the judgments made by i.

Of course even if we make the shift from talk of intuitions to talk of judgments there are serious concerns about what role such judgments should play in linguistics, or even whether they should play any at all. Are linguistic judgments reliable?

3.3 Linguistic Judgments are Reliable (enough)

I've already addressed some concerns about linguistic judgments and stressed that they need to be handled with care, but it certainly can be argued that they are altogether too volatile for use in serious scientific theorizing. This is clearly the position taken by Householder (1965) for example:

I . . . regard the "linguistic intuition of the native speaker" as extremely valuable heuristically, but too shifty and variable (both from speaker to speaker and from moment to moment) to be of any criterial value. (15)

Gethin (1990) is even less charitable, classifying linguistic judgments as "useless."

There are a number of concerns here, but chief among these concerns are worries that are inherited from traditional worries about introspection.

Here it would be useful to review the emergence of a similar concern in psychology—one that took root with the work of John Watson and the behaviorist tradition that subsequently emerged. Prior to behaviorism, the introspective method was very much standard fare in psychology, as the following passage from Tichner's (1912) "Prolegomena to a Theory of Introspection."

The movement towards qualitative analysis has culminated in what is called, with a certain redundancy of expression, the method of 'systematic experimental introspection'. Our graduate students—far better trained, it is true, than we were in our generation—sit down cheerfully to such introspective tasks such as we had not dreamed of. And it is when some second year graduate brings in a sheaf of reports upon Understanding of Belief, upon Recognition, or Judgement, that the director of a laboratory has his historic sense aroused, and wonders what he, at the same age, could have made of a similar problem. (427)

Just one year later, Watson (1913) published a paper entitled "Psychology as the Behaviorist Views It" in which he took strong exception to the introspective method.

Psychology as the behaviorist views it is a purely objective experimental branch of natural science. Its theoretical goal is the prediction and control of behavior. Introspection forms no essential part of its methods, nor is the scientific value of its data dependent upon the readiness with which they lend themselves to consciousness. (158)

Watson's position carried the day, of course, but why precisely? And do the considerations he raised also count against current linguistic methodology?

First of all note that the move to talk about judgments already seems to undercut Watson's position a bit. Try substituting 'judgment' for 'introspection' in the Watson quote. Is it really plausible to think that "judgment forms no essential part of psychology's methods"? (I will say more about this point in a bit.)

There are three basic worries about introspective data that appeared to concern Watson and subsequent behaviorists. First, the data are not public, and hence are not available to public scrutiny. Second, the experiments are not reproducible—that is, you can't reproduce my introspective experiment. Third, the introspective method is subject to error (and abuse) since the experimental parameters cannot be properly controlled.

Each of these concerns needs to be addressed. If I judge that 'Who did John see the boy that Bill hit' is unacceptable and use this as evidence that it is ungrammatical, one can naturally ask whether that act of judgment—which I consider to be a kind of experiment—is public, reproducible, etc.

The Reproducibility Objection

I think that the second objection—the reproducibility objection—can be dispensed with in short order. Appeals to linguistic judgments certainly *are* reproducible, and often without the usual expense associated with reproducing results in other sciences. If a team of physicists report results of an experiment at the Brookhaven Labs' particle accelerator, it is not an easy matter for others to reconstruct that experiment. Time on another particle accelerator must be purchased and reserved, the experimental conditions must be reproduced (up to a degree, obviously they can't be completely reproduced), etc. In the linguistic case matters are much more simple. You report that 'Who did John see the boy that Bill hit' is unacceptable. I simply judge whether or not that sentence is acceptable.

Of course linguistic experiments are never completely reproducible, but then neither are the experiments in, for example, physics. Subsequent experiments are conducted in different places, at different times of the day, with different equipment, and by researchers with different training and background. We generally suppose that these differences won't matter, although of course sometimes they do—in ways we hadn't anticipated. Strictly speaking no experiment is ever exactly reproduced, and probably there is no way to specify in advance what differences make the new experiment the same in kind or a completely different experiment. Linguistic experiments (even in the form of judgments) are no more nor less problematic than these other cases of experimental reproduction.

The Publicity Objection

This leads back to the first objection about introspection/judgment, which is that it is not public. The question is, if the experiments are reproducible does it matter if they are not public? The experiment at Brookhaven Labs envisioned above does not take place in public. Presumably only authorized personnel are permitted to watch the actual experiment. Yet this does not undermine the integrity of the experiment for the simple reason that other similarly equipped laboratories can reproduce the experiment. The public nature of scientific inquiry seems exaggerated here.

One might think that the notion of publicity relates to the question of whether the conduct of an experiment is "in principle" observable. The argument here is that while we may not be allowed into Brookhaven Labs, if we *were* allowed in we would in principle be able to observe the experiment, and that contrarily there is no way in which in principle you could observe my act of linguistic judgment.[1]

Three observations need to be made here. First, even if it were in principle possible to observe Brookhaven experiments but not the act of forming linguistic judgments would it matter? While there is a sense in which we *could* enter the Lab, the fact of the matter is that we don't, we never will, and the mere possibility that we could doesn't matter one bit to the conduct or value of the scientific experiments being conducted at Brookhaven.

Second, even if we enter the lab and watch someone make an observation (say they record where the meniscus of a fluid lies in a graduated cylinder) it does not follow that her actual observation is public. Imagine that I look at the fluid and record the meniscus as below 0.5. The lab assistant looks at the fluid at the same time, judges it to be above 0.5, but records it as below 0.5, perhaps as a recording error. We can't get into the head of the lab assistant to insure she is accurately recording what she is seeing.

Third, it is not clear that acts of linguistic judgment are completely private in principle or even in practice. Anyone who has worked with linguistic consultants

---

[1] Thanks to Axel Mueller for making this point salient to me.

(formerly called "linguistic informants") has experienced cases in which it was apparent that the consultant, having been asked for a judgment, was distracted by something, or in which their judgment was obviously being colored by semantic anomaly or in which they were apparently confused about the task demands. In some cases, acts of judgment involve saying a sentence out loud while we contemplate its acceptability, and observers can and do note phenomena like comma intonation and stress that can skew the judgment—in effect they can see (actually, hear) that the experiment is being conducted incorrectly. If the initial act of judgment is conducted in silence we can ask the subject to audibly articulate the sentence being judged in order to hear whether there are intonation breaks or stress involved. Acts of judgment are accessible to observers, not just in principle, but in practice! Nor should this surprise us once we reject the idea that linguistic judgments are episodes in a Cartesian mental theater. Judgments need not be exclusively private affairs, although of course judges have a kind of special (if sometimes mistaken) authority about the contents of their own acts of judgment.

The Fallibility Objection

Finally, there is the matter of error. But error is something that every science has to live with. The mere fact that multi-million dollar apparatuses are employed does not prohibit error from creeping in. And at some point judgment is going to be necessary. For example, at one point one had to study the photographic plates from the cloud chamber of a particle accelerator and decide whether a certain line was the track of a positron, a scratch, or a stray particle arriving from elsewhere. If two different laboratories came up with different results then one has to continue repeating the experiments to see if there was just random noise in one or both of the experiments, and then examine the two experimental setups in detail to see exactly where they diverged.

The situation is like this in linguistic theory, where diverse judgments about a particular linguistic form are possible. Perhaps the linguistic consultants are attending to different features of the linguistic form, or perhaps one of the consultants is unwittingly putting stress on one of the words, etc. The possible sources of trouble are doubtless unlimited, and it is the everyday job of the natural scientist to find the sources of trouble when judgments begin to diverge.

Of course it is also possible for consultants to be dishonest, or to be too compliant or too easily bullied into giving the desired judgment. This is not a situation unique to linguistics, however. Lab technicians throughout the world have the same human frailties that linguistic consultants do. Error is a basic fact of life in scientific practice. We naturally want to eliminate error, but it would be a gross meta-error to suppose that error can be eliminated or reduced by avoiding linguistic judgments of acceptability or judgments of possible meanings.

Of course it has been argued that the situation in linguistics is much worse than it is in other sciences—that linguistic judgments are just wildly unreliable. Indeed, as Schütze (1996) has chronicled, these worries go way back to the early days of generative linguistics. For example, Maclay and Sleator (1960) asked beginning rhetoric students (who for some reason they took to be linguistic experts), "Do these words form a grammatical English sentence?" The results were eye opening:

3 out of 21 said yes to 'Label break to calmed about and'

Only 4 said yes to 'Not if I have anything to do with it'.

2 of 10 who rejected the following changed their votes to yes when it was pointed out that it was strictly true: 'I never heard a green horse smoke a dozen oranges'.

Of course studies like this go directly to the issue of the competence of the experimenters and to the subjects themselves (who I take to be experimenters in their own right). One wonders if the task demands were explained correctly and one wonders what on earth people could be thinking when they say that 'Label break to calmed about and' is acceptable.

Pretty clearly we need some sort of notion of reliable judge, and apparently being a student in rhetoric is not a sufficient condition to be a reliable judge. Sometimes it is clear that the judges are simply being distracted by pragmatic effects. In the case of 'I never heard a green horse smoke a dozen oranges' it appears that some subjects were judging the sentence unacceptable because they found the described situation so anomalous. Pointing out its truth seemed to allow some people to filter out the anomalous nature of the described situations.

Similarly, as reported in Spencer (1973), Hill (1961) notes that sentences drawn from *Syntactic Structures* drew mixed results from experimental subjects. 'The child seems sleeping' was accepted by 4 of the 10 subjects *until* it was paired with 'The child seems to be sleeping' at which point all 10 subjects vote negatively. Establishing the contrast helped the subjects to see what the task demand was.

I've suggested that we need to distinguish between good and bad judges of linguistic phenomena, but of course this opens up the question of how we are to distinguish the good from the bad. One worry, raised in Spencer (1973), is that in cultivating "good judges" we are in effect cultivating a group of subjects that have an entirely different set of judgments from the average person and that such rarified judgments are in some sense suspect.

[I]n recent developments in linguistics the intuitions have become more and more subtle, and more difficult for nonlinguists to intuit themselves or accept. This disturbing development has led to the question of whether or not linguists' intuitions can be uncritically accepted as being valid and basic to the speech community. There are few points of contact between linguistic theory and natural speech phenomena except for the basic intuitions of linguists . . . It is possible that the behavior of producing linguistically relevant intuitions has developed into a specialized skill, no longer directly related to the language behavior of the speech community (Bever, 1970). (Spencer 1973, 87)

There are two problems with this worry. First, it is hardly unusual for scientific investigations to be opaque to those not trained in the science, and it is likewise not unusual that a person off the street would be unable to read an experimental apparatus, which might appear to be an unintelligible series of wires and lights and meters in many cases. Linguistic judgments are no different than judgments of experts with regard to a theoretical apparatus in the lab. One has to understand what the experimental situation is in order to provide reliable judgments. In any case it seems odd to think that there is something wrong with non-linguists being left behind on the matter of judgments in an experimental situation. To see why it is odd, simply swap the term 'chemistry' for 'linguistics' (and 'judgments' for 'intuitions') in the Spencer quote:

"in recent developments in ~~linguistics~~ *chemistry* the ~~intuitions~~ *judgments* have become more and more subtle, and more difficult for non ~~linguistics~~ *chemists* ~~to-intuit~~ *judge* themselves or accept. This disturbing development has led to the question of whether or not ~~linguists' intuitions~~ *chemists' judgments* can be uncritically accepted as being valid and basic to the ~~speech~~ community of *chemical based organisms.*

Perhaps we expect that non-linguists should be as good at judging linguistic facts as linguists because language is something that we all traffic in and in some sense "know", but this is a mistake on many levels. We all likewise are immersed in electromagnetic radiation, and are all exposed to the effects of gravity and the process of digestion more than language but that doesn't makes us experts in electromagnetic radiation or the theory of gravity or the process of digestion. Like these other phenomena, language is something with which we are acquainted, but only partially so, and we are quite capable of being in error about all of them if we do not have the proper scientific tools and training to investigate these natural phenomena with requisite care.

This leads me to the second objection to the worry expressed by Bever. His worry is grounded in a falsehood. It *could* have happened that only highly trained linguists could converge on a class of judgments, but it actually doesn't seem to take much training at all—certainly not the sort of training that would prejudice subjects towards one abstract formulation of generative linguistics versus some other.

Culbertson and Gross (in press) conducted an empirical study in which acceptability judgments were drawn from 42 test subjects, of whom 7 were linguists with Ph.D.s, 17 were students with at least one class in generative syntax, 11 were students with no syntax background but with experience in other areas of cognitive science, and 7 were people with a college level education but no background in cognitive science. The stimuli they used were 73 randomly selected sentences from an introductory textbook by Haegeman and Guéron (1999), including grammatical, ungrammatical, and "questionable" sentences.

Each subject was given a questionnaire and asked to evaluate the sentences for their acceptability, where this task was explained as follows:

A sentence sounds good if you think you would or could say it under appropriate circumstances. By contrast, a sentence sounds bad if you think you would never say it under any circumstances.

Subjects were then asked to read each sentence and rate it on a scale of 1–4 (1 = perfect, 4 = terrible).

The results? The judgments of the trained linguists, the students with *some* background in linguistics, and the subjects with *some* background in cognitive science converged. Subjects with no training at all in linguistics or the cognitive sciences had different judgments. So while it seems that some sort of training is necessary, it hardly seems to be the case that the training consists of being indoctrinated into a particular theoretical framework or position within generative linguistics. Indeed, you needn't have even had a course in linguistics!

Finally, it is worth noting that finding disputed examples from academic books and journals hardly undermines the reliability of judgments in general. Such work—in journal articles in particular—is designed to offer evidence in support of one of two evenly matched theories. Such evidence is often subtle. Obvious facts (for example, sentences like 'My car is faster than yours') don't enter into the debates for the simple reason that the theories already agree on the obvious facts, or at least advocates of each theory feel they have addressed the obvious facts or otherwise have reason to not abandon their positions in the face of these facts.

Our judgments about new and crucial facts are often subtle, but they find their way into the literature because they promise to help us decide between the theories. The thought that these judgments go unchallenged is therefore absurd. They have been entered into the debate precisely because they are being deployed to make the case against someone else's position! There is thus a ready band of critics who are not going to be happy with the judgment and will be more than happy to dispute the judgment if it falters in some way.

3.4 Linguistic Judgments as Scientific Experiments

The picture I am sketching here is one in which linguistic judgments are reliable if delicate and sometimes fallible tools for investigating the language faculty, and on this picture we can devise controlled experiments in which these judgments can hone in on specific questions about that faculty. Anyone with a modicum of experience in the practice of linguistic theorizing will tell you that the relevant data do not always jump out directly at us.

I'm going to illustrate this point by way of a particular argument that was initially offered in Fodor and Sag (1982), was responded to in Ludlow and Neale (1991), and remains in general a topic of discussion in semantic theory. My point here is not really about who is right or wrong about the claims in question, but rather to illustrate the kinds of moves that must be made to successfully cull manageable data from the noise.

The case here involves scopal readings. As we saw in Chapter 1, scope readings can be different from the surface scopes of operators, and sometimes the availability of the non-surface reading can jump out at us, as in 'An oak tree grew from every acorn'. Pretty clearly we can understand this as saying that every acorn is such that an oak tree grew from it.

Sometimes, however, we do not recognize possible scope readings immediately and they have to be pointed out to us. For example, it is very hard to find the intermediate scope reading of sentences like (1) and (2) and indeed, Fodor and Sag (1982) suggested it was impossible:

(1)   Each teacher overheard the rumor that a student of mine cheated

(2)   Each teacher thinks that for a student I know to cheat would be preposterous

In this case the intermediate reading of (1), for example, would be something to the effect that for every teacher x, there is a student of mine y such that x overheard the rumor that y cheated. So the operator 'a student of mine' has narrow scope with respect to 'every teacher' but wide scope with respect to 'overheard the rumor that'. Of course in using the phrase 'scope reading' I don't mean that quantifier raising and explicit scope taking account for the readings—this is precisely the question at issue. Perhaps there are better descriptors for the readings in question (descriptors that avoid talk of scope altogether) but for now we will make do with the terminology and the caveat that we don't want to presume that quantifier scope accounts for the readings in question.

The question Neale and I faced when we wrote our (1991) paper was whether in fact there was no intermediate reading in these cases. Now it is certainly true that it is difficult to "hear" the intermediate reading in (1) or (2), but many factors can contribute to confounding what might otherwise be clear judgments that such a reading is possible.

One problem is that it is very difficult to assess the relative scopes of definite and indefinite descriptions, and the argument being made by Fodor and Sag should generalize to any quantified noun phrases. Thus we offered that one might get clearer judgments if we considered alternative quantified noun phrases, as in (3) and (4).

(3)   Each teacher overheard **seven rumors** that a student of mine cheated

(4)   Each teacher overheard **many rumors** that a student of mine cheated

These examples had the same structure as (1), but it seemed that an intermediate reading was much easier to come by. We noted that in (3) for example, "we can imagine a situation in which each teacher overheard rumors about one of my students (perhaps not the same student that the other teachers heard about), and in every case the teacher overheard seven distinct rumors."

We then suggested that these examples could be improved further, because there is an additional confounding effect from the term 'rumor'. We noted that "one person might report to the teacher of hearing that Jackie wrote the answers on her sleeve, and another person might report (second hand) that Jackie wrote the answers on a stick of chewing gum. Given two such reports, it is not clear whether the teacher has heard one rumor of cheating or two."

To avoid this confounding effect we offered that a better example would deploy a noun like 'reports' or 'exclamations' instead of 'rumors'.

(5)   Each teacher overheard **seven reports** that a student of mine cheated

(6)   Each teacher overheard **many exclamations** that a student of mine cheated

I think this is fairly typical of the process that linguists undergo when dealing with data. In effect, one is conducting little experiments, attempting in each successive experiment to control for the confounding factors that might be interfering with our ability to get at the factual question of interest.

Indeed, students in my Northwestern graduate seminar have recently pointed out to me that we can help these examples a lot by setting up the background conditions correctly. Suppose, for example, that the school in question has a policy according to which teachers cannot reprimand students for cheating unless there is a corroborating report. So, for example, the episode of cheating cannot go on the student's permanent record unless there are two reports of cheating. Now suppose that I am called into the Dean's office because there are widespread reports about my advisees cheating. In fact, every teacher in the University has reprimanded one of my students for cheating—and they aren't a few bad apples, lots of my students have been reprimanded. The Dean insists that I need to speak with my advisees about this, and I ask whether the problem is really that bad and whether there was cause for *all* the teachers to be filing reports. The Dean responds as follows.

(7)   Every teacher heard two credible reports that a student of yours cheated

Notice first that in this case we probably don't understand 'a student of yours' as having maximally narrow scope. That wouldn't necessarily justify anyone being reprimanded (for example if the reports were never about the same person there is no administrative justification for issuing a reprimand). Notice second, that we don't understand 'a student of yours' as having maximally wide scope. I'm not questioning a claim that there is one student that was reported by everyone; I'm asking for justification for the claim that there is a cheating epidemic among my advisees. If I take (7) to be an attempt by the Dean to justify her reprimand, it seems like the only really salient reading is the intermediate one!

Of course in this and many other cases intuitions are still not entirely robust and the theory will admit of grades of acceptability. That needn't be considered a problem, and can even be taken to be just part of the data in some cases (there is no reason theories can't predict ambivalent judgments).

Examples like this clearly sink attempts to gloss intuitions or judgments as "fairly immediate" and "unreflective," as Devitt (2006) does. These judgments take great care and not a little bit of reflection on the conditions in play. Still, it is correct that once we control for the relevant conditions the judgment is non-inferential. That is, once the relevant conditions are controlled for, we don't reason to the judgment; we either have it or we don't.

Of course with or without graded judgments these techniques must be handled with care, but there is nothing prima facie problematic about them. For example, sometimes it needs to be observed that the addition of stress or comma intonation can flip a judgment of acceptability. For example 'John saw who?' is widely judged to be unacceptable, but with 'John saw WHO?' the judgment of acceptability flips (although an alternative "echo question" reading is usually assigned to the sentence).

Other times we may be concerned about the presence of interpretations that are actually the downstream product of pragmatic processing rather than what is delivered by the syntax and semantics alone. There is no handy guide to the kinds of filters and priming effects one wants to deploy, nor should there be. The toolkit is limited only by the imagination of the investigators and there are no guidelines that will assure us the toolkit won't be mishandled.

One might think that this is a very peculiar way for scientific experimentation to proceed; do other sciences involve this sort of fumbling around and these sorts of fits and starts? The answer is yes. In a detailed study of the process of scientific experimentation by figures like Faraday, Biot, and Davy, David Gooding (1990) describes the continual false starts, revisions, tinkering and kludging that goes on in constructing scientific experiments. In practice these scientists seldom got the results desired on the first pass of an experimental construction. It was only after many restarts that satisfactory results were achieved. Now, should we say that Faraday et al. were cooking the books? How did they know what could legitimately be filtered out? How did they know they weren't simply changing experimental conditions to achieve a result that they were seeking? The answer is that no one is completely safe here. Expectation bias is a danger even in physics, as reported in Jeng (2006).

Polanyi (1974) observed that the evaluation of an experiment also involves the evaluation of an experimenter, including the capabilities of the experimenter and the trustworthiness of the experimenter. In an experiment in materials science we might ask whether the experimenter knows how to read a density column. In the linguistic case we might ask whether the experimenter (here the person forming a judgment) knows how to correctly judge a relative scope fact. The easiest answer is simply that we come to trust certain experimenters as being reliable. Which ones? Well, in a graduate chemistry course we might say that the good experimenters are the ones that get the right results. But what do we say in a case where outcomes are uncertain—when we don't know what the right results are?

This leads to a classic puzzle in the philosophy of science—the *experimenter's regress*. As Collins (1981) puts the problem: "usually, successful practice of an experimental skill is evident in a successful outcome to an experiment, but where the detection of a novel phenomenon is in question, it is not clear what should count as a 'successful outcome'—detection or non detection of the phenomenon."

What happens when there is a dispute about the outcome of an experiment? Is this due to the experimenter's incompetence or to some fact of the matter? While in the end there is no way to be completely "safe" as regards the competence of an experimenter, we can point to certain ways of establishing competence. One way of doing this is by determining that the experimenter is reliable on certain easy cases or established cases. For example, do the experimenters converge with the trained subjects in the Culbertson and Gross study discussed in the previous section? If so, then we might be inclined to trust the experimenter on more subtle cases.

But we can do better than say some experimenters get it right and some get it wrong. We can often go further and explain *why* they consistently get it wrong and we can show that there are certain kinds of errors that they are prone to. For example, a chemist may get consistently bad results by failing to properly clean laboratory equipment (or failing to properly supervise the lab assistant assigned this task) thus allowing contaminants into the tested material. A physicist might fail to properly shield an experiment against outside radiation or vibrations. Likewise we might be able to explain why the Culbertson and Gross subjects without previous coursework in linguistics or cognitive science failed to converge with the others. For example, it might be that these linguistic experimenters chronically fail to screen against interference—some might be unable to ignore semantic anomaly and hence can't find 'I never saw a horse smoke a dozen oranges' acceptable. Others, under the spell of their training in logic, may be chronically too forgiving of constraints on LF operator movement. Perhaps they think 'I don't always go to parties' can mean that it is always the case that I don't go to parties. Still others might be so well indoctrinated into prescriptive grammar that they refuse to see that 'That is something I won't put up with' is perfectly good English (even in Winston Churchill's dialect!).

On the other hand, judges who are on the same page about these cases and simple scopal cases like 'Every man loves some woman' (i.e. they judge it has two readings) might then be enlisted in more subtle examples like whether there is an intermediate scope reading in 'Each teacher received two credible reports that a student of mine cheated'. Of course, sometimes equally reliable experimenters come to different results on an experiment. In these cases we need to look more closely at the difference in conditions between the experimental settings. Maybe the judgments are so subtle and the noise so intractable that even reliable judges fail to agree on a particular case. That can happen, in which case we may not have admissible data for our theory (unless the theory predicts ambivalence).

Parenthetically, while I believe that there are judgment failures and that these are not illuminating of linguistic facts, it does not follow that judgment failures are uninteresting.[2] First, the judgment failures are interesting as bits of data in cognitive science (even if linguists are not interested in the faculty of judgment itself, that doesn't mean no one else can be), and they are indeed important in our coming to understand systematic failures in experimental method. That is to say, if we understand that some experimenters chronically fail to screen out confounding factors (whether dirty test tubes, stray gamma rays, or pragmatic interference), then we can institute "best practice" policies and train experimenters so as to avoid these mistakes in the future. The point is that experimental failures

---

[2] Thanks to Gregory Ward for discussion here.

should not be discarded; we just need to understand that they are not illuminating of the object of linguistic inquiry, though they are certainly illuminating of many other things—some of them having to do with our limits as judges and experimenters.

Linguists may find this situation unhappy or frustrating, but it is a situation that every science has to face. Seeking a scientific method that affords perfect safety is a fool's errand, and attempts to avoid risk by reflexively ruling out classes of data that are not immune to error can be detrimental to scientific practice. The risk of being in error is part of any interesting scientific inquiry. Linguists may as well get used to it.

3.5 On the Alleged Priority of the Data

Sociologically, linguistic theory in general has been split since the 1950s between those linguists that are "data first" people and those that advocate "data in the service of theory." To some extent, this split was in the background of the Generative Semantics Wars that we discussed in section 1.1. The general split in attitude continues to this day, although it rarely surfaces in print. When it does surface, it does in an oblique way, as in McCawley's (1985) review of Fritz Newmeyer's *Linguistic Theory in America*.

Newmeyer's attitude here . . . resembles the traditional Christian attitude toward sex: the pleasure of gathering data is proper only within the confines of holy theory construction and when not carried to excess; recreational data-gathering is an abomination. (917)

Presumably no one—including Newmeyer—believes that data gathering shouldn't be done for fun. The real question is whether one should expect a research university to pay someone for doing recreational data gathering, and whether the recreational data gathering is the theory-free enterprise people think it is. What makes a piece of data interesting after all? Typically it is interesting because it stands out in some way—it flies in the face of our current theory, or alternatively, supplies unexpected support for some theory.

Of course, sometimes we don't see just how theory-laden our data gathering can be. Sally Thomason, while commenting approvingly of McCawley's remarks, inadvertently provides an example.

As for McCawley's comment, I take no stand on whether his charge against Fritz Newmeyer is justified, but it will resonate with those linguists who, like me, can get excited about the tiniest new fact that is recorded in their field notes or uncovered in their reading. ("They have a root that refers solely to the drumming of a ruffed grouse? Cool!")[3]

Thomason seems to think that this is an atheoretical fact. But is it? Notice that plenty of theoretical knowledge is required to even get her example rolling. For starters you have to know enough morphology to know what a root is. To a world class linguist and former President of the Linguistic Society of America like Sally Thomason that may seem like theory-free data, but it is worth noting that Claude Lévi-Strauss (1953, 350–351)

---

[3] http://itre.cis.upenn.edu/~myl/languagelog/archives/003890.html

compared the discovery of the morpheme and phoneme to the Newtonian revolution in physics. In other words, descriptions couched in terms of morphological elements (like roots), far from being raw data, pack into them one of the most profound theoretical discoveries in the history of western science. Beyond that, the example requires that you also have to know that roots are true of certain kinds of activities and that this one is true of drumming activities, and that the root only applies when the agent of the activity is a ruffed grouse.

Even with all that theoretical knowledge I personally don't have enough theoretical background to understand why this fact is cool. Is this rare? Is there something about standard linguistic assumptions that makes this surprising? Is this different from there being a word like 'gobble' which so far as I know (apart from the act of eating food rapidly and, I'm reliably informed by John Collins, an impolite meaning in British English) only applies to the noise made by turkeys? The point is that data are only really interesting against a backdrop of theory.

Of course the real issue here is not whether it is OK to do theory-free data gathering (assuming such is possible) but whether that is the best way to go about data gathering. Charles Darwin, in a letter to Henry Fawcett, thought not:

About 30 years ago there was much talk that geologists ought to observe and not to theorize; and I well remember someone saying that at this rate a man might as well go into a gravel pit and count the pebbles and describe the colors. How odd it is that anyone should not see that all observation must be for or against some view if it is to be of any service! (Darwin and Seward 1903)

Elsewhere, as reported in Mayr (1993, 9), Darwin wrote, "I can have no doubt that speculative men, with a curb on, make far the best observers."

Not only do they "make far the best observers," according to Darwin, but theory-driven observers needn't concede the "we have more fun" mantle to McCawley and Thomason. This time Julian Huxley comes to the defense of theory-driven observation in a remark in his book *Birds and the Territorial System*.

The man who is content to make records or to collect skins and eggs will, unless he spends years of his life in a systematic analysis of his own and others' facts, not get anything from his labours— save the very real pleasure of making the observations. But he who takes the trouble to think out new problems and new lines of attack upon the old will have the same pleasure, and in addition the joy of intellectual discovery. (1926, 170)

Should We Be Closer to the Data?

Of course critics of theory typically don't reject a role for theory altogether (McCawley and Thomason certainly didn't). Often the position is more nuanced—typically that there is a place for theory, but that data ought to drive the analysis (data is the ox, and theory is the oxcart). Others might reject this, but still hold that the field is too theoretical or that it is not paying enough attention to the data, or at least not respecting it enough. Let's consider both of these positions.

Data First?

Some linguists have argued that the traditional descriptive method in linguistics is more scientific because it begins with the data and only then proceeds to theory construction. For example, Absalom and Hajek (1997, 177) claim that "the data needs to drive theoretical analysis and not the other way around." In still other cases linguists have claimed to dispense with the theory-construction portion altogether, arguing that the extant theories all fall to counterexamples and the best we can do is to describe the linguistic data. In my view these positions are confused at best, and are potentially destructive *vis-à-vis* the goals of scientific inquiry.

The first problem is coherently formulating the thesis that one is beginning solely with naked data. This is the question we raised earlier: What *are* theory-free data? Simply assuming the existence of word boundaries assumes a lot of theory. Likewise, assuming that what one is perceiving is in fact language (as opposed to noises) is heavily theory-laden.

This is just a basic point about the philosophy of science. It is widely viewed since the work of Hanson (1958), Sellars (1949), Kuhn (1970) and many others that there is no such thing as raw data or raw sense perception. Everything is viewed, as it were, through the lens of some theory or other, whether that theory be learned, tacitly held and cultural, or a feature of our cognitive architecture.[4] Very simply, the issue is not whether one should begin with data and proceed to theory. The point is that when one begins gathering data one is already neck deep in theory—whether one realizes it or not.

This point exposes the pernicious aspect of these calls against theory. Those who advance such calls have theoretical assumptions of their own and they are asking us, in effect, not to examine those theoretical assumptions. For example, many linguists who rail against theory are all too happy to talk about sentences and words, but sentences and words are highly abstract theoretical constructs that were at one time theoretical discoveries. That they are now familiar to every grammar school student does not mean they are theory-free or pure data, but rather that the theory behind them has become so sedimented that we no longer notice it unless we sit back and actually think about it for a bit.

Data Trumps Theory?

There is a more subtle position. You might think that theory should be driving the enterprise (and of course concede that there is no such thing as data that is theory-free), but still argue that data *trump* theory. That is, ultimately, theory has to respect the data. Few people dispute this, but there is plenty of room to argue about what respect should consist in here. Does it mean that one piece of recalcitrant data kills a theory? Always?

---

[4]   I gather that even Fodor (1984), while arguing in defense of the observation/inference distinction, saves it by appealing to our shared cognitive architecture. That is, we come prewired with something like a theory that organizes our perceptual experience.

Falsificationism, of course, is the view championed by Popper (1969) in which theories are to be valued if they are more easily falsifiable—that is, if there are clear tests by which they can be refuted. The problem is that one turns the doctrine on its head when one asserts that theories should be modified or rejected because they are "falsified" by stray bits of data; this has the effect of creating Frankensteinish theories which cannot be falsified because they are forever being patched up to conform with the facts. Such theories are surely not what Popper envisioned.

Still, theories *can* be falsified. Or rather, they can be replaced by superior theories. The point is that the superior theory is not necessarily the theory that "covers" all the facts; it is the theory that does the best job of responding to all of our interests, and these range from covering the available data and making reliable predictions, to the preparation of the object of inquiry for reduction to more basic sciences, to the feasibility of utilizing our theoretical knowledge in other kinds of applications (engineering applications for example), and last but not least, helping us better *understand* the phenomena under investigation.

Thus, when Loporcaro (1989, 343) contends that "although descriptive simplicity is a desirable goal, it should not be attained at the cost of contradicting actual linguistic data," he is mistaken. If the "descriptive simplicity" enables the successful reduction of linguistics to more basic sciences then we should be prepared to take the "contradictory data" as puzzles remaining to be explained rather than grounds to abandon the theory.

The Minimalist Program discussed in section 1.4 is potentially a case in point. If the theoretical hunch behind the Minimalist Program is correct, then generative linguistics is being prepared for a reduction to more basic sciences—and the key aspects of linguistic theory (recursion, etc.) are going to be cashed out by basic biophysical mechanisms. But part of that preparation process is isolating core aspects of the FLN that are to be kept, and cutting loose other kinds of pre-theoretically linguistic phenomena that traditionally have been held to be part of the core of generative linguistics. In the extreme case, we could find that elements like binding theory, which played a central role in generative linguistics throughout the 1980s, would be separated out and treated as phenomena outside the core. Even something as basic as the head parameter (discussed in section 1.3) could end up being outside of the core.

If this is how the theory ultimately unfolds, then it will not be an unusual outcome for science in general nor even for the last 40 years of research in linguistic theory. Philosophers of science sometimes call the phenomenon "Kuhn loss," with the thought that sometimes data we had "explained" in a theory get orphaned when the theory moves out from under the data. Theory growth is not monotone—as it grows some explanations may be lost, and indeed our understanding of what counts as "linguistic" may change.

There is an excellent example of this phenomenon in the science of epidemiology. Originally, the term 'polio' was a covering term for a broad class of symptoms and conditions for which we had no clear explanation. Eventually, we developed the theory that polio was caused by a virus. However, the viral theory of polio did not cover all the phenomena that we took to be symptomatic of polio. Indeed, as reported in Assad and Cockburn (1972), Sabin (1981), and Gear (1981), we now know that there are dozens of other non-polio enteroviruses (NPEV) that are potentially capable of causing paralytic polio-like syndrome. It is generally agreed that at least some of the cases that fell under the rubric of 'polio' originally were in fact caused by NPEVs.

In response to facts like this, we might have moved in two distinct directions. We could have said that the viral theory of polio was a failure because it did not "cover the data" or that we are using a semantic trick to redefine polio (indeed the online website of the World Chiropractic Alliance claims just that[5]), or we could have said that there really isn't such a thing as polio, or we could have said that the viral theory accounts for polio and the other cases were conditions that we mistook for polio. If current work in generative linguistics including the Minimalist Program is ultimately successful we will face a choice similar to that in the case of polio, in effect a question about whether the emerging theory ought to be called 'linguistics'. It might alternatively be called 'the science of the FLN' or 'the science of the L-faculty'. No doubt there are political advantages to calling it 'linguistics', not least of which is the prospect of explaining where you should be housed in the university to one's deans and provosts.

Statistical Natural Language Processing

Finally, let's return to statistical natural language processing (NLP) which often characterizes itself as strongly situated in the "data first" camp. For example, in their introduction to statistical NLP, Manning and Schütze (1999) offer the following description of how their project contrasts with generative linguistics.

Chomskyan (or generative) linguistics seeks to describe the language module of the human mind (the I-language) for which data such as texts (the E-language) provide only indirect evidence, which can be supplemented by native speaker intuitions. Empiricist approaches are interested in describing the E-language as it actually occurs. Chomsky (1965: 3–4) thus makes a crucial distinction between linguistic competence, which reflects the knowledge of language structure that is assumed to be in the mind of a native speaker, and linguistic performance in the world, which is affected by all sorts of things such as memory limitations and distracting noises in the environment. Generative linguistics has argued that one can isolate linguistic competence and describe it in isolation, while empiricist approaches generally reject this notion and want to describe actual use of language. (1999, 6)

Obviously, if I am right about the conduct of generative linguistics, this description misfires badly. I've argued that we should dispense with talk of intuitions in favor of talk of judgments. As I have argued, we don't need to take texts as offering indirect evidence; I haven't privileged either corpora data or linguistic judgments. I have rejected the idea that thinking of linguistics as a chapter of psychology requires us to

---

[5]   http://www.worldchiropracticalliance.org/tcj/1989/aug/aug1989g.htm

think of linguistic facts as being "in the mind." I've also rejected the idea that we know a grammar, preferring to say that we cognize or, better yet, simply have it.

While it is certainly true that generative linguistics is interested in constructing a competence theory, it is weird to think such a theory could be "isolated" or "described in isolation". After all, the object of the competence theory (UG) contributes to the explanation of linguistic facts/phenomena, and these linguistic facts/phenomena provide evidence for our theories of UG. Nor is it clear why a generative linguist wouldn't be interested in describing the "actual use of language." The point is that actual usage would be *explained* by the competing actions of UG, memory limitations, pragmatic effects, salient events, ambient noise, perceptual and articulatory failures, etc. UG is just one piece of the explanation for the linguistic facts that data mining uncovers. Put another way, generative linguistics is involved in the construction of a theory for a system that does not explain everything, but which is a component in a symphony of elements that in concert might explain everything about "actual use of language." Manning and Schütze appear to be confusing the domain of inquiry (the explananda) with the object of inquiry (the explanans). Generative linguists are interested in language "as it actually occurs," but they are also interested in explaining why it occurs as it does. Part of that explanation is UG, and UG is the object of inquiry (the explanans) for many generative linguists.[6]

Setting aside the misunderstandings about generative linguistics, there is no question but that statistical NLP can be a powerful tool in the investigation of many aspects of language study, and it is easy to understand the excitement. Indeed, it is continuous with excitement throughout the sciences over the great success in application of statistical methods to large sets of data.

But just how excited should we really be? The popular magazine *Wired* ran a cover story in July 2008 entitled "The End of Science: The quest for knowledge used to begin with grand theories. Now it begins with massive amounts of data." (Interestingly the same issue noted (p. 56) that in the previous twelve years they had proclaimed the end of commercial web publishing (1996), the end of web browsers (1997), the end of online song swapping (2002), and the end of brands (2004)).

As its poster boy for the end of science, *Wired* used Craig Venter, who, in biology, has used supercomputers to statistically analyze the data resulting from his "shotgun gene sequencing" technique (see Venter et al. 2004). This has allowed Venter to "discover" thousands of previously unknown life forms (principally bacteria). 'Discover' is in scare quotes because Venter can't say much about the properties of these new species—they are just statistical blips in the data. Still, discovering new species—or

---

[6] My use of the terms 'explanans' and 'explananda' depart from other uses (perhaps Hempel's) in that I gather Hempel and others did not use 'explananda' to talk about phenomena but rather about statements of the phenomena. I do mean to be directly talking about the phenomena and the theory that purports to explain them.

perhaps we should say discovering *that* there is a species having a certain genetic sequence—is certainly something to be excited about.

But two questions are now salient. First, to what extent does the process piggyback on theory that wasn't and perhaps couldn't be extracted by statistical means alone? That is, without the theory of genes and without the DNA model and indeed without the theory of gene sequencing there would be nothing to run statistical methods over. Second, is it correct to think that Venter is applying statistical methods in a brute strength manner?

Despite being touted as someone who has used statistical methods with success, Venter (2008) is pretty blunt about the brute application of statistical methods:

Despite my urging that we always look for those big questions, data generation for its own sake continues to be a major impediment to real scientific breakthroughs in genomics. It is not hard to understand why investigators, particularly young scientists, are satisfied being data generators, as government agencies and some foundations continue to pay out hundreds of millions of dollars for just DNA sequencing or, even worse, microarrays, creating huge datasets but seldom any real scientific insight.

Venter also observed that rather than being engaged in passive data collection over existing sets of data, he is engaged in constructing combinations of genes in an attempt to understand what combinations are required for life:

Comparison of the *M. genitalium* and *H. influenzae* genomes raised an interesting question: If one species needed 1,800 genes and the other only 500 or so, was there a minimal genome that could sustain independent self-replicating life? Years of comparative genomics and gene knockouts have not answered completely the question, so we have turned to synthesizing genomes and varying their contents so we can find out just how little genetic information is necessary to make an organism work.

This is the experimental method in its classical form. Venter is not running statistical packages over existing data sets, but is rather tinkering with genomes in an attempt to understand their structural properties.

None of this is to diminish the value of statistical methods to Venter or to the rest of biology, but it is to suggest that these methods on their own do not answer the most interesting questions. Much of biology proceeds as it did before, decidedly theory-driven and relying on creative experimentation. And it is not hard to see why; we not only want to discover new species, we want to know what they are like, how and why they evolved, etc.

The situation is the same in linguistics. For example, statistical methods can confirm our judgments that violations of Ross constraints are unacceptable (they are very rare in corpora), but thus far it does little to help us to understand why they are rare. Statistical methods can also identify constructions that previously escaped our attention, but it is not clear that they can tell us why those constructions are present or what accounts for them. These are the kinds of questions that generative linguists are interested in, and at the moment, traditional investigative methods—for example constructing novel linguistic forms and judging whether they are acceptable and what their possible interpretations are—continue to be fruitful.

What Are Linguistic Judgments For?

In this chapter I've made the case that linguistic theories are not theories that axiomatize linguistic judgments, but rather that our judgments are evidence for linguistic facts and that our linguistic theories are designed to play a role in the explanation of these linguistic facts. But this raises the question of why we have any judgments at all about such things. Why should we have judgments about the acceptability of linguistic forms?

One possibility is that our ability to make these judgments is a fluke or a bit of luck, but there is another possibility. It might be that they play a role in our ability to follow the rules of our grammar—they might provide *normative guidance* for our linguistic performance. We can successfully comply with our linguistic rules because we are capable of judging whether what we are saying is acceptable (and what it means). The judgments thus could play a kind of regulative or optimizing role in our linguistic behavior at the same time that they provide insights into the language faculty.

This possibility opens up a great big can of questions. Does it make sense to think of the rules of generative linguistics being normative? And how could they be if we don't even know what those rules are? I take up these questions in the next chapter.

4

A Role for Normative Rule Governance?

Linguists and philosophers of linguistics don't often think of linguistic rules as being normative, but that doesn't mean the idea is a complete nonstarter.[1] One problem, of course, is that even rules of the sort envisioned in the 1970s are so abstract that few people would be in a position to consciously entertain them, much less reflect on their normative pull.

This, in effect, is why thinking about normative linguistic rules is not very attractive to linguists. It certainly doesn't make sense to think of us following these rules in any sort of reflective capacity. It is much easier to think of linguistic principles as being part of a project of *describing* linguistic competence, rather than *normatively guiding* linguistic competence.

But perhaps we can still make sense of the idea. In Chapter 3 we looked fairly extensively at linguistic judgments and the role they play in our linguistic theorizing. Could we also think of linguistic judgments as playing a role in *directing* or *monitoring* our linguistic performance?

For a prescriptive grammarian this makes perfect sense. Certain rules are ingrained in you (for example: "don't end a sentence with a preposition"), you come to have judgments that comport with those rules, and they guide your linguistic practice. Within generative linguistics as outlined in Chapter 1, this idea is so confused it would be a task to even sort out and enumerate all the mistakes. Clearly, we aren't interested in artificial prescriptive rules, and when we get to rules like subjacency or the tensed-S condition, or parameters like the polysynthetic parameter or the S/NP parameter for subjacency, it seems fairly implausible to think that we have transparent judgments about such things, much less that judgments of that form could provide normative guidance. So how can we be normatively guided by our grammar when it is construed as an abstract object that is the product of a parametric state of the language faculty?

---

[1] Thanks to Barry C. Smith for inspiring this chapter and to Barry, Sari Kisilevsky, and Peter Railton for comments on (and catching errors in) earlier versions of this chapter.

Consider the following passage from John Lawler's online course notes, where he discusses the role that Ross island constraints might play in our linguistic planning and performance:

Violations of Ross Constraints are very ungrammatical. Most people never encounter them. We appear to formulate our discourse to avoid them. Occasionally, we get in a bind and see one looming at the end of the clause, and have to do something quick. What we do is often illuminating about the relative importance of syntactic rules.

For instance, consider the following:

?That's the book$_i$ [that Bill married the woman$_j$ [who$_j$ illustrated it]].
★That's the book$_i$ [that Bill married the woman$_j$ [who$_j$ illustrated ___$_i$]].

Neither sentence is terrifically grammatical, but the first seems more appropriate (and common as a type) than the second, though the last word in the first sentence still feels strange. The ordinary rule of relative clause formation operating on the last clause should result in its deletion at the end of the clause (and thus the sentence). However, it appears inside another relative, an island, and is thus safe from such "movement" by the Complex NP Constraint.

Sentences like the first one are generated when, at the last minute, the speaker realizes what is going to result, and cancels the deletion, substituting an alternative relative-formation rule (called a *Resumptive Pronoun* in the trade), which merely pronominalizes the coreferential NP, instead of deleting it in the object position.

This is not the way English forms its relative clauses (though other languages use it frequently, e.g., Hebrew), and the sentence is thus ungrammatical. But this turns out to be a venial syntactic sin by comparison with a violation of a Ross constraint, which typically produces extreme ungrammaticality.

Lawler is not saying that we are consciously aware of Ross constraints, nor even that we judge that there has been compliance with such rules. Rather he is saying that we can see that something is wrong, and that we act so as to make it right. We make it as right as we can, and in so doing (and unbeknownst to all but theoretical linguists) we have acted so as to avoid a violation of the Complex NP constraint. What I am suggesting is that this is a case in which we are normatively guided by the Ross constraint even though we have no conscious knowledge of such guidance.

This is tricky. If it is true that we have judgments that play a role in the normative guidance of our linguistic performance, we don't want to be in a position that only true believers can be so guided. These should be judgments that not only are *available* to all competent linguistic agents, but in fact are *used* by them as ways of checking or regulating their linguistic performance. *All* linguistic agents. Even agents that believe their judgments are not grounded in cognized rules but are actually judgments about language construed as an external social object, even agents that believe the judgments are generated by high level central processing mechanisms, even agents that don't believe they have linguistic rules of any form.

Given all this, the idea of linguistic rules providing normative guidance must be pretty hopeless, no? I'm going to suggest that the problem is difficult but not necessarily hopeless. The puzzle is to figure out how can we have judgments that can guide us in producing linguistic forms that are well-formed according to a linguistic rule system even if we have no knowledge of the rule system. This might *seem* hopeless, but it is really a quite widespread phenomenon, or at least closely related to a widespread phenomenon.

An example comes from work in ethics by Arpaly (2003) and Railton (2006). They discuss cases where an agent is following an ethical principle, but does not recognize this, and even interprets their behavior as ethically unprincipled and indeed morally wrong. Arpaly illustrates this idea with a literary example from Mark Twain's book *Huck Finn*. In the example, Huck decides not to turn in the escaped slave Jim, even though he thinks the *moral* option is to do precisely that. Huck believes that Jim is someone else's property, after all. He judges that turning in Jim is not the thing to do, but he takes his judgment to have a non-moral etiology. Why does Huck refuse to turn in Jim? Well, Huck is really not able to articulate the reason. As Railton (2006) has described such situations, perhaps Huck just has a nagging feeling of discomfort at the idea of doing it. He doesn't feel that this discomfort or his decision of what to do is based on an ethical principle, but Arpaly and Railton argue that this is precisely what Huck is doing—he is following a moral principle, but he describes his action as being immoral. Indeed he thinks he is a bad boy for that very reason.

Now let's return to the case of judgments of acceptability for linguistic forms. We can imagine someone in the position of Huck, only with respect to linguistic rules rather than moral rules. Let's call this hypothetical agent 'Michael'. Michael has a grammar as part of his cognitive architecture, and he has judgments of linguistic acceptability that he uses to guide his linguistic performance. Yet Michael, like Huck, is deeply confused. Although his judgments guide him in such a way that he generally follows the rules/principles of grammar, he does not recognize that he is so guided. He doesn't believe that there is a grammar that is a feature of his cognitive psychology—to the contrary he takes language to be a social object, and he thinks that he isn't following rules at all, but rather thinks he has a kind of knowledge-how that accounts for his linguistic competence. He also misdescribes his judgments, taking them as being the by-products of high level processing over social linguistic facts.

Michael, like Huck who believes he is immoral, believes he is ignorant of language in the relevant sense. But on Arpaly and Railton's view we don't need to feel bad for either Huck or Michael. Huck really is acting on ethical principles; he is not really a bad boy after all. Similarly, Michael really is following grammatical rules—in spite of what even Michael himself insists.

As I said before, this gambit is subtle. One needs to develop a position on the normativity of language which can allow that linguistic rules are very abstract and currently outside the reach of our best linguistic theorizing yet have some normative pull on us.

It's interesting to note that Railton (2006) uses a linguistic case to illustrate the kind of rule governance he is attempting to get clear on.

Interestingly, such pressures for consistency can be triggered and felt even when the norm of the agent in question is one of which she herself is unaware. One intriguing piece of evidence for this is the phenomenon of over-regularization in children's speech. As their linguistic ability develops, some children who have previously mastered the past tenses of irregular verbs begin 'correcting themselves' by forming irregular past tenses using the ⟨verb stem + -ed⟩ rule for regular verbs, for example saying 'go-ed' instead of 'went'. This occurs despite the fact that these children have never heard 'go-ed' spoken by adult speakers, and have never been sanctioned for using 'went' as the past tense of 'go'. As adults, we feel similar pressures toward consistency in language use. We can sense that grammatical anomaly is creeping into a sentence we are uttering, and struggle to correct ourselves on the fly. We treat such anomalies as mistakes, even when they have no effect on—or even improve—sentence intelligibility, and even when we would be at a loss to identify the particular incompatibility with grammatical rules involved. (2006, 12)

But precisely what notion of rule governance works in cases like linguistics and the Huck Finn case we discussed earlier? Railton (2006) walks us through a series of accounts of rule governance until he gets one that he thinks fits the bill. He begins with the following formulation.

(RG1) Conduct C is guided by norm N only if C is in accord with N.

The problem with this formulation, as we all know too well, is that conduct can be rule guided but fall short of successfully being in accord with N. That is, I might be guided by a rule, try very hard to follow the rule, and yet fall well short of my goal. Rule guidance may fall well short of rule accord.

This leads us to Railton's second formulation.

(RG2) Conduct C is guided by norm N only if C is the manifestation of a reliable disposition to act in a way conducive to compliance with N.

This is better, but Railton suggests a problem. Consider the case of Harry the receptionist. He is disposed to dress in accord with company dress code, but is guided by his own sense of style rather than company dress code of which he is only vaguely aware. In this case we would say that Harry is disposed to act in a way that is conducive to compliance with N, but it does not seem that he is *guided* by the company dress code. We need to make it clear that one's disposition to be in compliance with N is somehow connected with one's being guided by N itself.

This leads us to the third formulation.

(RG3) Conduct C is guided by norm N only if C is the manifestation of a disposition to act in a way conducive to compliance with N, such that the fact that C conduces to compliance with N plays an appropriate role *in the explanation* of the agent's C-ing.

Obviously everything here turns on what would count as being explanatory in the agent's C-ing. Railton provides the following formulation: "A has a mental representation of N, judges that C-ing would conduce to compliance with N, takes this to be a reason for C-ing, and this judgment (partially) causes A's C-ing [in] virtue of its content."

The problem with this formulation is that most cases of norm guidance don't have this explicit character—in either the ethical or the linguistic realm. As Railton puts it, "in many cases of norm-guided behavior, individuals do not even form the belief that their conduct conduces toward normative compliance."

To see this, consider the case of Fred, who is disposed to validate his ticket whenever he gets on the bus. When he forgets to do so, he corrects his behavior.

Fred does feel discomfit upon discovering that he is riding without validating … Fred tends to treat departures from his usual practice as calling for correction.

Notice, however, that Fred may not be aware that he is motivated by some sort of rule. He may only be aware of the vague sense of discomfort that he feels. (As we have seen, linguistic cases and the Huck Finn case work like this too.) What we need is a notion of regulative behavior that allows that we can be guided by a rule without explicitly being aware of the content of the rule (under relevant descriptions). We could achieve this if the rule functioned as a kind of regulator in the sense deployed by engineers— something that regulates the system for error and corrects when necessary. More explicitly, Railton offers the following explication of regulative explanation:

regulative explanation: For an engineer, a regulator is a device with a distinctive functional character. One component continuously monitors the state of the system—the regulated system—relative to an externally set value, e.g. temperature, water pressure, or engine velocity. If the system departs from the set-point value, the monitor sends an "error signal" to a second component, which modulates the inputs into the system … until the set-point value is restored.

This helps us get closer to the notion of regulative behavior, and suggests the following formulation for rule governance:

(RG4) Agent A's conduct C is guided by the norm N only if C is a manifestation of A's disposition to act in a way conducive to compliance with N, such that N plays a regulative role in A's C-ing, where this involves some disposition on A's part to notice failures to comply with N, and to feel discomfort when this occurs, and to exert an effort to establish conformity with N.

The problem with this formulation is that regulative behavior isn't quite enough (this will be a key point when we look at the rule following arguments in Chapter 5). Not all regulated behavior counts as rule governed behavior. To illustrate this point, Railton offers another disposition of Fred's.

Fred usually has a snack around 10 a.m. every day. Typically, when he sees the clock strike 10, he goes and buys a snack. One day, however, buried under a pile of work, Fred works straight through to lunch. As Railton describes the situation, "Fred does not regard this failure as something that calls for correction. Instead, he thinks only, 'Funny, I didn't even notice'."

Railton calls this a non-consequential and unsanctioned failure to fit the standing behavioral expectations. The failure is non-consequential because, as it happened, Fred suffered no ill effects from the omission. The failure is unsanctioned (it might be better to say it is "not sanctioned") because no authority would take any interest in his missed snack or impose penalties.

In Railton's terminology, the morning snack is a *default plan*, and it plays a role in regulating Fred's behavior, but it isn't normative in the way that his ticket validating was. The clue to its not being normative is that Fred shrugs off the missed snack, whereas if, for example, he realized that he failed to validate his bus ticket earlier in the day his inner dialogue might invoke excuse-making and bargaining ("I've lost tickets before that I never used", or "I'll validate twice text time") even though his failure to comply with the validating rule has no real consequences when he realizes his omission.

Are linguistic cases like this too? We don't always exert effort to comply with our judgments of acceptability, but often enough we do, even when compliance is not required, and even when the editing gets in the way of smoothly communicating.

We need more than (RG4). Genuine rule governance is not just about following a default plan, it involves a felt need to fix things even when we are not under external pressure to do so. Thus Railton ultimately suggests we opt for (RG5).

(RG5) Agent A's conduct C is guided by the norm N only if C is a manifestation of A's disposition to act in a way conducive to compliance with N, such that N plays a regulative role in A's C-ing, where this involves some disposition on A's part to notice failures to comply with N, to feel discomfort when this occurs, and to exert effort to establish conformity with N *even when* the departure from N is unsanctioned and non-consequential.

Railton's formulation here is a bit misleading because it seems to suggest we might be in a position to consciously recognize we are complying with N, but this can't be what Railton intends, since he expressly states that we may not have access to N. So let's try the following more austere formulation.

(RG5′) Agent A's conduct C is guided by the norm N only if C is a manifestation of A's disposition to act in a way conducive to compliance with N, such that N plays a regulative role in A's C-ing, where this involves some disposition on A's part to feel discomfort at failing to C, and to exert effort to C *even when* failing to C is unsanctioned and non-consequential.

Even on this austere formulation, there are a couple of assumptions built into Railton's analysis that we may not want to buy into. For example, Railton is focused on the discomfort one might feel after failing to comply with a rule. Must it always involve such discomfort? For example, one might feel no discomfort at all from a failure to comply with rules but plenty of satisfaction from compliance. To illustrate, consider Church Lady (borrowed from the old *Saturday Night Live* routine), who is puffed up with moral pride. Let's suppose she never feels guilt or discomfort at failure to follow a rule (indeed she cannot recognize that she fails to be moral). She never forgets to validate her bus pass. On some days, however, the bus is very crowded and it becomes inconvenient to validate. She realizes that on such days she will not be sanctioned for failing to validate. Nevertheless, she validates her ticket and feels a sense of satisfaction with herself and her conduct.

Railton is showing his Kantian stripes here in thinking that Church Lady is not ethically rule guided. Kant would say that Church Lady is not acting out of respect for the law; she is merely acting out of the sense of pride she feels in her action. I'm not an expert on moral psychology, but I am suspicious of theories that take actions motivated out of moral pride to not be cases of behavior that is governed by moral rules. Church Lady was puffed up with moral pride, but I have trouble thinking that she was not for all that often guided by moral rules.

Now to be sure if we allow that cases like these are instances of rule governance we need to rethink the weight put on the notion of a regulator in Railton's proposal.[2] A regulator, after all, detects that something is wrong and attempts to return the system to equilibrium. That works in the case of someone who feels discomfort at not validating their ticket (validating returns the system to equilibrium by eliminating the sense of discomfort) but it doesn't seem to work for Church Lady, who is not trying to return to a state of equilibrium but is attempting to accumulate as much satisfaction as she can.

Regulators aren't the right metaphor for this, but there are other metaphors that can be employed here. Obviously, there are systems that strive to maximize for certain properties (for example consider a system that attempts to absorb as much sunlight as possible). Let's call these systems *optimizing systems*.

Here is how we might have to structure the theory for Church Lady.

(RG5-CL) Agent A's conduct C is guided by the norm N only if C is a manifestation of A's disposition (i) to act in a way conducive to compliance with N, such that N plays a role in A's C-ing, where this involves some disposition on A's part to notice that C-ing will optimize for her sense of pride, and (ii) to exert effort to C *even when* failure to C is unnoticed and non-consequential.

If we wanted, then we could construct a disjunctive analysis that would allow either route to normative guidance—one where the primary moral sentiment is discomfort at failure to comply and one where the primary moral sentiment is pride at compliance. But does this analysis have to be hooked to a particular moral sentiment at all? That is, does normative rule guidance involve a distinctive phenomenology?

Consider Zombie Girl, who is phenomenologically impaired as regards her rule compliance. If she fails to validate her ticket she feels no discomfort. If she goes out of her way to validate her ticket, even when it is inconvenient to do so, she feels no satisfaction. She validates, alright, but there is no moral sentiment involved. She simply judges that it is the thing to do, and that is why she does it.

---

[2] Thanks to my Spring 2009 graduate seminar participants for pointing this out.

Humeans like Prinz (2007) might argue that these sorts of cases aren't possible—that normative judgment necessarily involves some emotional content. But again I wonder if this is right.

For example, there is a version of Kantianism described by Korsgaard (1996) according to which not only is Church Lady not acting morally (she is acting out of pride rather than respect for the law) but the same might be said of the person who is acting merely so as to ease discomfort. After all, how is acting to ease discomfort the same as acting out of respect for the law? On this view the phenomenology attending our acts of rule governance might provide *evidence* that we are acting in a rule governed way, but the sentiment is not *constitutive* of our so acting.[3]

I am pressing against the role of moral sentiment here because if we want to extend Railton's analysis of rule governance to the linguistic case there is a very serious question as to what the relevant sentiments might be. In the case of traditional prescriptive grammar there is an easy answer: I might feel shame or embarrassment at not speaking properly. That's fine for learned linguistic rules like using 'whom' not 'who' in dative case, but it's less clear how to make sense of the kinds of linguistic rules generative linguists are concerned with. It also isn't clear that the sense of embarrassment one feels at failure to comply with prescriptive linguistic rules is about failing to comply with a linguistic norm—it might simply be due to telegraphing one's social or educational status. The prescriptive rules are just like secret handshakes in this case. If you don't know the prescriptive rules then you are marked as an outsider or a social inferior and thus you feel bad. Obviously these sorts of prescriptive norms are established by power relations, and obviously they have nothing to do with the individual norms that would be operative in the context of generative linguistics.

Take the pending violation of the Ross Constraint the agent sees in the example discussed by Lawler. Does the agent correct and add the resumptive pronoun because she sees that she would have felt shame or embarrassment at failure to do so? Just what is the attending phenomenology? And is there any reason to believe that her phenomenology is shared by other agents? That is, even if there is some sentiment that she has when she sees an impending violation of a Ross Constraint, why should she suppose that others have a similar sentiment in similar circumstances? Maybe violations of Ross Constraints are like fingers on a blackboard to her but like a dull headache to me. Or maybe like Zombie Girl there is no phenomenology at all attending my insertion of a resumptive pronoun.

If we want to extend the analysis to at least allow such possibilities then it seems we want to revise Railton's analysis to something like (RG6):

(RG6) Agent A's conduct C is guided by the norm N only if C is a manifestation of A's disposition to act in a way conducive to compliance with N, such that N plays a role in A's C-ing, where A judges that her efforts to C, whether successful or not, are the thing to do—particularly when so acting is difficult and unsanctioned, and even when

---

[3] Once again, thanks are due to my Spring 2009 seminar participants for discussion of this point.

inconsequential. Some of A's failures to try and C may give rise to A's feeling discomfort and A's efforts to C, whether successful or not, may have led A to feel a sense of satisfaction—of having "done (tried to do) the right thing." These sentiments may signal to A that she is acting appropriately but they are not constitutive of her being rule governed.

While this unlinks rule governance from moral sentiment there is a sense in which it falls short of some of the goals of Railton's proposal. Notice that to escape talk of moral sentiments we are now leaning on the idea that A is judging that C is the thing to do, and thus it looks like our analysis of rule governance has normative judgment packed within the analysis. Is this OK?

If we were looking for a completely reductive analysis of rule governance then it isn't OK as it stands. On Railton's proposal we had a reduction in which the analysis of rule governance bottomed out with a particular sentiment—a particular feeling of discomfort. Now we bottom out with a normative judgment.

Still, we might think that there is a difference between bottoming out in a normative judgment and bottoming out in rule governance. That is to say, maybe it was never part of the game to expunge normative elements from the analysis—maybe the goal was to have the analysis of normative rule governance bottom out with the right kinds of normative elements. In this case it bottoms out with our judgment that something is either right or not right.

For the record, it's not clear that Railton has a clean reduction to the non-normative either. After all, we might ask how moral sentiments are to be individuated. Not every physical affect is a candidate (for example the need to sneeze); only special affects are— the emotions that are distinctively *moral*. So we might think that the relevant sentiments can't be basic.

Meanwhile, if we are engaged in a reductive project, perhaps the detour through moral *judgments* is necessary to get the reduction. For example, these normative judgments could be given an analysis in terms of expressivism. When I judge that C is the thing to do, perhaps that just comes to me having a Pro-attitude about C-ing in this instance (I would express this attitude as "yay C-ing!"). Or to use Mark Schroeder's (2008) formulation, perhaps I am "*for* C-ing." In the linguistic case, this invites the formulation that I have a grammar that establishes rules *for me*, and when I am normatively guided by those rules I am *for* acting in a way conducive to compliance with those rules.[4]

Alternatively, there is the Gibbard (2003) formulation in which I *plan* to do C or have a kind of contingency plan according to which I would do C. Personally, I like the Schroeder formulation better, because it does a better job of handling the case of Fred and his morning snack. Recall that we did not want to say Fred is normatively guided, but surely he did *plan* on a morning snack. It is not at all clear, however, that he is *for* having a morning snack. In fact, if we asked him we can imagine him saying "of

---

[4] Thanks to Barry C. Smith for this very clever formulation.

course I *planned* on having a morning snack, but it's not like I was *for* it—it was just something I always do."

Whichever formulation we eventually end up with, the point is this: If we are interested in giving a reductive account of rule governance we might find the move to normative judgments a more productive first step than attempting to make the reduction directly to moral sentiments. (Notice that we are not necessarily talking about a reduction of normative facts here, just a reduction of the normative judgments.)

Whatever we might say about standard moral cases, I have to say that I like this approach better for accounts of individual normative governance in the case of linguistic rules. We encounter a subjacency violation and we reject it, not because we have a feeling of discomfort about it, but rather because we simply are *against* saying that sort of thing. And that is the end of it. Similarly, we are *for* there being a binding relationship between 'himself' and 'John' in 'John saw himself', but we are *against* such a relationship in 'John's mother saw himself'.

So far I've been supposing that the kinds of moral judgments made in cases like Huck Finn are parallel to those cases in which we judge a particular example to be unacceptable or we judge a particular interpretation to be possible for a structure. But the parallel is inexact.

Recall that in Chapters 2 and 3 I made a distinction between the grammar, linguistic facts/phenomena, and our judgments about those linguistic phenomena. In the Railton proposal there doesn't seem to be a place for moral facts/phenomena. Suppose we tried to introduce that element before we developed our general theory of individual normative guidance.

The parallel moral case would be something like this:

Moral rules/principles → moral facts/phenomena ← ethical judgments
       (establish)   (provide evidence for)

So in the case of Huck Finn, let's suppose that the moral principles are something like "always treat persons as members of the Kingdom of Ends" or some other version of the categorical imperative. This general principle establishes and explains the moral fact that Huck ought not to turn in Jim. Huck's judgment is that turning in Jim is not the thing to do; we can formulate this in various ways—for example that Huck is *for* not turning in Jim (Schroeder's formulation), or he *plans* to not turn in Jim (Gibbard's formulation). As in the linguistic case Huck has no access to the deep underlying principle (it took a genius like Kant to discover that, after all). Huck does not even have direct access to the explanatory description of the moral fact—this too is a deep and important discovery. Huck merely judges that turning in Jim isn't the thing to do. We as theorists can take this as evidence for the fact that turning in Jim is morally wrong. Obviously Huck doesn't take it as evidence for this fact. But it is not necessary that he do so in order to be morally guided by the categorical imperative.

We are still short of having a satisfactory notion of rule governance, however, since we may want to incorporate the Lawler case in which some norms trump others (and in which we correct ourselves on the fly). In linguistics, rule ordering is standard fare. Kant and Peter Geach famously argued that moral conflicts just don't happen, but this seems optimistic to me. I see no reason why the notion shouldn't be employed in ethics. We might also allow that circumstances can make conduct conforming with N imprudent (e.g. validating may require muscling aside a street gang).

(RG7) Agent A's conduct C is guided by the norm N (where N is an element in the set of norms N*) only if C is a manifestation of A's disposition to act in a way conducive to compliance with N, such that N plays a role in A's C-ing, where this involves some disposition on A's part to judge that C is the thing to do unless there are extenuating circumstances and/or conflicting actions C′ that are conducive to compliance with higher ranked norms in N*, and to exert effort to C even when any failure to C would be unsanctioned and non-consequential.

(Norm Ranking) Given conduct C that is conducive to compliance with N (where N plays a role in A's C-ing), and conduct C′ that is conducive to compliance with N′ (where N′ plays a role in A's C′-ing), N is higher ranked than N′ only if A has a disposition wherein having to choose between C-ing and C′-ing A judges that C-ing is the thing to do, all other things being equal.

This formulation not only works in the ethical case but also seems apt for the sorts of linguistic rule following cases we are interested in. Agents may not be aware of the linguistic rules—indeed, how could they be?—but their behavior is nonetheless guided by the rules. Like Lawler's agent, we judge that something is not right and we repair it, or do the best we can to repair it, even though our failure to do so is unsanctioned and inconsequential.

We may have formulated a coherent notion of individual normative rule governance in generative linguistics, but there is a penalty for that—we now run straight into the teeth of Wittgenstein and Kripke's rule following argument. I take up this problem in the next chapter.

5

Worries about Rules and Representations

We concluded the previous chapter by exploring the idea that agents are normatively guided by individual linguistic norms—that is, that each person has a grammar that establishes linguistic norms for them and which provides normative guidance for them. As we will see in this chapter, this idea raises some interesting philosophical worries.

Beyond the possibility of individual linguistic norms, however, there are philosophical worries that extrude simply from supposing that our language faculty can be described in terms of rules and representations (and by extension, principles and parameters). That is to say, quite apart from issues of rule following, there is an issue of whether we can appeal to rules of the form introduced in Chapter 1.

For example, Quine leveled an early critique of grammatical theory with a version of his indeterminacy argument. We take this up in section 5.1. More recently, Kripke has introduced considerations from the later Wittgenstein that purport to show that rule following in general is problematic. As we will see, there are a number of elements to the Kripkenstein argument, some of which seem to target rule following, but others of which seem to target the more general possibility of positing rules and representations. In effect, the latter arguments contend that there is no brute fact about a system in isolation by virtue of which we can say it is following a particular rule (or, for that matter, is in a particular syntactic state). We take up these concerns in section 5.2.

As we will see, there are a number of reasons to resist Kripke's argument, but what follows if we are persuaded by it? One option is to reject the idea of rules and representations altogether, but another option that we will explore in section 5.3 is the idea that environmental embedding conditions could contribute to the determination of syntactic states—i.e. not only that it makes sense to be externalists about semantic content, but that we should also consider being externalists about syntax! According to this provocative thesis, the syntactic (computational) state of an information processing system is not determined solely by facts about the system in isolation, but also by the social and physical world in which it is embedded. As we will see, a number of interesting consequences extrude from this idea.

5.1 Quinean Indeterminacy Arguments

Quine's (1970) arguments against rules have their roots in the indeterminacy of translation argument, which is essentially intended as an argument against meanings. In that argument, Quine (1960a, 1972) asks us to consider the case where an anthropologist parachutes into an exotic culture and attempts to construct a .translation manual for the language of that culture. Suppose that the anthropologist is standing with a denizen of this culture when a rabbit hops by. The native points towards the rabbit and says "Gavagai." Should the anthropologist conclude that 'gavagai' means rabbit? Or should the anthropologist conclude that it means connected rabbit parts? Or rabbit stage? Or fuzzy animate object, or . . . According to Quine, there can in principle be no answer to this particular question.

Before we examine whether this argument, as alleged, undermines linguistic meaning, we need to see its relation to questions about syntactic rules. Similar sorts of scenarios can be constructed. Consider, for example, the following two phrase structure grammars for a very restricted fragment of English.

Grammar 1
S → NP VP
VP → V2 NP
VP → V1
V1 → barks, walks
V2 → sees, likes
NP → every N
NP → some N
NP → Smith, Jones
N → man, woman, cat, dog

Grammar 2
S → NV2 NP
S → NV1
NV1 → NP V1
NV2 → NP V2
V1 → barks, walks
V2 → sees, likes
NP → every N
NP → some N
NP → Smith, Jones
N → man, woman, cat, dog

These two grammars have the same weak generative capacity. That is, they can generate exactly the same set of terminal strings. It appears that there can be no way to decide between these alternatives on the basis of the sentences uttered, therefore it seems that there is no fact of the matter about which of these two analyses is correct.

Notice the similarity between the argument for the case of meanings and the argument for the case of rules. In the case of meanings, there were several candidate meanings for 'gavagai' and allegedly no evidence that would help adjudicate between them. In the case of the two grammars, there is allegedly no apparent way to decide which of the two grammars was the correct one, hence there is no real fact of the matter.

Let's return to Quine's (1960a, 1972) argument about meanings. Gareth Evans (1975) has raised a number of considerations that suggest that the task facing the anthropologist is not as daunting as Quine suggests.

For example, consider cases where additional predicates are introduced. Just given one word sentences like 'rabbit*' we might find it difficult to determine whether the speaker is talking of rabbits or rabbithood, or rabbit stage, but consider the case where the native says 'white* rabbit*.' Here it hardly seems to be the case that this utterance could be about rabbithood. Even more telling is the case when we string together several predicates as in 'dirty* white* rabbit*'. Suppose that when this is said with a gesture at a group of rabbits, some of which are white and others of which are dirty, the native speaker of the language dissents from the utterance. From this and cases like it, we can eventually deduce that 'rabbit*' refers to individual rabbits and not rabbit stages or parts or rabbithood in general. It takes time to get the meaning right, but should this come as a surprise?

Even if we grant Quine the point about meanings, we need not feel compelled to grant the point about grammars. (Quine himself eventually came to see this; see Quine 1987.) Part of the problem with the argument as constructed above is that it supposes the only concern we have in constructing a grammar is weak generative capacity. But as we saw in section 1.1, generative linguists have long contested the adequacy of such an approach. Rather, they have argued that we ought to be concerned with strong generative capacity—that we need to be concerned not just with the terminal strings but with the form of the phrase markers generated. Among the considerations underlying this idea appears to be the assumption that the goal of linguistics is not just to generate all of the spoken strings, but to deliver form/meaning pairs.

Consider the following famous example from Chomsky's earlier work.

(1)   Flying planes can be dangerous

This sentence is ambiguous between a reading in which the activity of flying planes can be dangerous, and a reading in which planes in flight are dangerous (perhaps because they might bomb us or crash on us). These two meanings are thus reflected in two distinct structures.

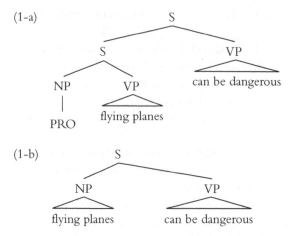

(1-a)

(1-b)

If we adopt this standard assumption about strong generative capacity, then we immediately gain a number of important probes into the question of the correct form for a grammatical theory. For example, syntactic movement involves constituents, and only a theory of strong generative capacity allows us to identify constituents like NP and VP. As I noted in section 1.1, we also rely upon constituent structure to tell us where adverbs might be inserted. Thus, we can see why the examples in (2) are much better than the examples in (3).

(2)   Often, flying planes can be dangerous
      Flying planes often can be dangerous
      Flying planes can often be dangerous
      Flying planes can be dangerous often

(3)   *Flying often planes can be dangerous
      *Flying planes can be often dangerous

Chomsky (1969, 1975b, 1980a) has made several other responses to Quine's argument. In the first place, Chomsky takes Quine's argument to be a rehash of the standard scientific problem of the underdetermination of theory by evidence. So, for example, even if there are several grammars that are consistent with the available linguistic facts (not linguistic behavior, for Chomsky, but judgments about acceptability and possible interpretation) we still have the additional constraint of which theory best accounts for the problem of language acquisition, acquired linguistic deficits (e.g. from brain damage), linguistic processing, etc. In other words, since grammatical theory is embedded within cognitive psychology, then the choice between candidate theories can, in principle, be constrained by those theories. But further, even if we had two descriptively adequate grammars, each of which could be naturally embedded within cognitive psychology, there remain standard best theory criteria (simplicity, etc.), which can help us to adjudicate between the theories. In sum, it is the standard situation in science where there are numerous competing theories with reasonably good data coverage.

5.2 Kripke/Wittgenstein Concerns about Rules

One of the most influential recent challenges to rules and representations in linguistic theory has been a position articulated by (although not necessarily endorsed by) Saul Kripke in his *Wittgenstein on Rules and Private Language*.[1]

The Skeptical Argument and its Import

What fact can one appeal to in order to determine that a particular rule used in the past is identical to the rule being used now? Take Kripke's example of someone (let's say Jones) who determines that $68 + 57 = 125$. The skeptic then asks Jones how she knows that the rule denoted by 'plus' right now is the same rule she was using in the past. Suppose that Jones has never before added two numbers totaling greater than 57. Is it not possible that in the past Jones was using 'plus' to refer to another rule altogether, perhaps one which we might call 'quus', which is like plus in all respects except that when two numbers totaling greater than 57 are quused, the answer is 5, not 125? Jones would surely be right in saying that the skeptic is crazy. But what fact about Jones (or the world) could we point to, to show that she was in fact using the rule plus before? If we cannot succeed, then there is a problem not merely for past uses of 'plus' but for current ones as well. When we say that we are using a rule, what fact does our assertion correspond to? As Kripke puts the problem ...

Since the sceptic who supposes that I meant quus cannot be answered, there is no fact about me that distinguishes my meaning plus and my meaning quus. Indeed there is no fact that distinguishes my meaning a definite function by 'plus' (which determines my responses in new cases) and my meaning nothing at all. (1982, 21)

It is natural to think we can get around the skeptical argument by saying that the addition function is in turn defined by the rule for counting, and the quus rule violates the counting rule at a more basic level. But here the Kripkean skeptic can reply that there will be a non-standard interpretation of the rule denoted by 'count'. Perhaps Jones is really using the rule quount.

There is some temptation to say the skeptical argument is nothing more than Goodman's (1955) puzzle about 'grue' in a different guise. Recall that given a predicate 'grue', which is true of objects that are green before the year 2100, and blue thereafter, any evidence we find which confirms that all emeralds are green will also confirm all emeralds are grue. Applied to the case of Jones, we could say the following. Until she begins to add numbers greater than 57, any evidence that confirms that Jones is following the rule addition, will also confirm that she is using the rule quaddition.

---

[1] There is now a fair bit of secondary literature that addresses the question of whether Kripke is faithful to Wittgenstein in his exegesis. I will pass over this question and will consider the view presented on its own merits.

Kripke thinks there is an important difference in these cases. According to Kripke, the key difference is that Goodman is interested in induction, while Kripke/Wittgenstein is interested in meaning. Goodman, after all, presupposed the extensions of 'grue' and 'green' to be understood. Hence, to get off the ground Goodman needs to assume that we know the correct rule for the interpretation of 'grue' and 'green'.

Moreover, Kripke thinks that Goodman would have to appeal to the Wittgensteinian skeptical argument to counter a possible criticism of his "riddle of induction." Recall that Goodman attempts to head off a distinction between 'grue' and 'green' on the basis of grue being temporal and green not, arguing that there is no non-question begging way to distinguish them. But Kripke points out that one might appeal to how these predicates are learned, noting that 'green' can be learned without reference to time. The way out for Goodman would be to ask "who is to say that it isn't grue that we learn by ostension (and call 'green')?" thus effectively introducing Kripke's problem. Kripke concludes that the rule following problem is something different and deeper than Goodman's new riddle of induction.

Wittgenstein has invented a new form of scepticism. Personally I am inclined to regard it as the most radical and original sceptical problem that philosophy has seen to date, one that only a highly unusual cast of mind could have produced. (1982, 60)

But what are the consequences of the argument if it is sound? One conclusion that one could draw from the argument is that talk of rules and representations is somehow illegitimate, and should be exorcised from the cognitive sciences. Kripke suggests that the argument may have just such consequences for research in generative grammar:

[I]f statements attributing rule-following are neither to be regarded as stating facts, nor to be thought of as *explaining* our behavior... it would seem that the use of the idea of rules and of competence in linguistics needs serious reconsideration, even if these notions are not rendered meaningless. (31 n. 22)

But does the argument hold up? To answer this question we need to take a closer look. There are three different elements that commentators have found (or think they found) in the argument. Let's label them as follows.

(i) The normativity question
(ii) The knowledge question
(iii) The determination question

The normativity question comes to this. Even if you could show that an agent like Jones has a disposition to act in conformity with a clearly identifiable rule (for example addition and not quaddition), there is a serious question about finding some fact that makes it true she is rule guided. Here is how Kripke puts the point.

What is the relation of this supposition [the supposition that I mean addition by '+'] to the question how I will respond to the problem '68 + 57'? The dispositionalist gives a *descriptive* answer of this relation: if '+' meant addition, then I will answer '125'. But this is not the proper account of the relation, which is *normative*, not descriptive. The point is *not* that, if I meant addition by '+', I will answer '125', but if I intend to accord with my past meaning of '+', I *should* answer '125'. (37)

For a number of generative linguists, this won't be an issue, because they don't take linguistic rules to be normative. But in the story I sketched in the previous chapter, we made sense of the idea of linguistic competence by appealing to the idea that we have linguistic rules and that they have a certain kind of normative force. On the other hand, it also seems that, following Railton, we had a plausible story about the facts that underwrite the normative aspect of rule following.

Recall Railton's example of Fred and his morning snack. Fred had a disposition to have a snack every day mid-morning, but on occasion he failed to have a snack. In Railton's terminology Fred had a "default plan," and his behavior was certainly rule *described* but it wasn't rule *guided* because on those cases when Fred failed to have his morning snack he merely shrugged his shoulders ("Oh well, I guess I forgot"). Had it been a case of normative rule guidance Fred would have judged that he was in some sense *against* this having happened. Perhaps he would feel a sense of moral discomfort at failing to have his morning snack (as he does when he fails to validate his bus ticket), or perhaps his inner monologue would involve attempts to justify or bargain his omission ("I'll have two snacks tomorrow" or "I was extra super busy").

If this is right then there is an ingredient to rule following beyond the merely having a disposition to act in a way conducive to compliance with a rule. Indeed, in the previous chapter we saw precisely the role that this normative element played in concert with having a disposition to act in compliance with a rule.

The second component—the epistemic question—may or may not be a component of Kripke's argument (there is some dispute about this), but we can frame the worry like this: Surely if I am following a rule (say plus) I must be in a position to know that I am doing so.

Now it is certainly the case that for some kinds of rule following we do know that we are following the rule (the rule plus is a case in point), and maybe it is even *crucial* that we know we are following the rule in order to follow it (this would be difficult to establish), but the linguistic rule following cases do not appear to be structured in this way. As we saw in Chapter 4, linguistic rules like subjacency are the product of scientific investigation and not known to the vast majority of language users, but we still can make sense of those rules normatively guiding us.

Now there is another way of taking the epistemic question—one deployed by Crispin Wright—by which it is not really about whether we know the rule, but about whether we could know—in principle—the facts that ground the rule itself.

Roughly, the conclusion that there are no facts of a disputed species [i.e., about meaning] is to follow from an argument to the effect that, even if we imagine our abilities idealized to the point where, if there were any such facts to be known, we would certainly be in possession of them, we *still* would not be in a position to justify any particular claim about their character. So we first, as it were plot the area in which the facts in question would have to be found if they existed and then imagine a suitable idealization, with respect to that area, of our knowledge acquiring powers; if it then transpires that any particular claim about those facts [about meaning] still proves resistant to all justification, there is no alternative to concluding that the 'facts' never existed in the first place. (Wright 2001, 94–95)

This is a fairly powerful philosophical tool. If sound, it appears it would also be quite capable of defeating epistemicism in epistemology, for example. Whether or not this is a component of Kripke's argument, the question leads us directly into the determination question of Kripke's argument: What fact about an agent metaphysically determines that the agent is following a particular rule N, and not some other rule N′ which has the same result for all previously analyzed cases?

Here we really do get to a worry that directly targets the linguistic case, and indeed the analysis of rule governance that we borrowed from Railton. Let's look at our formulation (RG6) again.

(RG6) Agent A's conduct C is guided by the norm N only if C is a manifestation of A's disposition to act in a way conducive to compliance with N, such that N plays a role in A's C-ing, where A judges that her efforts to C, whether successful or not, are the thing to do—particularly when so acting is difficult and unsanctioned, and even when inconsequential. Some of A's failures to try and C may give rise to A's feeling discomfort and A's efforts to C, whether successful or not, may have led A to feel a sense of satisfaction—of having "done (tried to do) the right thing." These sentiments may signal to A that she is acting appropriately but they are not constitutive of her being rule governed.

Now we can concede that any number of dispositions might be consistent with previous conduct (say addition or speaking a language) but we must be careful not to overlook the norm N, which is represented by the agent and which plays a role in A's conduct. So, to turn to the mathematical example, what separates Jones the adder from Jones the quadder is that there are different norms that are represented in the two cases. To a first approximation, we might think of this as involving two distinct lines of code or two distinct computer programs. Let's call this the *computationalist response* to the rule following problem.

Of course, as I suggested in Chapter 2, this talk of lines of code is not stable. And, as we will see, this answer does not skate around the Kripkenstein argument, for Kripke and Wittgenstein both argued that one cannot even freely appeal to the representation of the rule. This might seem the most surprising claim, because it seems there must surely be a fact about what rule is represented (especially thinking of the rule in terms of a line of code in a computer program). But as Kripke and Wittgenstein argue, this is far from clear.

The Computationalist Response and Kripke's Reply

The computationalist response to the skeptical problem states that there *is* a fact of the matter about which rule Jones is using and that the rule corresponds to the computational state that she realizes when she added in the past. As I argued in Chapter 2, it doesn't really matter if we think of the rule of addition being explicitly represented or if we think of Jones as executing an addition program in which the rule is not explicitly represented. Either way the idea is that once we get down to the level of the circuitry of the computer (or in this case, down to neural activity), we will see that an addition operation is being called and not a quaddition operation.

This sort of solution is suggested by Fodor in *The Language of Thought*. Fodor's formulation:

The physics of the machine thus guarantees that the sequences of states and operations it runs through in the course of its computations respect the semantic constraints on formulae in its internal language. What takes the place of a truth definition for the machine language is simply the engineering principles which guarantee this correspondence. (1975, 66)

...it is worth mentioning that, whatever Wittgenstein proved, it cannot have been that it is impossible that a language should be private in whatever sense the machine language of a computer is, for there *are* such things as computers, and whatever is actual is possible. (68)

Let's rehearse the argument in broad form. Any time we attribute rule following behavior to a system, computer or otherwise, we are offering, in part, a theory about the program that the system is executing. Since there is a brute fact about what program the system is executing, then that is the fact about the world that underlies our attribution of the rule to the system.

But matters are not so simple. Kripke reviews a number of worries about the computationalist alternative. The most potentially damaging objection can be put as follows: Is there really a fact of the matter about which program a system (computer or not) is executing?

I cannot really insist that the values of the function are given by the machine. First, the machine is a finite object, accepting only finitely many numbers as input and yielding only finitely many as output—others are simply too big. Indefinitely many programs extend the actual finite behavior of the machine. Usually this is ignored because the designer of the machine intended it to fulfill just one program, but in the present context such an approach to the intentions of the designer simply gives the skeptic his wedge to interpret in a non-standard way. (Indeed, the appeal to the designer's program makes the physical machine superfluous; only the program is relevant. The machine as physical object is of value only if the intended function can somehow be read off from the physical object alone). (1982, 34)

In this, Kripke echoes an earlier passage from Wittgenstein's *Philosophical Investigations*:

The machine as symbolizing its action: the action of a machine—I might say at first—seems to be there in it from the start. What does this mean?—If we know the machine, everything else, that is its movement, seems to be already completely determined.

We talk as if these parts could only move in this way, as if they could not do anything else. How is this—do we forget the possibility of their bending, breaking off, melting and so on? (§ 193)

The upshot is that appeal to computers will not work, for the skeptical argument can be extended to them as well. In short, there is no fact of the matter about what rules and representations they are using.

Let's return to Crispin Wright's suggestion that we consider whether even an ideal knower could determine the facts for rules of this form, and consider a series of thought experiments. Suppose that I program a computer to parse sentences of some fragment of English, and I ask you to reconstruct the program simply from the behavior of the machine. We know of course that if we are just provided with input and output from the system the task will be daunting, but suppose that I make things easier. Suppose I use a machine that you are familiar with—in the sense that you know the microprocessors in it like the back of your hand. Suppose further that I allow you to open the machine and I provide you with the ability to study the logic gates of the computer while it is in operation. What I will not tell you is what language I originally wrote the program in, nor will I allow you knowledge of my favorite programming techniques or my favorite grammatical theory. Could you reconstruct the program?

A second thought experiment makes the task more difficult. Suppose that this time I have designed my own microprocessor, and suppose you have no idea about what kinds of microprocessors I am familiar with or would be likely to design. *Now* could you determine the program my machine was running? How informative would it be for you to be able to observe the logic gates in such a machine?

Finally let's consider a case where the machine is not designed by me, but simply drops from the sky (perhaps it was found in an alien space vessel). Could we (in principle) determine the program that such a machine was executing? For that matter, could we even determine if it was a computer at all? But this is exactly the position that cognitive scientists find themselves in. Their task is to study the rules and representations utilized by systems of unknown origin. If the skeptic is right, such an enterprise will be impossible, for there is no fact of the matter about such systems.

But if Kripke and Wittgenstein are right, there is an additional problem in the case of the computer from the sky. Suppose that after studying the alien computer we actually *can* infer the program it is executing on the basis of studying the behavior of the machine and its inner workings. Suppose we *can* actually offer a proof that a machine of such and such construction must be executing a specific program. But suppose that just as we are about to announce our analysis of the machine, a wire melts causing the machine to behave differently. "Obviously a malfunction," we say, but the Kripkean skeptic disagrees. "This is not a malfunction at all, but is merely part of the design of the machine."

Actual machines can malfunction: through melting wires and slipping gears they may give the wrong answer. How is it determined when a malfunction occurs? By reference to the program of the machine, as intended by the designer, not simply by reference to the machine itself. Depending on the intent of the designer, any particular phenomenon may or may not count as a machine "malfunction". A programmer with suitable intentions may even have intended to make use of the fact that wires melt or gears slip, so that a machine that is "malfunctioning" for me is behaving perfectly for him. Whether a machine ever malfunctions and, if so, when, is not a property of the machine itself as a physical object but is well defined only in terms of its program, as stipulated by its designer. Given the program, once again the physical object is superfluous for the purpose of determining what function is meant. (Kripke 1980, 34–35)

It seems that the appeal to the physics of the system has come full circle. One cannot determine what program a system is executing until one is clear on whether it is functioning properly, but one cannot determine if the system is functioning properly until one has the program that the system is executing.

The skeptic claims that we could not determine the program being executed by the alien computer, but is the skeptic right? This remains to be seen. I've put the above questions to a number of computer scientists through the years, and the answers are mixed. Perhaps the most interesting answer came from Allen Newell, who said that determining the program is impossible, but we do it all the time. I gather that Newell's point was that we often "reverse engineer" computers. But it might be argued that while we can reverse engineer a computer from Silicon Valley, reverse engineering a computer from the sky is an entirely different matter.

If we have intuitions in the case of the computer from the sky, it is hard to know what to make of them. But perhaps if we simplify the problem a great deal we can make some headway. The basic problem is this. Can we determine the possible syntactic states of a machine simply by studying the machine in isolation from the intentions of the designer?

Suppose that the machine we find is exceedingly simple. In fact, let's suppose it looks like a simple toggle switch. Could we determine that it is a machine with two discrete syntactic states? Surely it is logically possible that the designer intended to utilize a continuum of possible states (say as a device to test finger strength up to a certain threshold).[2]

But suppose that the skeptic disagrees with this assessment and insists that we cannot so easily dismiss the possibility that the designer of the machine intended that it have a continuum of possible states up to a certain limit, or intended that the switch should break upon being flipped. Is there any way to respond to the skeptic?

Extending the Skeptical Argument to other Sciences

Chomsky's (1993, 1994b, 1995b) response to the Kripkean argument is to concede that there is no fact of the matter about computers, but arguing that there nevertheless *is* a fact of the matter about objects which are part of the natural order (and not the

---

[2] I owe this point to Noam Chomsky (p.c.).

product of human—or Martian—intentions). The principles and parameters of the language faculty are embedded within cognitive psychology and ultimately facts about human biology. Therefore the structure of the language faculty is no less grounded than, for example, the human genome. Even if we allow Kripkean skepticism, it stops at the door of naturalistic inquiry.

The trick to playing Chomsky's gambit here is to secure the distinction between objects and artifacts. Suppose that we discovered the language faculty was genetically engineered and implanted in humans by visiting Martians several millennia ago. Would it then be the case that the language faculty is an artifact after all and therefore that there is no fact of the matter about its organization? For that matter, Martian naturalists may come and visit us and may find our computers no less a part of the natural order than beehives and birds' nests. If the artifact/natural object distinction eludes them, why should we put so much stock in it?

Even if the distinction between natural and non-natural (artifactual) systems was stable, is it really the case that natural systems are immune to these kinds of skeptical arguments? The first thing to observe about Kripkean skeptical arguments is that they apply not just to the kinds of rules and representations one finds in computers and simple machines like toggle switches, but to any way of describing objects which relies upon the form or organization of those objects, and (as a corollary) to any science which employs the notion of information and information transfer.[3] To see that this is so, we need merely reflect on where the skeptic focuses the attack. In the case of determining what program a machine is executing, the task is simply to determine how the system is organized. There are, of course, many possible theories of how the system might be organized, all of them compatible with what we observe, but this is true when we go about describing the organization of *anything*. So, for example, if we are presented with a pattern of dots like the following, there are any number of ways in which we might describe its organization.

We might describe this as three rows of dots, or three columns of dots, or as any number of other possibilities. It may be that we would be hard pressed to show that there is a fact of the matter about patterns like the above, but a number of sciences identify patterns in nature on a routine basis. In the remaining portion of this section, I will survey two such sciences—mineralogy, biology—and show that the Kripkean skeptical argument can be leveled against these sciences as well. The conclusion will be

---

[3] Since information is characterized in terms of the organization of a system.

that skeptical arguments don't pose a greater problem for linguistics than these other sciences, and I'll suggest further that thinking about the skeptical problem in terms of a broader range of sciences can also help us to see our way to a solution to the problem.

Kripkean Skepticism in Mineralogy

Emerton (1984) notes that there was a time when it was supposed that it was legitimate to attribute underlying form or organization to the human mind, but not to things like crystals.

[M]ost medieval writers on mineral subjects continued to follow Aristotle, Theophrastus, Pliny, and Avicenna in confining themselves to the material and efficient causes. Precedent is always an important factor in scientific explanation. Some felt that the form, like the soul, should be reserved for biological and mental processes, not for inorganic phenomena. If a need was felt for formative causes in the mineral realm, astrological or alchemical forces seemed more accessible than philosophical concepts, in the view of most writers on mineral subjects. And as time went on, the gradual enlargement of knowledge about stones, gems, ores, and metals encouraged a belief that enough was known to explain minerals in physical terms alone. (27)

The idea that the study of crystals should concern itself with the *form* or organization of crystals was dismissed as unscientific, and there was a drawn out conflict in mineralogy that introduced a number of arguments that are now being directed against the attribution of rules and representations to the cognitive systems.

The debate centered around Aristotle's four causes (efficient, formal, final, and material), and the question of which causes could be relevant to scientific explanation. To illustrate the role that these causes played, we can consider a famous example (from Aristotle) of a bronze statue. The efficient cause of the statue is the sculptor, the formal cause is the design or pattern that the sculptor used. The final cause is the end or use of the sculpture, and the material cause is the bronze itself. While since Descartes most scientific explanation has appealed to the notion of efficient cause, the notion of final cause appears in biology as teleological explanation, and one might think of the explanations in cognitive science as appealing to formal cause.

The notion that formal cause might play a role in mineralogy was not seriously entertained until the early part of the seventeenth century. Among the early advocates of formal cause in this domain was the German physician Sennert, whose remarks, with modification, might be adapted to a discussion of the merits of cognitive psychology over behaviorism.

Always in vain does anyone resort to external causes for the concreation of things; rather does it concern the internal disposition of the matter.... On account of their forms ... things have dispositions to act.... They receive their perfection from their form, not from an external cause. Hence also salt has a natural concreation ... not from heat or cold, but from its form, which is the architecture of its domicile. (1650, 765)

The introduction of form obviously posed problems for seventeenth-century mechanistic philosophers and chemists, who were for the most part committed to particle theory. Crucially, they eventually found it necessary to incorporate form into their theories.

In a philosophy that claimed to explain all phenomena in terms of matter and motion there might seem to be no place for either the salt principle or the formal cause, but when crystals were taken into account the formal cause could not be dismissed.... Study of the well-known writings of de Boot and Sennert raised the question of how the specific form might be understood in relation to corpuscular and saline theories of crystallization, and this led to new interpretations of the form concept in particulate terms. (Emerton 1984, 42)

Another difficulty that arose in the practice of approaching crystallography in this fashion was that there were any number of possible basic geometrical shapes that could give rise to the external crystalline structure that might be observed by the naked eye. The eighteenth-century naturalist Comte Georges de Buffon seems have raised this point in objection to Linnaeus' classification of crystalline minerals by shape, arguing that "crystal form is more equivocal and more variable than other characteristics."[4]

With proper modification, Buffon's criticism of Linnaeus could take the form of a Kripkean skeptical challenge. "You say that the underlying crystalline form is such and such a polyhedron, but how do we know that it isn't really this *other* form which is so far consistent with all our observations?" Note that the problem here is more pressing than in typical worries about induction. The alternative crystalline structures are not grue-like—they are not time-sensitive properties. They are simply forms that are consistent with everything we have thus far observed, and we may even have reason to suppose that future observations are not likely to resolve the matter.

Kripkean Skepticism in Biology

Most people know that contemporary molecular biology frequently talks about organization and information. So, for example, by virtue of how certain proteins are organized, a DNA molecule can encode and transmit information. One of the key projects in molecular biology then, is to study this organization. It is interesting to note that some of the resources developed in linguistics have been employed for this task. So, for example, Cudia (1988) describes a set of context free grammars that can be used for characterizing the information in the genetic code.

As I suggested earlier, anytime a science is concerned with the organization of a system, a Kripkean skeptical argument will be possible. For example, is there some way to look at a strand of DNA in isolation and determine what the genes are? Not very likely. Contemporary research casts doubt on the idea that a single gene will correspond to a single location (coding sequence) on the DNA strand. For example, Spilianakis et al. (2005) have noted that the control regions do not necessarily have to be continuous coding sequences on the linear molecule or even on the same

---

[4] *Histoire naturelle des minéraux*, vol. 1, pp. 242–243.

chromosome (the regions only come into close proximity in the nucleus). Similarly, Kapranov et al. (2005) have shown that some proteins can be composed of exons from far away regions and even different chromosomes. This type of data has prompted Gerstein et al. (2007) to offer a definition of a gene as "a union of genomic sequences encoding a coherent set of potentially overlapping functional products." Their new definition effectively categorizes genes by functional products, whether they be proteins or RNA, rather than specific DNA loci. All regulatory elements of DNA (whether they are proteins or RNA) and not just specific locations on the DNA sequence can therefore be classified as gene-associated regions.

How is this relevant to Kripkean skepticism? In effect, the individuation of genes cannot take place by looking at strands of DNA in isolation but is inherently tied to our understanding of biological function and salient morphological properties of the organism, and these in turn are tied to the environment in which the organism is embedded (we will explore this idea more closely in Chapter 6).

It is of course open to the skeptic to say that the argument infects all these sciences—to say that we are deluded if we suppose that there is a fact of the matter about the systems we study (or even to suppose that there is a fact of the matter about their being systems). The idea would be that all of science is an interpretive enterprise. There are philosophers (maybe even scientists) who believe some version of this thesis. But the key point is that linguists need take it no more seriously than the mineralogist or the biologist.

The Soames Objection

In the previous section we showed that Kripkean skepticism does not exclusively target non-natural systems like computers (assuming that a natural/non-natural distinction even holds up) but extends also to natural sciences like mineralogy and biology. Assuming information-theoretic approaches to physics, it could extend all the way to physics. On the other hand, this suggests a reductio of the skeptical argument (at least given our interests in securing generative linguistics; linguistics is no worse off than these other sciences). But extending the problem out to other forms of naturalistic inquiry also suggests a broader solution. Just as we anchored biological form in features of the broader environment—e.g. functional properties and environmentally individuated morphological properties—so too we can cast our net wider in the case of linguistic rule following.

Keep in mind that we are currently focused on the metaphysical determination problem and that the skepticism about metaphysical determination is driven by the assumption that even as ideal epistemic agents we can't imagine having facts at our disposal that would determine which rule is being represented. But is it really plausible to think that an ideal agent would not have sufficient information once our net is cast this broadly? More urgently, if we expunge the talk of knowledge and just think in terms of whether there might be some set of non-intentional facts that metaphysically determine our computational states, it is difficult to see why there can't be. Is it really plausible to think that there is a possible world in which all the relevant non-intentional facts hold and I am not in the same computational state? Soames (1998a), addressing this question for conscious rule following, puts the problem like this.

Would the result change if we enlarged the set of potential meaning-determining truths still further to include not only all truths about my dispositions to verbal behavior, but also all truths about (i) the internal physical states of my brain, (ii) my causal and historical relationships to things in my environment, (iii) my (nonintentionally characterized) interactions with other members of my linguistic community, (iv) their dispositions to verbal behavior, and so on? Is there a possible world in which someone conforms to all those facts—precisely the facts that characterize me in the actual world—and yet that person does not mean anything by '+'?

I think not. Given my conviction that in the past I did mean addition by '+', and given also my conviction that if there are intentional facts, then they don't float free of everything else, I am confident that there is no such world. Although I cannot identify the smallest set of nonintentional facts about me in the actual world on which meaning facts supervene, I am confident that they do supervene. Why shouldn't I be? (229)

According to Soames, Kripke's skeptical argument incorporates two different notions of determination (as in what it is that *determines* that I meant plus instead of quus). The first is an epistemological notion of determination and the second is a notion of determination that is grounded in metaphysical necessity. That is, in the former case it is supposed that meaning is grounded in nonintentional facts that Jones knows (and that Jones could not *know* any facts which determine that she meant plus). In the second case it is supposed that meaning is determined by metaphysical necessity (and it is argued that there are possible worlds in which all of the relevant nonintentional facts hold and in which she does not mean plus). Soames reconstructs the overarching argument as follows:

P_1) If in the past there was a fact about what I meant by '+', in particular, if there was a fact that I meant addition by '+', then either:

    (i) this fact was determined by nonintentional facts of such and such kinds—facts about my past calculations using '+', the rules or algorithms I followed in doing calculations involving '+', my past dispositions to respond to questions 'What is $\underline{n} + \underline{m}$?', the totality of my past dispositions to verbal behavior involving '+' etc.

    or

    (ii) the fact that I meant addition by '+' was a primitive fact, not determined by nonintentional facts.

P_2) Nonintentional facts of type (i) did not determine that I meant addition (or anything else) by '+'.

P_3) What I meant by '+' was not a primitive fact.

C_1) Thus, in the past there was no fact that I meant addition (or anything else) by '+'.

C_2) By parity of reasoning, there never was a fact about what I, or anyone else, meant by any word; *ditto* for the present.

The argument is valid, but what reason do we have to believe the premises—particular (P_2) and (P_3). According to Soames there are problems with both of these premises, since, on the metaphysical determination, (P_2) is false (just because the meaning is necessarily determined it doesn't follow that I know *how* it is determined) and on the epistemic determination (P_3) is false (if the meaning is determined by a primitive fact, there is no reason why I couldn't know this primitive fact a priori). We need to shift between our notions of meaning determination (and in just the right ways) in order to get the argument to work. If we hold the notion of meaning determination fixed, the argument fails.

Soames is particularly vivid in his characterization of why the argument fails if we take the relevant notion of meaning determination as being metaphysical—i.e. the fact that I meant addition could be *necessarily* determined by nonintentional facts without my knowing what those facts are.

[the skeptics] try to establish that no collection of nonintentional truths will allow us to *demonstrate* the truth of the relevant intentional claims. This, I have suggested, is tantamount to an attempt to convince us that claims about meaning (and propositional attitudes) are not a priori consequences of any set of nonintentional truths.

On this point it must be admitted that the skeptic has a strong case. . . . I don't know how to give such a derivation and I am not sure that any is possible . . .

If it were clear that any necessary consequence of a set of claims P was also an a priori consequence of P, this admission would provide the skeptic with just what he needs; for then he could force me to admit that claims about meaning may not be necessary consequences of nonintentional truths. That would conflict with my conviction that meaning facts must supervene on nonintentional facts, and so would threaten my pretheoretic commitment to meaning facts. However, this argumentative strategy fails. Thanks to the work of Kripke and others, it has become clear that many necessary consequences of propositions are not apriori consequences of them. Consequently my admission that claims about meanings may not be a priori consequences of nonintentional truths need not undermine my belief that they are necessary consequences of those truths. (230–231)

In effect, if there are some nonintentional facts that necessarily determine the rule I am following, it does not follow that I should be in a position to know these facts (as we are taught by Kripke 1980). A remarkable error for Kripke, of all people, to have made.

5.3 Externalism about Syntax?

If we block the Kripkean considerations raised in the previous section, by casting our net widely on the determination question, we move to a position where meaning facts supervene on nonintentional relational facts. For example, the fact about what rule I am utilizing may supervene on (among other things) nonintentional facts about my environmental embedding. If the Kripkean argument applies to all forms of rule following (as it is supposed to) this seems to push us to a view in which syntactic states, like semantic states, are sensitive to embedding environmental conditions. That is, we could be pushed towards externalism about syntax.

Externalism is usually characterized as the doctrine that the contents of our mental states and the semantic contents of our utterances are determined at least in part by the external environment. But why should externalists stop with psychological and semantic *contents*? Why can't the *forms* of those mental states and the syntax of our utterances be sensitive to environmental conditions as well? There is, of course, a standard supposition that even if the contents of our mental states are externally fixed, the forms of our mental states supervene directly on our physical microstructure, but this supposition seems to be directly called into question by the Kripkean arguments of the previous section. If they are persuaded by Kripkean considerations, why can't externalists take the further step and argue that the logical form of our *utterances* are also sensitive to external conditions? In this section I will explore the possibility of being an externalist about syntax in this sense, and I'll argue that the position needs to be taken seriously, and indeed, that it offers some interesting perspectives on at least one long-standing philosophical puzzle. I will conclude, however, with some potential troubles for the position.

Can the syntax of an utterance really be tied to properties that are partly external to the speaker? It has to be conceded that the thesis I am describing here is a fairly radical thesis. This is not like the wide computationalism explored in Wilson (1994) and Clark and Chalmers (1998). The kind of wide computationalism they are interested in involves computations that incorporate the environment into the system (e.g. using your fingers or a note pad to help solve a cognitive problem). For them, the part of the computation that takes place intracranially is stable across Twin-Earth scenarios. *This* story, alternatively, is one in which the intracranial computations and syntactic states *are* sensitive to Twin-Earth scenarios. The thesis may be radical, but I would suggest that the externalist has good grounds for asserting that the syntactic states of a system can be and often are determined by environmental considerations—even for systems like digital computers and mechanical adding machines. What is the case for this?

Notoriously, Searle (1980, 1990) and Putnam (1988) argued that any physical system can instantiate any Turing machine program (more accurately, in Putnam's case, any finite state machine). Bontly (1998) and Chalmers (1996) have effectively critiqued this view, but the moves they (particularly Bontly) make to block Searle and Putnam move us towards understanding that computational states are environmentally sensitive.

First, what reason do we have to think that any physical system can instantiate any program (or strictly speaking, any finite state automaton)? The full argument is complex, but the basic idea is simple enough. To illustrate, a simple rock lying on a desk might be used to perform computations of arbitrary complexity. Suppose that the input consists of my pushing the rock with my finger and the output consists of the final resting place of the rock. Then the syntactic states of the machine (here taken as the system including the table and the rock) supervene on those inputs and outputs and the surface friction and irregularities of the rock and the table. Hypothetically, there could be creatures for whom making the appropriate finger movements and "reading" the final resting positions of the rock on the table would be simple. Perhaps less persuasively, Searle has argued that even a wall can instantiate a program like Microsoft Word.

Chalmers has offered that what we are really interested in here is whether a physical system instantiates a *combinatorial state automaton*, or CSA. Such automata differ from finite state automata in that the internal states of a CSA have combinatorial structure. In particular, as Chalmers puts it, its internal state is a *vector $[S\hat{}1, S\hat{}2, \ldots, S\hat{}n]$*, where

the ith component of the vector can take on a finite number of different values, or *substates*. . . . The substates correspond to symbols in those squares or particular values for the cells. . . . State-transition rules are determined by specifying for each component of the state vector a function by which its new substate depends on the old overall state vector and input vector (it will frequently depend on only a few "nearby" components of these vectors), and the same for each element of the output vector.

This is a reasonable way to think about the kind of computational systems we deal with in cognitive science (the language faculty being a case in point) where the complexity of the systems and the way the components interact can be quite rich. Chalmers then offers the following way of thinking about what it means for a physical system to instantiate a CSA.

A physical system implements a given CSA if there is a decomposition of its internal states into substates $[s\hat{}1, s\hat{}2, \ldots, s\hat{}n]$, and a mapping f from these substates onto corresponding substates $S\hat{}j$ of the CSA, along with similar mappings for inputs and outputs, such that: for every formal state transition $([I\hat{}1, \ldots, I\hat{}k], [S\hat{}1, \ldots, S\hat{}n]) \rightarrow ([S'\hat{}1, \ldots, S'\hat{}n], [O\hat{}1, \ldots, O\hat{}l])$ of the CSA, if the system is in internal state $[s\hat{}1, \ldots, s\hat{}n]$ and receiving input $[i\hat{}1, \ldots, i\hat{}n]$ such that the physical states and inputs map to the formal states and inputs, this causes it to enter an internal state and produce an output that map appropriately to the required formal state and output.

If we think about the implementation conditions of CSAs in this way then Putnam and Searle type arguments are certainly more difficult to get up and running. For example, the physical system would not only have to mirror the structure of the CSA, but the sub-states of the physical system would have to be connected in the right way. For example, in the example above where we pushed a rock across the table, it is not enough that there be states of the table that are isomorphic to those of the CSA and that the system pass through those states in the right order. Those states would have to be causally connected in the right way. This also means that the dependencies between the states would have to be non-accidental. There have to be laws connecting the state transitions of our rock/table computer. On top of all this Chalmers emphasizes that the parts of the internal state of the system must be independently variable (like, for example, switches are).

Given these constraints it seems implausible to think that *any* physical object could instantiate any computer program, but it does seem too strong to suggest, as Chalmers does, that "the right sort of complex structure will be found in very few physical systems." Every physical system is astoundingly complex, and I see no reason to doubt that there are subsystems contained in many of them that are lined up in the right way (combinatorially and causally) so that the CSA could be instantiated. But of course, the real issue is not how many physical systems can instantiate a program, but whether the system in isolation is enough to determine *which* CSA is being instantiated. One problem here is that if a system is complex enough to instantiate one CSA it is certainly complex enough to instantiate many others, and thus we are led to ask which of these is the one actually being computed.

One answer, of course, is that they all are. But another answer would be that it depends upon how the physical object lines up with other physical systems in its environment. There might, by some freaky artifact of how walls are made, be a kind of complex structure within sheetrock walls that not only is isomorphic to the structure of the Word program, but actually satisfies the CSA constraints given by Chalmers. Still, we are not apt to think it instantiates the Word program unless the input and output are accessible to us (or to something intelligent). That is, unless this complexity is harnessed to accept input from us (a keyboard would be helpful) and generate usable output (a monitor would be nice). We aren't interested in inert computational systems.

For this reason, Bontly (1998) has suggested that the view that any physical system can instantiate any computation is too liberal. For example, he holds that one constraint on whether a physical system can instantiate a program is the function of the physical system. That is, in the ordinary course of affairs the rock and table could not possibly serve as a computer, and hence could not instantiate just any computer program. Of course, for the creatures that we envisioned earlier, the system *would* instantiate a program. What the externalist might argue is that the external environment determines *whether* a computation is being performed by the system and also fixes the allowable inputs and outputs so that the environment also fixes *which* computation is being performed.[5] In short, whether the rock or the wall instantiates a program and, if so, which program, will depend upon its embedding conditions.

This point extends to biological systems as well. Human DNA is very complex, and presumably it can instantiate many CSAs. As we saw earlier, we can't simply read genes off of linear coding sequences of the DNA molecule, but we have to consider the (sometimes discontinuous) features of DNA which underwrite salient properties of the organism, which just means we have to consider properties that are of interest to us and properties which help the creature to navigate and function in our world. Had the world been radically different, genetics would have been radically different.

If this general position holds (and it seems a natural position for an externalist to adopt in any case), then syntactic states do not supervene exclusively on individualistic properties of the system. It would follow that this holds not just for computers, but for any system that can be attributed syntactic states.

---

[5] For some criticism of externalist theories of computation, see Egan (1992).

An Application

If we adopt externalism about logical form, we find that we are offered some new ways of approaching at least one long-standing philosophical puzzle. Since Russell (1905) the descriptive theory of names has offered a tantalizing if (to date) elusive solution to the problem of empty (non-referring) names. If empty names can be taken to be denoting expressions—expressions standing proxy for descriptions (e.g. if 'Santa Claus' can be taken as proxy for 'The fat jolly elf who lives at the north pole etc. etc.'[6])—then we have a natural account of how a sentence like 'Santa Claus delivered the toys' can be meaningful (and false) even though 'Santa Claus' does not refer.[7] Unfortunately, there appear to be fatal problems for descriptive theories of names as a general thesis about names. In particular, Kripke (1980) has shown that among other limitations the descriptive theory simply cannot account for our intuition that most uses of names rigidly designate.

Kripke's positive proposal, of course, was to say that names are referring expressions. While that proposal works well for most uses of names it at least appears that it cannot be extended to the analysis of empty names. Barring attempts to treat such names as referring to fictions or to nonexistent objects, one is left with the alternative of saying that sentences with empty names fail to express a determinate proposition or that they express some sort of "gappy" proposition or "propositional radical." Such strategies can certainly be carried out, but one wonders if it has to come to this.

One possible way out is to hold that some names are referring expressions and that others are descriptive. That is one could allow that names like 'Bill Clinton' are referring expressions and names like 'Santa Claus' are descriptive. This would allow us to treat names like 'Bill Clinton' as rigid designators and at the same time allow that names like 'Santa Claus' are purely descriptive. The problem is, how do we know in general which names are referential and which are descriptive?

One possible answer is that we simply don't know. We make certain utterances and the logical forms of those utterances are what they are as fixed by the external world, completely independently of facts about our linguistic intentions. Accordingly, the logical form of an utterance of 'Santa delivered the toys' depends entirely on whether Santa exists. If Santa exists, then 'Santa' is a referring expression. If Santa does not exist, then 'Santa' is a denoting expression. This move—let's call it "bald externalism about logical form"—arguably solves the problem, but many philosophers, myself among them, have not been prepared to sever the link between the logical form of an utterance and our linguistic intentions.

---

[6] Here I am ignoring more sophisticated versions of the descriptive theory of names, such as that in Searle (1958). Nothing I say here turns on the choice between a theory like Searle's and the classical Russellian theory of descriptive names. There may, of course, be independent reasons for favoring Searle's version.

[7] Here I am ignoring the possibility, discussed in Kripke (1980), that 'Santa Claus' might refer to some actual historical saint. For purposes of discussion let's suppose that there is no individual relevantly linked to the name 'Santa Claus'.

Russell's (1910–1911) take on the matter was that whether a name was a genuine referring expression (a "logically proper name" in Russell's terminology) or a denoting expression (and hence a description in disguise) was tied to the speaker's psychology.[8] If the speaker had knowledge by acquaintance of a particular individual, then he was able to employ a genuine referring expression to refer to that individual. If the speaker had only knowledge by description of an individual, then the speaker would have to employ a denoting expression and would have to speak about the individual under a description. The idea is that we have singular and general thoughts, and when we express those thoughts linguistically the logical form of our linguistic expressions will depend upon the nature of the thoughts being expressed.

The problem, of course, is that some names that we take to be referential turn out to be empty, and often we may wonder whether a particular name (like 'King Arthur') is referential or not (i.e. whether there exists an individual to which the name refers). Accordingly, if there is some room for doubt about whether I am directly acquainted with some individual answering to a particular name, then the name cannot be a referring expression in my idiolect but must be a denoting expression. Problem: isn't there always room for doubt about whether we have knowledge by acquaintance? Historical names, which we take to have a causal history linking them with some particular individual, may in fact be unanchored; they may turn out to be the invention of a past storyteller. Names and demonstrations that appear to refer to individuals in the perceptual environment may in fact not do so at all, given the possibility of illusions and hallucinations. One can see how Russell (1985) was driven to the extreme position that we are only acquainted with sense data and with "egocentric particulars." Correlatively, it is also easy to see how Russell was driven to the position that genuine referring expressions (logically proper names) are deployed only on rare occasions and that denoting expressions are rather the norm. Such are the dangers of linking logical form to the speaker's psychology.

The problem of empty names thus presents a dilemma for the philosophy of language. One can take the first horn and argue that all names are in fact descriptive, but then one is skewered by Kripkean rigidity arguments.[9] One can take the second horn, and argue that all (or most) names are referring expressions, but then one is skewered by the counterintuitive conclusion that many sentences containing empty names fail to express a determinate proposition.[10] Finally, if one attempts to escape between the horns (à la Russell) by distinguishing referring expressions and denoting expressions psychologically, one gets forced back towards the first horn. Meanwhile, if

---

[8] See Evans (1982) and Neale (1990) for discussion of this point.

[9] One can try to follow Dummett (1973, 110–151) and hold that rigidity effects can be accounted for if we think of descriptions as taking mandatory wide scope in these cases, but see Soames (1998b) for extended criticism of this strategy.

[10] Alternatively (following the Meinongian route) one can say all (most) names are referring expressions that in the case of so-called empty names refer to non-existent objects. See Parsons (1980) and Zalta (1983, 1988) for examples of this strategy. I pass over that strategy here.

we choose bald externalism about logical form, we are forced to sever the link between logical form and our linguistic intentions.

But the externalism about syntactic form that we are exploring in this chapter provides an alternative way to escape between the horns. Suppose that Twin-Earth is a world that is just like the actual world except that Socrates was an invention of Plato (here we ignore differences in the causal history between Earth and Twin-Earth that are due to the agency of Socrates). On Twin-Earth everyone assents to the same basic utterances involving the name 'Socrates' that we do ('Socrates taught Plato', 'Socrates drank hemlock', etc.). In the version of externalism I have in mind, my twin—a molecular duplicate of me—has thoughts that not only differ in content from mine, but also differ in form. So, for example, my thought that I express as 'Socrates was a philosopher' is a singular proposition containing Socrates as a constituent. The thought that my twin expresses as 'Socrates was a philosopher' is a general proposition. More, the linguistic expressions of our thoughts will differ in ways correlative to the ways in which the thoughts differ in form. So, for example, the logical form of my utterance of 'Socrates was a philosopher' contains a referring expression. My twin's utterance of 'Socrates was a philosopher' does not contain a referring expression but rather a denoting expression. The idea is that the logical form of an utterance is tied to the speaker's psychology, and that the wideness of the speaker's psychology allows the environment to help fix the syntactic form of the utterance.

If we are drawn to the idea that the formation of linguistic intentions involves forming mental representations having standard syntactic forms, then a similar story holds. Oscar has a mental representation containing a referring expression. Twin-Oscar has a mental representation with a denoting expression in place of a referring expression. Oscar's mental representation is in effect syntactically simpler than Twin-Oscar's representation.[11] The syntactic forms of those mental representations in turn fix the syntactic forms of the utterances.

In effect, one can say that Russell was right. Some names are logically proper names, others are denoting expressions in disguise, and which are which depends upon the speaker's psychology. Russell's mistake was the residual Cartesianism in his psychology. Once that is discarded we appear to make great headway in dissolving this puzzle about names.

The type of strategy I just outlined is not married to a Russellian theory of names; it can be extended to any theory that has two logically distinct kinds of names. For example, if one held that some names are genuine referring expressions and that others are fictive names, one could argue that these two kinds of names are distinct in form and that the forms are environmentally sensitive in precisely the same way as I outlined above. Likewise one could hold that some utterances contain genuine syntactic names and others do not (perhaps non-referring expressions just contain noises in the name-position)

---

[11] See Neale (1993) for a discussion of the idea that referring expressions are syntactically simple and that quantified expressions (including denoting expressions) are syntactically complex.

and whether they contain genuine syntactic names or not can be environmentally sensitive. The strategy can be generalized across a wide number of theories about names.

One might object that while environmental factors could anchor representational structures, they cannot plausibly account for whether or not a particular sentence has one logical form or another. That is to say, while it is plausible that the environment can establish the kinds of representational states being computed, it cannot plausibly be said to fix a particular instance of a representation in this way.

After all, even if the environment determines (or enters into the determination of) the program of a system, it seems that we should be able to tell whether a proper name in a given sentence is represented as a description or a referring expression without our knowing whether there is an individual answering to the name. That is, surely we don't need to need to know whether Santa Claus exists to know what kinds of data structures we are computing over.

This objection trades on a confusion, I believe—the idea that features of logical form like this correspond to the sorts of data structures familiar from work in natural language processing. We can grant that every proper name comes complete with a data structure or file, but this doesn't answer the relevant question of what the logical form of the sentence is and in particular whether a particular name is an individual constant or a description.

Now clearly there is some intuitive pull to think that if a name is a descriptive name then there must be a data structure associated with the name that encodes the relevant properties associated with the denoted individual and if the name isn't a description in disguise then the lexical entry for the name must be austere—perhaps just the name and some metaphysically essential properties. The problem is that the distinction between lexicon and data base in natural language processing is not particularly stable—at best one can gloss the distinction in terms of whether the information associated with a name is in some sense immediately at hand (for example in a memory buffer). These days, computational speeds being what they are, this is more of a convenience for people who are tasked with updating lexical information and data bases than an actual difference in processing efficiency. But even if processing efficiencies did turn on such choices, there is no really interesting logical difference between lexical information and data base information. This shouldn't surprise us; it's not like the analytic/synthetic distinction somehow manages to come back to life when we start doing computer science.

So what then does a difference in logical form involving names and descriptions come to? Just this: whatever data structures may be in play, whether the content of those data structures gets bundled into the name itself (as part of a descriptive name) or not depends entirely on whether there is something out there corresponding to the name (linked information-theoretically or causally). If there is nothing corresponding to the name, then the content of relevant data structures is built into the name (as part of a descriptive name). If there is something answering to the name, then the content associated with the name is austere. Notice that we aren't talking about some difference in the low level description of the machine itself in these cases; at the lowest level of the machine precisely the same thing is going on in the two cases (*general* embedding conditions might contribute to fixing these facts). What is being affected are higher level descriptions of the operation of the machine. This is not the sort of issue that a computational linguist even needs to worry about until she starts to develop systems that model other agents. But when we think about other agents then the difference becomes salient.

Consider first, an omniscient agent interpreting the utterances of others. An omniscient agent will be in a position to correctly identify the logical form of an utterance because such an agent will know whether or not there is an individual answering to the names in question. The logical form, assigned in this way, will cross-cut the way in which the computational linguist might think about the data structures associated with names, but this is not really an issue; the computational linguist has other interests here. However, the logical forms, determined in this way, are not inert. Getting the logical form right allows our omniscient agent to make correct predictions about entailment relations, the modal profile of these sentences, etc.

Outstanding Problems

There are obviously a number of anti-externalist arguments that can be raised against this position (we will address some of them in the next chapter), but for now I think it is more interesting to consider how the position holds up assuming externalism to be true. Let me conclude with a couple of theory-internal worries that the externalist about logical form must face. The first problem is related to what Schiffer (1992b) has called the "meaning intention" problem, but it is closely related to the knowledge question that was raised in section 5.2.

The Meaning Intention Problem (The Knowledge Question Revisited)

Notice how we preserved the link between linguistic intentions and logical form. By allowing that the forms of our thoughts and intentions can co-vary according to external conditions we can re-secure the link between linguistic intentions and syntactic form. That is, following the usual Twin-Earth considerations, Oscar might have one linguistic intention and Twin-Oscar may have quite another, despite their both having the same physical microstructure. Oscar, when he utters 'Socrates taught Plato' does so with the intention of expressing a particular singular proposition. Twin-Oscar (who lives in the Socrates-free world), when uttering words of the "same form," does so with the intention of expressing a particular general proposition.

But now the meaning intention problem rears its head. If linguistic intentions are environmentally determined, then it appears we cannot *know* our linguistic intentions without investigating the environment, and in some cases the kind of investigation necessary (say, to determine whether Socrates or King Arthur existed) may not be open to us. For example, when Oscar utters 'Socrates taught Plato' on this theory he may have the intention to express a particular singular proposition, but he cannot *know* that he has this intention without first investigating the environment to see if Socrates exists. In short, it would appear to follow that we cannot always know our linguistic intentions. Since we rarely are in a position to undertake such an investigation, it follows that we rarely have a handle on what we intend to say. Or so the objection would go.

This problem should sound familiar. It is simply a special case of the general problem of externalism and authoritative self-knowledge.[12] What the externalist can argue in response is that the contents and forms of second order thoughts (and their corresponding expressions) are *also* fixed by the environment. Thus, the linguistic intention that Oscar reports when he utters, 'I intend to say that Socrates was snub-nosed' is an intention to express the singular proposition that Socrates was snub-nosed. The linguistic intention that Twin-Oscar reports when he utters 'I intend to say that Socrates was snub-nosed' is the intention to express the general proposition that (for example) there is a unique teacher of Plato who drank hemlock etc. and that he was snub-nosed. In effect, this problem is familiar to the externalist, and the externalist will not find it a persuasive objection.

Perhaps we can retreat and go after the externalist again, this time focusing on the talk of logical form here. The strategy would be to concede that one can know that one intends to express the singular proposition that Socrates is snub-nosed, but deny that it is credible that one can know that one intends to utter something that contains a referring expression. In effect, the standard externalist strategy may work for contents, but it cannot be extended to forms.

But is it really impossible for the externalist to extend this strategy to forms? It could be argued that you do indeed intend to utter a sentence that has such and such form. It does not follow that you must know that it has such and such form, and it does not follow that you have the ability to individuate utterances on the basis of their forms.[13]

The answer is analogous to what one says about knowledge of contents; you are thinking that water is wet, and you know that you are thinking that water is wet, but it does not follow that you can differentiate water thoughts from twater thoughts.[14] In the case of form, one can know one is intending to utter a sentence with a referring expression without being able to distinguish utterances having referring expressions from utterances having denoting expressions. Of course, this *is* to concede that (unless we are philosophers of language) we are simply indifferent to the logical forms of what we say. And if we *are* philosophers of language—perhaps uttering a sentence with 'Santa Claus' in the subject position and (quote-unquote) *intending* to employ a referring expression, well, we are simply trying to do the impossible. Again this is

---

[12] See Ludlow and Martin (1998) for a survey of the literature on this topic.

[13] Part of the misunderstanding here may stem from a failure to specify what lies within the scope of the verb 'intends'. Here's another way to put it. You intend to utter a sentence S. S has form f. You do not know that S has f.

[14] This is a point stressed by McLaughlin and Tye (1999).

exactly parallel to the discussions of content externalism and self-knowledge, where one is indifferent to the individuating conditions of a thought, yet one can still know what one is thinking. (As Davidson would put the point, one can know what one is thinking/saying, but it doesn't follow that one knows what one is thinking/saying under all descriptions.)

The Environmental Sensitivity of Logic?

If the logical forms of our utterances are environmentally sensitive, then it appears that there are some strong consequences for the nature of logic. In a way this should not be surprising; it has already been observed that externalism about content has unusual consequences for logic. For example Boghossian (1992a, 1992b) and Schiffer (1992b) discuss cases in which an agent unwittingly slow-switches from Earth to Twin-Earth, and reasons thus:

I fell in water at t0
<u>I just fell in water at t1</u>
I have fallen in water more than once

The problem is that the agent is equivocating without realizing it. The first use of 'water' picks up water, and the second picks up twater. (If we say that the first use no longer invokes the water content but only the twater content, then the argument fails by virtue of the first premise being false.)

Externalism about syntactic form raises the ante somewhat. Not only will there be cases of equivocation, but the very notion of what counts as a logical inference will come unhinged. Here is the problem: Suppose that the forms of proper names like 'Socrates' depend upon environmental embedding in the ways outlined above. If we live in a world with Socrates, then 'Socrates' is a referring expression. If we live in a Socrates-free world, then 'Socrates' is a description in disguise—perhaps something of the form 'the teacher of Plato who drank hemlock . . .'. Then in the Socrates world the following inference will be invalid, but in the Socrates-free world it will be valid!

<u>Socrates was a snub-nosed philosopher</u>
A snub-nosed philosopher taught Plato

Obviously the analytic/synthetic distinction also comes unglued in ways that even Quine did not anticipate. If forms are environmentally sensitive, then an utterance of 'Socrates was a philosopher' may be analytic in some worlds but synthetic in others.

The Collapse of Sameness of Form

While I think that the first (and perhaps also the second) objection can be answered in a way that is consistent with basic externalist assumptions, it may be that the answers given lead directly to a third problem for the externalist about logical form. Consider the case where Oscar and Twin-Oscar separately utter 'Socrates was snub-nosed'. Earlier I said that in such a case "Oscar and Twin-Oscar use expressions *of the same form*."

But do they use expressions of the same form? Clearly they do not, since at a minimum the syntactic forms of those expressions will be quite different. Strictly speaking, we can no longer say that they make utterances of the same form. At best, Twin-Oscar produces the same acoustical signal as does Oscar (he may not even do that, depending upon how acoustical signals are individuated). If the considerations raised in this section are right, then our standard ways of reporting Twin-Earth happenings may be careless. Our twins do not utter the same expressions as we do for the simple reason that the forms of our respective expressions are quite different. The problem could actually be much more serious than this. If forms are sensitive to the environment, we may also wonder if we really have the same microstructure as our twins. Microstructure, as we saw in section 5.2, is arguably a matter of form. The question is, can microstructure be sensitive to local environments, or is the only environment that matters to microstructure the entire physical universe (or at least large regions of it)? Obviously if microstructure is sensitive in this way it makes a hash out of standard Twin-Earth thought experiments and may well undermine the internal/external distinction altogether.

6

Referential Semantics for Narrow Ψ-Languages

In Chapter 2 I argued that one can endorse a conception of Ψ-language without buying into the idea that Ψ-language is individualistic—that is, a chapter of narrow psychology. Let's continue to call a view of Ψ-language (like Chomsky's) in which Ψ-language is construed individualistically, either "I-language" or "narrow Ψ-language." Let's call a conception that individuates Ψ-language states widely "broad Ψ-language."

In the last chapter we explored the coherence of certain accounts of broad Ψ-language—in particular, the coherence of the idea that syntactic states could be individuated widely. The central issue in *this* chapter is the question of whether there is room within the narrow Ψ-language conception of language (Chomsky's I-language conception) to allow a semantic theory that provides language/world relations. Following standard philosophical terminology, let's speak of such a semantic theory as a "referential semantics." Can there be a referential semantics for narrow Ψ-language?

In Ludlow (2003) I argued that there could be such a semantic theory, and Chomsky (2003a) has responded negatively to the proposal. In this chapter I will develop the case for the possibility of a referential semantics for I-language (developing what I will call a "bite the bullet" strategy), review Chomsky's case against compatibilism, and finally offer a rebuttal to Chomsky.

6.1 The Compatibility of Referential Semantics and Narrow Ψ-Languages

Prima facie, the idea of a referential semantics for an I-language seems problematic—at least on Chomsky's individualistic conception of I-language and in particular the FLN. In Chapters 2 and 5, I suggested that the individualism could be jettisoned, but if we adhere to individualism about the FLN then it initially looks like one has a strong case against referential semantics. If the FLN supervenes on narrow properties of the mind/brain then how could it be otherwise?

But there is no reason we need to take semantic theory as being a component of the FLN—indeed on the prevailing view of the FLN in generative linguistics it simply makes no sense for it to include semantic theory. At best, a semantic theory speaks to what Chomsky has called the Conceptual/Intentional system and establishes interface conditions for the FLN. Put another way, what the FLN does is construct form/meaning pairs that are legible to the interfaces, and one way to understand this is as saying that the FLN computes representations (LF representations, for example) that are visible to the semantic theory. But the semantic theory itself could involve properties that involve relations between the agent in isolation and the world in which it is embedded. Thus it is entirely coherent to say that the FLN could be individualistic even if the related semantic component is relational.[1]

In Ludlow (2003) I argued that the general phenomenon of individualistic and relational sciences informing each other is fairly common. One example I drew on was the contrast between primate physiology and primate ecology, and I offered that the former draws upon individualistic facts (about, for example, the skeletal structure of the primate) and the latter addresses relations between the primate and its environment. Despite the apparently distinct properties under investigation, it is possible for facts about primate physiology to support a particular claim about the relation of the primate to its environment and vice versa.

My favorite illustration of the general phenomenon is Webster and Webster (1988), in which it is observed that individualistic anatomical structure can place constraints on the types of (relational) environmental functions that are possible, and vice versa. One such case involves the study of the anatomy of the kangaroo rat, where it has been useful to make inferences from physical structure to organism/environment relations, and vice versa. For example, when kangaroo rats were first studied, biologists noted that they had particularly large middle ear cavities. According to Webster and Webster, subsequent biologists posited a number of hypotheses about the function of the cavity, and the hypotheses based on anatomy alone appeared to have been the weakest. For example Hatt (1932) argued that the enlarged cavities shifted the weight of the head to the posterior and thereby assisted upright saltatorial locomotion. An alternative and productive assumption, however, was that the enlarged cavities served the function of improved hearing. Webster and Webster (1971) showed that the function was to pick up low frequency sound waves typically generated by predators like owls and snakes.[2]

---

[1] This is a bit more complicated than I've made it sound, since, if the semantics is externalist and if the FLN computes efficient ways to wire up phonological representations with semantic representations, then it would seem the computations made by the FLN will have to be environmentally sensitive. However, one could concede that some semantic rules (say the basic lexical rules) are relational and that others (say the composition rules) are individualistic, and that the composition rules are what put constraints on the FLN (as, for example, they did in my proposal in section 1.4). I don't mean to say that this safely retires the issue; I only mean it to table the concern for the time being.

[2] I recognize that this looks more like a case for methodological wide individuation than constitutive wide individuation (cf. section 2.1). In this case, however, the level of grain of description of the anatomical features is effectively at the functional level, so that in worlds without owls and snakes (or other predators making low frequency noises) the same creature would, in effect, have a different functional anatomy. That is, environmental facts not only help us figure out what the anatomical function of the cavity is; in some sense they also metaphysically determine it.

Even Chomsky (1995b, 28) seems to concede that relational and individualistic sciences can inform each other:

Naturalistic study is of course not limited to such [internalist] bounds; internalist inquiry into a planet or an ant does not preempt or preclude the study of the solar system or an ant community. Non-internalist studies of humans can take many forms: as phases in an Oxygen-to-Carbon Dioxide cycle or gene transmission, as farmers or gourmets, as participants in associations and communities, with their power structures, doctrinal systems, cultural practices, and so on. Internalist studies are commonly presupposed in others with broader range, but it should be obvious that the legitimacy of one or another kind of inquiry does not arise.

Of course, as I noted in Ludlow (2003), it is important to be cautious in making inferences from individualistic properties to relational ones and back. One can be misled by familiar morphological features of an animal, and too much attention to the environment may mislead about the actual internal structure of the animal. There are no rules that guarantee one can't be misled in making these inferences. Turning again to Webster and Webster (1988), they summarize the situation rather nicely:

Implicit in many morphological studies is the idea that structure determines, and therefore can reveal, function. Unfortunately this is an oversimplification. A more realistic view is that structure—whether of an entire organism or its parts—places constraints on what functions are possible (Gans, 1985) and may, to the observant, suggest some that are plausible.

As plausible as this may sound, Chomsky has raised a number of objections to the extension of this form of compatibilism to the linguistic case.

6.2 Chomsky's Incompatibilist Arguments

In Ludlow (2003) I cataloged Chomsky's objections to referential semantics as involving three different objections:

   (i) The Implausible Commitments Argument
   (ii) The Type Mismatch Argument
   (iii) The Misbehaving Object Argument

Each of them was designed to show that a referential semantics forces us into some uncomfortable if not implausible metaphysical positions. Each argument is worth revisiting.

The Implausible Commitments Argument

Chomsky (1981, 324) has drawn attention to the fact that a referential semantics commits us to what he considers to be implausible entities, flaws for example, and suggests that we really can't take seriously a theory which commits us to such entities.

If I say "the flaw in the argument is obvious, but it escaped John's attention," I am not committed to the absurd view that among things in the world are flaws, one of them in the argument in question. Nevertheless, the NP <u>the flaw in the argument</u> behaves in all relevant respects in the manner of the truly referential expression the coat in the closet. . . .

Pursuing a similar line of attack, Hornstein (1984, 58) has drawn attention to constructions like (1).

(1)   The average man is concerned about his weight

Hornstein contends that "no one wishes to argue that there are objects that are average men in any meaningful sense."

The "Type Mismatch" Argument

In addition to his reservations about entities like flaws, Chomsky (1995b) argues that there is an apparent mismatch between the type individuation that objects and substances intuitively have, and the type individuation that a referential semantics will provide.

To try and get clear on this issue, I offered a terminological distinction between an I-substance on the one hand and a P-substance, where a P-substance was the sort of substance that would have a role in physical theory (H_2O for example), and an I-substance was the stuff that we are intuitively talking about when we use language (the intuitive referent of 'water'). To put the point in a more theory-neutral way, the I-substance is what it appears we are talking about based upon our (individual) understanding and use of language. To be fully consistent with earlier chapters of this book I will hereafter use the expression 'Ψ-substances' to talk about these kinds of substances.

As I understand Chomsky's worry, Ψ-substances and P-substances just don't match up right. For example, if 'water' refers to H_2O, then a referential semantics will assign a P-substance (H_2O) as the semantic value of 'water'. But the problem is that the stuff we are actually talking about when we use the term 'water'—the Ψ-substance—is something else altogether. To see this, consider the fact that what we find in the Chicago River is called 'water' though it could hardly be considered H_2O (it actually caught on fire during the great Chicago fire). Also problematic is the fact that there are substances like ice tea which chemically approximate H_2O much more closely than Chicago River water, yet we don't call them 'water'. According to Chomsky, the situation is even more problematic than this. If someone at the water company poured tea leaves into the system so that what came out of the tap was chemically identical to Lipton Ice Tea, we would still call it 'water'—although we might complain about its impurity.

So, here is the situation. What we are talking about when we use the term 'water'—the Ψ-substance—depends upon the social setting in which we find that substance. But according to referential semantics, the meaning of the term is supposed to depend upon the chemical composition of the substance referred to—it's supposed to be a P-substance. Conclusion: referential semantics will not track the intuitive notion of meaning.

One might think it possible to get off the hook if one appeals to social theories of external (referential) content (in the sense of Burge 1979). Rather than P-substances, we might posit S-substances, substances that are individuated according to community norms. So, while my concept of water might not accord with H_2O, it might still accord with a certain socially determined object, which has the property of being water when it comes from the faucet, but not when it is served at a restaurant. The problem here is that there are plenty of cases where such S-substances (if there could be such things) would not track our judgments about the extension of terms—Burge's own examples about tharthritis and brisket are cases in point. That is, there is also a mismatch between Ψ-substances and S-substances.

The Misbehaving Object Argument

There are a number of interesting features to the water/tea story, one of which can be broken out as a separate objection to referential semantics.

The type mismatch argument showed us that Ψ-substances don't track P-substances, but there is another problem. The water/tea story also seems to show that the Ψ-substance we are talking about when we use the term 'water' is a most ill-behaved sort of substance. Something may cease to be water even if no internal physical changes have taken place. For example, the same chemical compound is water when it comes from the tap, but ceases to be water when it is served at a restaurant.

If that's the intuitive character of Ψ-substances, then there is really little hope that referential semantics can "give the reference" of what we talk about when we talk about 'water' and 'tea', since referential semantics is supposedly going to say that the content of these terms is H_2O in the first case and H_2O plus certain other elements in the latter. That is, Ψ-substances are so unruly that it is wildly implausible to suppose that they could have any counterparts in the physical world. Hence they have no counterparts that a referential semantics could utilize as their referents.

A related, if somewhat more general point, is made in Chomsky (1975b, 203), where Chomsky notes that the very notion of whether we are talking about a single object or a collection of objects turns on any number of social and institutional factors.

We do not regard a herd of cattle as a physical object, but rather as a collection, though there would be no logical incoherence in the notion of a scattered object, as Quine, Goodman, and others have made clear. But even spatiotemporal contiguity does not suffice as a general condition. One wing of an airplane is an object, but its left half, though equally continuous, is not. . . . Furthermore, scattered entities can be taken to be single physical objects under some conditions: consider a picket fence with breaks, or a Calder mobile. The latter is a "thing," whereas a collection of leaves on a tree is not. The reason, apparently, is that the mobile is created by an act of human will. If this is correct, then beliefs about human will and action and intention play a crucial role in determining even the most simple and elementary of concepts.

Moving that discussion into the current debate, we might say that it is implausible for even very simple semantic concepts like object and collection to correspond in any interesting sense to P-substances.

6.3 The "Bite the Bullet" Strategy and Chomsky's Response

In Ludlow (2003) I argued that these arguments were not really aimed at referential semantics so much as they were aimed at a doctrine that I called "Language/World Isomorphism" (or LWI). The examples don't show that language can't hook up with the world in any way whatsoever, but rather that we can't expect to find a one-to-one match between linguistic categories and fundamental ontological categories.

Beyond that, however, I argued further that there is nothing implausible about a "bite the bullet" strategy in which one simply concedes that there *are* entities like flaws in arguments, coats in closets, and the average family.

This isn't the only option. Higginbotham (1985) suggested a strategy in which we think of 'average' in 'the average family' as working like an adverbial element, so that a sentence like (2) has an analysis along the lines of (2′).

(2)   The average family has 2.3 children

(2′)   On average, a family has 2.3 children

Chomsky (p.c.) has observed that this won't work in the case of more complex cases like (3).

(3)   Your report on the average family fails to make it clear that it has 2.3 children.

Here there are two problems. First, as Stanley (2001) has noted, there is the matter of the anaphor (what does the 'it' in 'it has 2.3 children' refer to), but beyond that there is also the issue of our needing to reintroduce the adverbial element, as in (3′).

(3′)   Your report on what on average the state of the family is, fails to make it clear that on average it has 2.3 children.

This single example has spawned a fair bit of discussion, including Ludlow (1999), Stanley (2001), Stanley and Kennedy (forthcoming), and Carlson and Pelletier (2002), and all have attempted to dodge the conclusion that there is an entity like the average family—an entity that has 2.3 children.

This is an interesting example because it shows the tension that the language faculty and metaphysics can place upon each other. In effect, we are left with three options. First, we can follow Chomsky and sever the connection between grammar and ontology. Second, we can follow Higginbotham, Stanley, and others and argue that the syntax and semantics of these constructions is much more robust than appears on the surface, or we can "bite the bullet" and say that there really are entities like the average family.

There are also hybrid strategies. I am persuaded by Stanley and Kennedy (forthcoming) that a good number of cases involving 'the average family' can be treated with average as a kind of operator. However, there remain recalcitrant cases (not least Chomsky's 'Joe Sixpack' example) where I think the bite the bullet strategy lines up with the data more cleanly. But is the bite the bullet strategy a viable option even if only applied to a limited class of cases?

First, I'm not entirely sure I should call this last strategy a "bite the bullet" strategy, since the kind of entity being posited doesn't seem particularly unusual to me—the average family is simply an abstract object that statisticians speak of as having fractional values (2.3 children, for example).

In fact, the notion of "the average man" and "the average family" is a theoretical entity—an invention of the nineteenth-century statistician Adolphe Quetelet. The notion of 'the average man' (*l'homme moyen*) was introduced in Quetelet (1835), and the motivation was that it would be a useful theoretical tool in statistics and social science. Or as Stigler (1986, 171) put it, "the average man was a device for smoothing away the random variations of society and revealing the regularities that were to be the laws of his 'social physics'." It was a theoretical posit, and we can choose to not be realists about it, but that is a bit like not being realists about atoms—it is just a form of scientific anti-realism and not really the rejection of an obviously absurd entity.

One might think that our contemporary use of 'the average man' has nothing to do with Quetelet's invention, but in fact one can probably reconstruct the introduction of the concept by Quetelet and connect it to our use of the locution 'the average X' today. This is a case where a scientific discovery caught the public imagination and quickly made its way into mainstream common usage.

The average man was a fictional being in his creator's eye, but such was his appeal that he underwent a transformation, like Pinocchio or Pygmalion's statue, so that he still lives in headlines of our daily papers ... The idea of the average man caught the imagination in 1835 as it does now. As a psychological ploy it was a brilliant device. It captured the egalitarian idea of the common man in a precise and apparently scientific way that was quite congenial to nineteenth-century political thought, and it served a valid and useful statistical purpose. (Stigler 1986, 170–171)

On the other hand, there was probably more to the average man concept than the public knew.

But Quetelet's average man was in fact a more complex creature than naive accounts would indicate. He was Quetelet's device for allowing a beginning of a "social physics," the gate-keeper to a mathematical social science. (171)

When people invoke expressions like 'the average man' and 'Joe Sixpack' they may have peculiar ideas about what they are doing (they may think they are talking about something having morally ideal properties for example) or they may think they are not talking about anything at all (this must be Chomsky's view), but of course a referential semanticist should not be troubled by this. There is a causal or information-theoretic chain linking us to the theoretical entities that Quetelet discovered, and *that* is what we are talking about. It is similar to when we talk about atoms or quarks. We may know very little about these entities and we may know even less about the origin of these terms and our beliefs about them will contain plenty of errors, but we are still talking about those entities for all that.

What made the concept of the average X prima facie suspect is that the average family can have properties that ordinary things don't have—2.3 children, for example—but once we understand that the average family is a scientific construct (and that fractional children are theoretical posits as well), the worries should subside. But what about other cases (like 'coats in the closet'), which clearly do not have the scientific pedigree that 'the average family' does. Is there any reason to think that there simply can't be such things? Is there any reason we can't bite the bullet?

Chomsky has responded to the bite the bullet strategy, but not entirely productively, in my view. According to Chomsky (2003a, 289),

There is a sense in which sounds, flaws, books, . . . "are clearly not logically absurd entities, nor . . . particularly odd entities" (Ludlow). Sounds, for example are perfectly robust things. We have no problem assigning sounds to the expressions of (1), or none of the above, in a vast range of normal cases. If we are satisfied with this result, we can avoid the hard problems of experimental phonetics.

Proceeding, we can quantify over flaws and average guys; also sounds and books. We use a nominal phrase X, we can usually say, intelligibly, that the X's are the things we are talking about: flaws, books, the darkening sky, Joe Sixpack, the bank that was burned to the ground after rejecting the loan application, the threat of global warming, a biochemical process that is tragic (life), *The Purpose of America* (the title of a book by one of the founders of realist international relations theory), . . . Again, if satisfied with this result we can avoid the hard problems of the study of meaning, reference, and language use generally.

Even more contentiously (2003a, 290):

These moves should, I think, be understood as registering lack of interest in the problems. That may be entirely reasonable; no one seeks to study everything. But we should not mislead ourselves into believing that by invoking sounds, flaws, John Doe, attention, escaping, . . . or rivers, water, cities, books, trees, . . . and taking them to be related to pronouns and other words by an invented technical notion called "reference," we have even begun to investigate, let alone to have solved, the problem of how people use language to refer to things in the world, or any other kind of language–world relation. That's taken for granted in the study of sound, and should be in the study of meaning and referring as well, I think.

What should we say about this?

6.4 The Compatibilist Bites Back

The above remarks by Chomsky seem to be based on a failure to make a distinction between (i) and (ii).

(i) Semantic theory is interested in a four-place relation that holds between expressions, speakers, contexts and external objects.

(ii) Semantic theory is interested in a four-place relation that holds between expressions, speakers, contexts and external objects and is therefore not the least bit interested in the nature of the relations—it is only interested in stating the relata, and furthermore insists that no one else should study the relata further.

Clearly it is absurd to think that studying relations to externalia precludes the investigation of the nature and origin of those relations and why they have the character that they do.

Let's take the case of the expression 'water'. A referential semanticist will probably say that people use that expression to refer to a class of liquids. I would maintain that it refers to a very interesting Ψ-substance that is sensitive to social context (what might be called 'water' in one context could be called 'tea' in another). But what sort of semanticist would say that this is where inquiry must end? To the contrary, it should be just the beginning.

Granted, some investigators are big on disciplinary bookkeeping, and don't want to get their hands dirty with investigating certain questions, like how or why our semantics of 'water' is the way it is. They might say "that isn't my job, it's the job of the psychologist or lexical semanticist." As Chomsky says, "no one seeks to study everything," and there is no accounting for what one might be interested in studying, but who would say that such questions shouldn't be investigated by anyone? More strongly, why on earth should the positing of a four-place relation involving expressions, speakers, contexts, and things in the world preclude the study of the nature of that relation—the specifics of the relation, why it is the way it is, how it came to hold, etc.?

In a certain sense, it is not the referentialist but the internalist that seems to be registering a lack of interest in these questions. If we are internalists and there is a concept WATER, there isn't much to say about the concept—it is what it is. But if we reject internalism then a number of interesting questions arise. For example, why does our application of the term 'water' come apart from the concept of water used in the physical sciences? This is only a puzzle and worthy of our attention if we expect our linguistic expressions to pick out well-behaved objects. Chomsky is right to point out that the object picked out by our use of 'water' is a misbehaving object, and the fact that it is misbehaving is what makes the question interesting. If we cut the link between language and the external world we simply have an internal data structure that doesn't seem to be in any way special.

These cases can be multiplied. Consider Chomsky's example of the pronoun 'it' as used in a sentence like 'I bought John's book, started to read it but lost it, then bought it again, but hated it so I burned it'. If we aren't attuned to the metaphysical issues here it is not clear why this should be an interesting puzzle at all, but of course for the externalist it is indeed a puzzle: Why is it we are able to smoothly shift between talking about types and tokens here? We don't expect anaphoric relations to work this way, but apparently they do. We now have a couple of options available to us. We can try to come up with an explanation for why and how anaphora can shift between types and tokens, or we could try a more radical solution, arguing that the things we call books are these strange objects that morph between types and tokens. (A book is something that many people can own and read and that we can also "destroy," even as people continue to buy and read it.) This latter view seems implausible on the face of it, but it may still be worth investigating. Whether the view holds up is beside the point here—what is relevant is that standard externalist assumptions are driving the investigation rather than closing it off.

In point of fact, current semantic investigations into the nature of anaphora are much more robust than Chomsky's remarks reflect. Consider his claim that the pronoun in (4) is "referentially linked."

(4)   The flaw in the argument is obvious, but it escaped John's attention

Or consider the following passage in which we confront a Martian linguist who is interested in how human language works.

we can account for everything by invoking the metaphysical thesis that among the things of the world are sounds, flaws, books, . . . saying that words like "it" *refer* to these things, and so on. But M wants to know more: What are sounds, flaws, books, . . . and what is the relation "refer" that has these curious properties? Suppose we assure M again that there's no problem: we all understand very well what sounds, flaws, books, . . . are and how to use "it" to refer to them. (Chomsky 2003a, 291)

The problem is that for even hard core referentialists there is an open question as to whether the pronouns in question refer. A standard view, advanced by Parsons (1978), Cooper (1979), Evans (1977), Neale (1990), Heim (1990), Ludlow (1994) among many others is that discourse pronouns like these are "E-type" pronouns and best analyzed as descriptions in disguise, not as "devices of reference."

This illustrates two points. First, when we call an expression a "referring expression" we are making certain predictions about how the expression should behave when embedded in modal environments, propositional attitude environments, and many others. For example, if the expression can be understood as taking intermediate scope between two operators then it cannot plausibly be taken to be a referring expression. To illustrate this point, consider the following example.

(5)   John found a flaw in the argument. Fred believes that Mary found it first.

In the second sentence it is possible to understand the pronoun as having wide scope with respect to Mary, but narrow scope with respect to Fred. For example, suppose Fred takes a dim view of John's originality and supposes that everything John discovers was already discovered by Mary. Fred doesn't know what the flaw is, he just heard that John found one, and conjectures that Mary must have found it (whatever flaw John found) already. If the pronoun was truly referential we would only expect it to have the widest possible reading—one where Fred too must know which flaw was discovered. Indeed we might also insist that the speaker and audience in some way be acquainted with the flaw in question.

Not everyone will agree that the pronoun can't refer in this case, but those people need to adopt a "cheaper" view of reference—one where acquaintance and salience are not required for us to successfully refer to something.

Second, however, once we accept the idea that the pronoun is a referring expression (or an E-type expression) in these cases it merely opens the door to further very interesting questions involving the generative mechanisms that underlie our use of referring (E-type) expressions.

It is also worth reflecting on Chomsky's invocation of the Martian linguist here. We are told that the Martian linguist will opt for a representational stance towards ants:

What we can know is determined by the "modes of conception in the understanding," in Cudworth's phrase. That led to illuminating work in the theory of meaning by neoplatonists, empiricists from Hobbes to Hume, and others, influencing Kant, with later resonance until today.... The Martian scientist would be well advised to pursue a similar course, adopting the ethological perspective that seeks to discover the organism's *Umwelt*, its particular mode of interpreting the world.

For non-human animals, so it is alleged, internal computational systems are "representational" in something like the sense of technical referential semantics. Introducing a series of experimental papers, Gallistel (1990) argues that representations play a key role in animal behavior and cognition; here "representation" is understood as isomorphism, a one–one relation between mind/brain processes and "an aspect of the environment to which these processes adapt the animal's behavior," as when an ant "represents" the corpse of a conspecific by odor. For humans, this notion is completely inappropriate, as we see by inspecting even the simplest words, criteria of individuation, the basic mechanisms of intended referential dependence, and other elementary properties of language and its use, even the concept of "nameable thing" (as noted in comments that Ludlow quotes).

Pursuing this course we can learn a lot about humans, and about how the expressions of the I-languages related to language-external entities—sounds and things in informal usage. But we do not arrive at "substantive metaphysical theses," except about the nature of the human mind and the "modes of conception in the understanding" that enter into constructing the *Umwelt* in which we live and act. Non-human representational systems might yield directly a kind of mind-independent "metaphysical thesis" if Gallistel is correct, but not human language, which does not seem to be a "representational system" in anything like this sense, in either its sound or meaning aspects. (Chomsky 2003a, 292)

Can it really be that a Martian version of Gallistel is going to treat humans as radically different from ants? We find it natural to suppose that ants are "representational" in Gallistel's sense because their representational states form a subset of the representational states that are available to us. The Martian Gallistel might find that the ants pick out a subset of his representational states as well, or he might find the ants positively mysterious. For example, the Martian may have no concept of species. It may not see how the representational states of the ants map onto reality at all. After extensive investigation it may come to hypothesize a theory very much like Gallistel's, but reject the idea that anything is represented—it may take the ant communication system to be a calculus of chemicals not linked to any natural kinds in the ants' world.

Let's suppose that humans are just as mysterious to the Martian. It simply can't make out what we are on about when we utter 'water' etc. If the Martian finally figures out what 'water' refers to—the Ψ-substance that depends upon contextual issues like whether it comes from a restaurant waiter or a faucet—the Martian may or may not be charitable and call it a real property—there is no reason Martians should be above chauvinism here. But let's think a bit about *how* the Martian figures this out. The quickest way to sorting things out would be for the Martian to find some reliable consultants who can tell it under what conditions someone might call something 'water'. It will construct a theory that successfully predicts when something will be called 'water'.

The Martian is of course in a different position than we are. If its cognitive architecture is different from ours it has to ask or, less fruitfully, observe what we are up to in our linguistic practices. The Martian doesn't know in advance the range of things that 'water' refers to and it may just give up before it knows. We aren't in that position. We already know, up to cases of significant complexity.

If the Martian doesn't get that far it hasn't paid the price of admission to the interesting and fun part of the exercise—how do humans come to apply a term like 'water' to that strange class of substances across diverse contexts? What are the mechanism(s) that underlie this and other aspects of the human lexical semantics? If the Martian does get this far, we no longer have an advantage over the Martian—both we and the Martian have to do our best to reconstruct the cognitive system that explains this linguistic fact.

In this sense Chomsky is right about the mentalist aspect of the exercise; that is where the action is. Where I disagree is that I take these investigations into "modes of conception in the understanding" to be investigations into the mechanisms that underwrite our representational states—or, if one prefers, give us the representational states that we have. Mental facts supervene on relational facts, as do the mechanisms, rules, representations, and principles that we posit to explain these relational facts.

Chomsky presumably wants to say that the Martian investigator doesn't care about whether there really is a substance like our water, but let's face it, the Martian will have to talk about it just the same, because it stands to reason that the Martian will come to know the Ψ-substance (let's say it calls it 'blarg' in Martian) before it figures out the mechanisms at work by which we come to use 'water' to refer to blarg/water.

But now let's consider what happens when the Martian begins investigating our use of terms like 'shadow', 'flaw', or 'the average family'. Like us, the Martian will have a choice as to whether to take these to be basic nominal expressions, or whether they are really something else in disguise. Once again, if the conceptual apparatus of the Martian is different from ours it may give up before it figures out the semantics of 'shadow', 'flaw', etc. On the other hand, the Martian may hypothesize that if these crazy creatures represent the world as having species, food supplies, predators, etc., maybe they represent it as having flaws and shadows too.

The question is, will the Martian feel the pull to avoid reference to things like flaws and shadows and so forth? Clearly, metaphysical intuitions are driving the initial arguments from Chomsky and the defenses from Higginbotham, Stanley, and others. Obviously, Chomsky supposes we have a less secure grip on shadows and flaws than we do on coats and shoes.

The Martian scientist has the same suite of options that we do, of course. It might fail to see a difference between coats and flaws and posit both entities without a second thought. Alternatively, the Martian might see them as a distinct class of objects, and will look for ways to analyze away one class (the Martian, of course, could be happy with flaws and shadows, but be suspicious of coats and shoes). In this case the Martian undergoes the same exercise as Higginbotham and Stanley in seeking an alternative analysis. Whether the analysis works depends upon how well it embeds within linguistic theory (not very well, or at least not without some outstanding puzzles, it would seem).

The Martian may or may not choose to be chauvinistic about this. Maybe it will concede that the world is furnished with such things, or maybe it will just take these as being so much loose talk.

Chomsky seems to think that the Marian scientist who engages in figuring out human Ψ-substances (or we, when we do the same) is doing a form of ethnography—it's not really a study of what there is, so much as a chapter of anthropology and what people *think* there is. But this isn't right. The kind of metaphysical exercise I'm proposing and what the ethnographer are up to will come apart in significant ways. For example, the ethnographer will overlook certain kinds of errors; if her subjects think that a ritual turns water into wine or blood then that is what the ethnographer will record. The metaphysician isn't going to be on board with this. It is still water, which these people call 'blood' or 'wine' in the relevant ritualistic circumstances. (This distinction can come under pressure, but the ethnographer is not going to argue that the waiter is performing a kind of ritual, turning dirty water into tea.)

Another reason to think this isn't ethnography is that many of the metaphysical posits that come from such investigations would not surface in an ethnographic study. Would events be posited, for example? Would surfaces? Would the distinction between types and tokens? Most of the posits of metaphysics fall outside the ken of the average person; they are the product of investigation.

Posits like flaws and the average family are cases in point. If we are driven to acknowledge such entities it is not because the average person is prepared to say that they exist or even because we have robust highly trained metaphysical intuitions that they must. It is rather because our semantics must quantify over such entities in order to account for a broad class of natural language phenomena (for example, the case for events is made in part by appeal to entailment relations holding between action sentences). The ontology is tied to the demands of our scientific theory of the semantics of natural language, and not to the kinds of entities and objects that members of a particular culture might believe in.

6.5   The Prospects for a Non-referential Semantics

So far I've been attempting to defend the compatibility of referential semantics with an I-language conception of the language faculty. But this isn't the only position that needs defending. If one is going to reject referential semantics, then what is the alternative? The question can no longer be idly dismissed. As we saw in section 1.4, the best way we have of making sense of legibility requirements imposed by the Conceptual/Intentional interface is to think that the semantic theory is imposing these legibility constraints. If the semantic theory remains inchoate, then it is difficult to imagine that it could place any legibility constraints, and this threatens to undo the Minimalist Program—claims about legibility would become vacuous.

What we need is an alternative to a referential semantics that is still rigorous but which does not deploy referential primitives like truth and reference. Is this possible? A number of researchers, ranging from Chomsky (2000b, and numerous other publications) to Horwich (1998, 2003, 2005), have suggested that the C/I system might be likened to a linguistic use theory. Of course, a use theory could also lapse into a theory of everything, so without a constrained picture of the mechanisms of language use, a use theory puts few legibility constraints on the interface. Again, we need a concrete story here if talk of "legibility" is to be non-vacuous.

One problem in any attempt to resolve this situation is that there has been a great divide in Anglo-American philosophy over the past 50 years between use theorists on the one hand (Wittgenstein, Austin, Searle) and truth-conditional semanticists on the other (Montague, Kaplan, Kripke). The traditional view has been that use theories resist formalization. When use theories *are* formalized, as in Kaplan (2001), it is done by assigning truth-conditional content where we might be surprised to find it. As Kaplan frames the move space, on Wittgenstein's view 'I am in pain' means 'ouch', while on Kaplan's view 'ouch' means 'I am in pain'. The underlying assumption of Kaplan is that the raw use theory cannot be directly formalized; formalization is only possible if we posit truth-conditional content.

Horwich (a use theorist) has resisted this conclusion, going so far as to suggest that the formalization of the use theory is a trivial matter, basically only requiring that we understand the contribution of the components.

[O]ne might wonder how it can be that the content of SEM(E) [the semantic object associated with an expression] is determined by the contents of its parts—i.e., why there is no possibility that the underlying property in virtue of which a complex mental expression has its meaning fails to square with the properties in virtue of which the lexical items have their meanings (given the way these items have been combined). But this can be explained trivially—in a way that has nothing to do with truth conditions. It suffices to suppose that the content-property of a complex mental expression, SEM, is *constituted by*—one might even say *identical to*—its property of being constructed as it is from LIs [lexical items] with certain meanings.

... compositionality is accommodated without making any assumptions whatsoever about what sort of property of a primitive is responsible for its embodying the concept it does. (2003, 174–175)

Chomsky, on the other hand, is more cautious:

Similar uneasiness is elicited, at least for me, by Horwich's account of compositionality. We have to account for the fact that "the content of SEM(E) is determined by the contents of its parts..." This "can be explained trivially," Horwich suggests, if we recognize that understanding an expression, "is, by definition, nothing over and above understanding its parts and knowing how they have been combined." It is true that we could understand the expressions (1)–(10) when we understand their parts and know how they are combined, but to work this out seems anything but trivial. One could also say that perception of a cube in motion should be explained in terms of firing of cells in the visual cortex and the way the effects are integrated, but there's nothing trivial about the task of explanation, even for perception of a straight line. It might be true that the task can be carried out for language without reference to truth conditions, as Horwich suggests, just as it might be true that it can be carried out with reference to truth conditions. But it has to be shown, which doesn't seem easy, in either case. (2003b, 303)

As we will see, Chomsky is right to be cautious here. As semanticists know, understanding how meanings combine is far from trivial in the truth-conditional case (indeed, you could argue that trying to figure this out is precisely what semanticists do for a living). But as we will also see below, the move to a use theory of meaning does not necessarily preserve the hard won discoveries of truth-conditional semantics.

Recent work in philosophy has explored the prospects of developing an expressivist semantics for natural language. Expressivism (which we briefly touched on in Chapter 4) has its roots in attempts to naturalize normative discourse in ethics. For example, Stevenson (1944) proposed that when we make moral claims to the effect that 'x is wrong', we can be understood as expressing something without cognitive content (non-cognitive here means that there is no truth-conditional content)—we are "emoting" in Stevenson's terminology. We could also say we are expressing an attitude of disapproval towards the contemplated action or (following Gibbard 2003) are expressing a commitment or plan to act in a particular manner.

Obviously there are a number of forms that expressivism could take and a number of ways we could describe the relevant attitudes, but let us use the term 'Pro!' with an exclamation point '!' to signify the attitude that is expressed when approving a certain action and/or committing ourselves to a certain course of action (possibly a linguistic action). Similarly, we can use 'Con!' with an exclamation point to signify the attitude that is expressed in disapproving a certain action or making a commitment not to act in a certain manner.

One outstanding problem with treating the varieties of normative discourse expressivistically is the so-called Frege–Geach problem (Ross 1939, 33–34; Geach 1958, 1960, 1965; and Searle 1962, 1969). The basic problem is this: If sentences expressing normative discourse don't have traditional truth values and only express attitudes, then how is it that we can embed those sentences within larger sentences that clearly *do* have truth values?

For example, consider an utterance of the following sentence:

(6) If eating foie gras is wrong, then I don't want to be right.

It is one thing to say that one is merely emoting in the utterance of a sentence like 'eating foie gras is wrong', but the conditional is usually taken to have a definitive truth value. But this only makes sense if truth values can be assigned to both the antecedent and the consequent. What is one to do?

One strategy is to extend our expressivist account to conditionals as well (for example they might express conditional attitudes), but we might also suppose that the mistake was trying to apply expressivism piecemeal. Perhaps what we really need is a generalized expressivist semantics for natural language. In this way, there is nothing special about the semantic value of the antecedent of (6) or (6) itself. *Everything* has expressivist content.

In the remainder of this section I want to explore the general expressivist strategy— i.e. to attempt the construction of an expressivist (or expressivist-friendly) semantic theory that is finitely axiomatizable, and in some interesting sense compositional, and which is robust enough to be able to tackle the formidable logical complexity of natural languages as explored by natural language semanticists. This may sound like the sort of project that could be executed in a brute strength manner, and is, at the end of the day, philosophically trivial (as noted above, this is a view that appears to be held by Horwich). As we will see, however, this is far from the case. But before we get into the problems, let's look at the positive side of this project.

The basic idea is the following. Assuming we are constructing an expressivist semantics for an agent that is hyperdecided (an agent that has an opinion about every proposition), we can simply swap out our basic notions <e> (for entities) and <t> (for truth values) and replace them with expressivistically kosher basic elements.

For example, instead of truth values, we will introduce the attitudes Pro! and Con!. Instead of entities, we will introduce what I will call referential intentions. These are the attitudes we express when, for example, pointing. The remaining semantic types will be built from these basic notions and will in effect be "functional attitudes," or "classificatory attitudes."

To keep our two approaches to semantics separate then, let's use 'i' to indicate a referential intention and 'A' to indicate a Pro-attitude. Instead of indicating the semantic value of an element a thus: $[[a]]$, we can use the following notation to indicate that we are talking about an attitude expressed: !!a!!. Strictly speaking, we will be talking about an utterance of a by an agent a, in a context c etc., and we can annotate our notation accordingly—!!a!!$_{a,c}$ but I will abstract from that in the discussion that follows.

We can then translate our basic semantic types as follows.

Syntactic category	Semantic type (extensionalized)	Expressions
ProperN	$<i>$	names (*John*)
S	$<A>$	sentences
CN(P)	$<i, A>$	common noun phrases (*cat*)
NP	$<i>$	"referential" NPs (*John, the king, he$_i$*)
	$<<i, A>, A>$	noun phrases as generalized quantifiers (*every man, the king, a man, John*)
	$<i, A>$	NPs as predicates (*a man, the king*)
ADJ(P)	$<i, A>$	predicative adjectives (*carnivorous, happy*)
	$<<i, A>, <i, A>>$	adjectives as predicate modifiers (*skillful*)
REL	$<i, A>$	relative clauses (*who(m) Mary loves*)
VP, IV	$<i, A>$	verb phrases, intransitive verbs (*loves Mary, is tall, walks*)
TV	$<i, <i, A>>$	transitive verb (*loves*)
is	$<<i, A>, <i, A>>$	*is*
DET	$<<i, A>, <<i, A>, A>>>$	*a, some, the, every, no*

The semantic rules, PM, PA, etc., also remain unchanged except that, as I said before, we swap out the $[[a]]$ notation for !!a!!. So technically everything operates as it did in section 1.4. There just remains the problem of interpreting the formalism.

Let's work our way into this by looking at the sentential connectives first. Rather than having truth values as our basic semantic values we have the attitudes Pro! and Con!.

(7)   !!and!! $= \lambda p \in D_A. [\lambda q \in D_A.$ Pro!, iff $p = q =$ Pro!]

(8)   !!or!! $= \lambda p \in D_A. [\lambda q \in D_A.$ Pro!, iff $[p =$ Pro! or $q =$ Pro!]]

(9)   !!not!! $= \lambda p \in D_A.$ Pro!, iff not $p =$ Pro! (and because the agent is hyperdecided $p =$ Con!)

At the subsentential level, a function like $<i, A>$ indicates a functional/classificatory attitude. When you express this attitude you are expressing an attitude about mappings from referential intentions to pro-attitudes. For example, consider the noun 'food'.

I am *for* applying this noun to some of my referential intentions, but not all of them. The attitude is a "functional attitude" in the sense that it maps from referential intentions onto Pro!. When I use the word 'food' I am expressing that attitude.

And so it goes with progressively more complex attitudes. Adjectives are higher order attitudes that map from functional attitudes onto functional attitudes and so on. Fans of truth-conditional semantics might object at this point; after all, how do we make sense of these higher order attitudes? Do they correlate with recognized psychological attitudes? This is a reasonable place to drop a flag, but without development it is hard to see the worry as a program killer. There is no reason why a semantic theory shouldn't introduce complex attitudes that are not found in our folk psychology, and, as we will see, there is at least some empirical payoff from the resulting taxonomy of higher order attitudes.

Staying with the conceit that all agents are hyperdecided, let's revisit our taxonomy (from section 1.4) for what semantic rules are required for various recursive structures to be legible.

PM: required for noun–noun recursion, and NP–PP recursion

PA: required for relative clause recursion

Type reflexive lexical rules: required for [adj [adj [. . . [N]]] recursion, logical connective recursion, etc.

Derived type reflexive theorems: required for sentential complement recursion

Can we say more about the semantic precondition hypothesis if we assume an expressivist semantics? The answer appears to be yes. First, since as expressivists we are now thinking about semantic rules in terms of operations on attitudes we can see that certain kinds of attitudes are involved in these different semantic rules. Or better, the rules just describe attitudes and operations on attitudes.

For example, what I have called reflexive lexical rules involve the ability to map from attitudes of a particular type onto attitudes of the same type—it involves our having second order expressivist attitudes.

PM involves what we might call a kind of attitude fusion. It is an operation that takes two functional expressivist attitudes and fuses them into a new expressivist functional attitude. Crucially, then PM not only involves our having attitudes about attitudes, but it introduces the ability to merge them.

PA involves the ability to take something for which we might have a Pro-attitude (say a sentence) and convert it into a functional attitude. We might be inclined to say that it involves our ability to take basic attitudes of type A, and create more abstract attitudes of type $<i, A>$.

Finally, our derived type reflexive theorems involve our ability not only to operate on higher order attitudes, but to chain them together. So our new taxonomy is something like this.

PM: involves second order attitudes and attitude fusion

PA: involves second order attitudes and abstraction on them

Type reflexive lexical rules: involve second order attitudes, and mapping from att to att

Derived type reflexive theorems: involve second order attitudes, attitude mapping, and chaining

Putting this all together we have the following correlation between kinds of recursive structures and cognitive abilities.

Second order attitudes and attitude fusion: required for noun–noun compounds, and NP–PP recursion

Second order attitudes and abstraction on them: required for relative clause recursion

Second order attitudes, and mapping from att to att: required for [adj [adj [. . . [N]]] recursion, logical connective recursion, etc.

Second order attitudes, attitude mapping, and chaining: required for sentential complement recursion

Some Predictions

If this story is correct, then several predictions fall out immediately. First and foremost: If these cognitive abilities are preconditions for linguistic recursion, then there should be a correlation between linguistic recursion and second order reasoning—for example the false belief tests. So far so good; as de Villiers (2007) has reported, this appears to be the case. There *is* such a correlation.

But there are also opportunities for probing some finer grained questions here. If there are certain kinds of aphasia that would target some of these cognitive abilities (for example the ability to abstract functional attitudes from basic attitudes), then the result would be not the loss of recursion altogether but rather the loss of relative clause recursion only. Similarly, the loss of the ability to fuse attitudes might wipe out certain kinds of N–PP recursion. Presumably if the maturation of these cognitive abilities happened at different rates, then we could predict the correlative onset of competence with different classes of recursive structures at different times (a prediction that appears to be supported by Roeper and Snyder (2005) among others).[3]

---

[3] Less clear is the question of whether this has consequences for cross-linguistic variation. Examples in Roeper (2005) for example illustrate that the kinds of recursive structures allowed vary significantly across languages. French, for example, does not allow recursion on possessives, so that constructions like 'John's mother's dentist's cousin' are not happy. Is it feasible to think that these variations are the result of variation in the kinds of cognitive operations employed? This is certainly doubtful, given that the semantic rules deployed in the interpretation of possessive recursion are active elsewhere in the semantics. This linguistic variation appears to have its source in parametric variation in the FLN that is not tied to the C/I interface. Options are limited here; presumably one looks for constraints driven by differences between the English and French perceptual/articulatory systems.

Expressivist Semantics as Use Theory

One interesting feature of the program developed thus far is that it appears to provide us with the ingredients for a formalized use theory of meaning. Why? A standard conception of semantics since Frege has been the idea that linguistic expressions have referents and truth conditions. As Austin and others cautioned, however, it seems more apt to say that we *use* expressions to refer, etc., but that they do not in and of themselves *have* referents or truth conditions. By shifting our perspective to an expressivist semantics this admonition hardly seems necessary. It might seem plausible to think that words have referents, but the idea that words have referential intentions is borderline nonsensical. Likewise, while it might seem plausible to think that an utterance has truth conditions, it is hard to imagine that it (the expression) could, in isolation of us as speakers, express an attitude.

If we reconfigure semantic theory as I have suggested, then what we get is a kind of tool kit for using language to recursively construct and express complex attitudes. This isn't the kind of use theory envisioned by Austin and Wittgenstein. For one thing, there is nothing social about this use theory. The basic ingredients could be part of our biological endowment, and indeed the basic level components could be continuous with the systems that animals use to express attitudes (our system happens to have additional resources like higher order attitudes which in turn allow recursive structures and these in turn enable the expression of attitudes of unlimited complexity).

Two concerns must now be addressed. First, given the broad range of attitudes that we can express, there is a question of how attitudes are to be individuated. What makes one attitude distinct from another one? The concern is that when we try to answer this question we will be tempted to say that the attitudes correspond to different states of affairs, and this suggests that the whole project rests on a truth-conditional semantics at its foundations. This tracks a traditional worry about expressivism in general: what is going on when people are disagreeing about something? If the first party to the disagreement is simply saying "Yay! p," and the second party is simply saying "Boo! p" then it's not clear what sense we can make of the disagreement (two fans can cheer for different teams, but we don't suppose they are disagreeing).

The traditional response to this worry is to say that when we disagree we disagree "in attitude," but this response seems a bit thin. What does it mean to disagree in attitude? And how are the underlying attitudes individuated? Gibbard (2003) has argued that we might think of a disagreement in attitude as akin to a disagreement in plans (plans not individuated by truth conditions, obviously). Here is one way to think about the matter (not attempting to be faithful to Gibbard). Suppose we have a shared referential intention. You point and say 'that is food'. I point and say 'that is a predator'. On the theory I have sketched we are expressing different attitudes, and with Gibbard's proposal the difference in attitude will be manifest in the kinds of plans they give rise to. For example your attitude might be manifested in a plan to chase, and mine in a plan to flee.

This picture can also help us make sense of the disagreement we are involved in. Our disagreement is not characterized in terms of our attitudes having different truth conditions, but rather in terms of our having different plans—we *disagree in plan*. Indeed our disagreement in plan may lead to conflicting actions. In some cases the disagreement may be subtle and the difference in plan might be hypothetical. Suppose we are looking at a newly painted wall and I say the color is "off white" and you say it is "egg shell." Our discussion might end there, but our difference in attitude can be brought out in the following way: I plan that *if* I want to recreate the color of that wall I will ask for "off white paint" and you plan that *if* you want to recreate the color of that wall you will ask for "egg shell."

If attitudes are individuated in terms of plans in this way, then the use theory is now deeply infused into our semantics. The semantic theory is a theory that allows us to express complex plans. But it can also serve as a tool for *constructing* complex plans—the linguistic structures legible to the semantics serve as scaffolding by which we are able to recursively construct plans and express them to each other and ourselves.

So far, the expressivist project for the semantics of natural language sounds like a winning program. Let's take stock of what it can do.

(1) It gives us a tightly constrained picture of what the C/I interface conditions must be. LF structures (or the outputs of syntactic derivations) must be visible to the semantic theory—either merge-by-merge or phase-by-phase or as a whole. Whatever the chunk handed to the interface it must be legible to the semantic theory—construed as a formal semantic theory.

(2) It gives us a way of situating semantic theory within the C/I system and thus provides a foothold for any attempt to construct a modular theory of the C/I system. It gives us a well defined component of that system.

(3) The introduction of expressivism gives us a plausible strategy for naturalizing semantic theory.

(4) Correlatively, it gives us an account that shows that natural language is continuous with animal languages on one level—it is fundamentally expressivist—but that human language may be distinctive in that complex attitudes are built by recursion.

(5) It gives us a picture of the kinds of cognitive abilities that are preconditions for recursive structures to be legible.

(6) In turn, this gives us a powerful tool for exploring correlations between specific recursive structures and diverse cognitive abilities.

(7) If we think of the semantic theory as stating constraints on the expression of attitudes (or, following Gibbard, as expressing plans) then in effect we have the makings of a formal and naturalizable use-based theory of meaning.

As I said, this sounds like a winning program, but there are difficulties with executing the details of any such effort.

The Problem with Expressivism

Thus far I have been operating under the fiction that agents are hyperdecided. Clearly, that hypothesis can't be maintained, and this is the fundamental problem with expressivism—it breaks down (or appears to break down)—with agents that are not hyper-decided.

To see this, consider again the direct translations of our rules for sentential connectives into our expressivist semantics:

(10) $!!and!! = \lambda p \in D_A. [\lambda q \in D_A. Pro!, \text{ iff } p = q = Pro!]$

(11) $!!or!! = \lambda p \in D_A. [\lambda q \in D_A. Pro!, \text{ iff } [p = Pro! \text{ or } q = Pro!]]$

(12) $!!not!! = \lambda p \in D_A. Pro!, \text{ iff not } p = Pro!$

Initially the rule for 'and' seems unproblematic, but the rules for 'or' and 'not' seem to fail.

Consider the rule for 'or' first. I might approve of 'S1 or S2' but it does not follow that I either approve of S1 or approve of S2. To make this vivid, suppose that S2 is simply the negated form of S1 and suppose that S1 is some complex logical proposition. Then it is entirely reasonable that I approve 'S1 or S2', even though I am not ready to approve either S1 or S2.

Do we want to expand our basic attitudes to include Indifferent!? That won't do, because we are not *merely* indifferent towards both of the conjuncts. We are ready to be Pro! towards one of the conjuncts. We just don't know which one. One option is to introduce a disjunctive attitude, but this seems to be non-compositional. What would the disjunctive attitudes be built out of? Or to put it another way, what are the semantic values of the components of a disjunctive attitude?

As Blackburn (1984, 1988) and Unwin (1999, 2001) argued, problems also arise for negation. Suppose again that S is some claim that I am decidedly opposed to and I assert 'not S'. The problem is that not being Pro! doesn't seem to be strong enough. In this case I am not merely not Pro! I am Con!

To a first approximation it looks like we need to introduce additional basic attitudes into the mix. For example it looks like we need a negation rule like the following.

(13) $!!not!! = \lambda p \in D_A. Pro!, \text{ iff } p = Con!$

But if we make this move then now we have a problem with conjunction, for what are we to say in a case where we are Con! a particular conjunction? I might be Con! the sentence 'S and ~S' but it doesn't follow that I am Con! one of the conjuncts. Not surprisingly, we here revisit the problem we had with disjunction.

So far I've not spoken about conditionals, but obviously if disjunctions are a problem then conditionals are as well.

Consider the following attempt:

(14) !!**if-then**!! $= \lambda p \in D_A. [\lambda q \in D_A. \text{Pro!, iff } [\text{not } p = \text{Pro! or } q = \text{Pro!}]]$

The problem is that we now inherit both our negation problem and our disjunction problem.

Even if we can work out an expressivist semantics for the basic conditionals there is the question of whether we can extend it to modals, quantification, etc. For the record, Schroeder (2008) thinks the worries just surveyed are surmountable but that modals and certain quantifiers can't be given a viable expressivist treatment.

I'm not claiming that an expressivist semantics can't be made to work. My concerns with non-referential semantics are more philosophical than technical. On the other hand, it may be that the expressivist program fails here and takes the formal use theory down with it, and it may be that we need to pursue the idea that a truth-conditional semantics can be a part of naturalistic inquiry.

Are Non-referential Semantics Metaphysically Noncommitting?

As we have seen, one can develop alternative approaches to semantic theorizing like an expressivist semantic theory in which the basic primitives of a linguistic theory are Pro-attitudes and referential intentions instead of notions like truth and reference. Alternatively, one might opt for an approach in which truth conditions are replaced with assertability conditions. The problem at the moment is that these approaches have technical difficulties that have not been resolved yet.

I for one am not going to argue that these technical difficulties can't be resolved. My real concern is this: If we successfully construct a non-referential semantics is it really so clear that it won't be metaphysically committing? For example, Brown (2009) has observed that such theories have metaphysical commitments of their own. For example, if I say that a certain linguistic expression is assertable under conditions c, those conditions will invariably involve reference to externalia.

Consider again the case of the tea. We might ask what the assertability conditions of 'tea' are, and to a first approximation the answer is that it is assertable in the presence of the Ψ-substance tea. It won't do to try and stipulate all the assertability conditions in some other way because we won't know how to proceed. The best way—perhaps the only way—of stating the assertability conditions is by reference to external objects and substances.

Metaphysical commitments don't extrude from our having a referential semantics for natural language; they extrude from our having any semantics that comes close to stating what our semantic rules are.

7

Best Theory Criteria and Methodological Minimalism

It is widely held that in addition to the explanatory power of a linguistic theory, the theory's data coverage, and the embeddability of the theory into more basic sciences, there are additional metrics by which we can evaluate competing linguistic theories. Two of these proposed evaluation metrics are theoretical simplicity (or theoretical elegance) and formal rigor.

In this chapter I examine both of these alleged desiderata, and suggest that despite their prima facie appeal, on closer inspection it is far from clear what either simplicity or formal rigor are. I argue that the clearest sense we can make of these notions is by thinking of them in terms of "simple to use and understand" and "rigorous enough for current purposes." More generally, these notions are special cases of the general principle that we ought to adopt those methods that allow us as theorists to accomplish our goals with the minimal amount of cognitive labor.

7.1 Simplicity Criteria

Since the beginning of generative linguistics, appeals to simplicity have played a central role in discussions of theory choice. But what *is* simplicity and why is it a good thing to have in a linguistic theory?

In asking this question, I am not so much concerned with technical uses of the term 'simplicity' within particular linguistic theories. While there have been a number of formal definitions of simplicity within specific linguistic theories (see, for example, Chomsky 1975a, Chomsky and Halle 1968, and Halle 1961), for the most part these efforts have not been (and were not intended to be) utilized in theory choice across linguistic frameworks.[1] My interest in this section is not with such technical uses of the term 'simplicity', but rather with appeals to simplicity that are designed to argue for one theory over another—with simplicity as a criterion for theory choice.

---

[1] Consider for example the simplicity measurement found in Chomsky and Halle (1968), which measures simplicity on the basis of the number of symbols contained in a phonological rule.

Much writing in linguistic theory appears to be driven by a certain common wisdom, which is that the simplest theory either is the most aesthetically elegant or has the fewest components, or that it is the theory that eschews extra conceptual resources. This common wisdom is reflected in a 1972 paper by Paul Postal entitled "The Best Theory," which appeals to simplicity criteria for support of a particular linguistic proposal. A lot of linguists would wholeheartedly endorse Postal's remark (pp. 137–138) that, "[w]ith everything held constant, one must always pick as the preferable theory that proposal which is most restricted conceptually and most constrained in the theoretical machinery it offers."

This claim may seem pretty intuitive, but it stands in need of clarification, and once clarified, the claim is much less intuitive, if not obviously false. As an alternative, I will propose that genuine simplicity criteria should not involve appeal to theoretical machinery, but rather a notion of simplicity in the sense of "simplicity of use." That is, simplicity is not a genuine property of the object of investigation (whether construed as the human language faculty or something else), but is rather a property that is entirely relative to the investigator, and turns on the kinds of elements that the investigator finds perspicuous and "user friendly."

Let's begin by considering Postal's thesis that the simplest (and other things being equal the best) theory is the one that utilizes less theoretical machinery. It may seem natural to talk about "theoretical machinery," but what exactly *is* theoretical machinery? Consider the following questions that arise in cross-theoretical evaluation of linguistic theories of the sort discussed in Chapter 1. Is a level of linguistic representation part of the machinery? How about a transformation? A constraint on movement? A principle of binding theory? A feature? How about an algorithm that maps from level to level, or that allows us to dispense with levels of representation altogether? These questions are not trivial, nor are they easy to answer. Worse, there may be no theory neutral way of answering them.

The problem is that 'machinery' can be defined any way we choose. The machinery might include levels of representation, but then again it might not (one might hold that the machinery delivers the level of representation, but that the level of representation itself is not part of the machinery). Alternatively, one might argue that levels of representation *are* part of the machinery (as they are supported by data structures of some sort), but that the mapping algorithms which generate the levels of representation are not (as they never have concrete realization). Likewise one might argue that constraints on movement are part of the machinery (since they constrain other portions of the machinery), or one might argue that they are not (since they never have concrete realizations).

Even if we could agree on what counts as part of the machinery, we immediately encounter the question of how one measures whether one element or another represents *more* machinery. Within a particular well-defined theory it makes perfect sense to offer objective criteria for measuring the simplicity of the theoretical machinery, but measurement across theories is quite another matter.

For example, if we concede that both mapping algorithms and levels of representation are candidates for being theoretical machinery, is there some reason to suppose that a level of representation counts as more machinery than a mapping algorithm which allows us to avoid that level of representation? If so, then by what measurement?

To illustrate the problem, following Williams (1986) and other authors,[2] one might argue that scope relations among operators can be accounted for via scope indexing rather than moving the operators to form LF representations that encode those relations as we saw in section 1.1. That is, rather than represent the scope possibilities of (1) via the two LF representations in (2) and (3),

(1)   Every man loves some woman

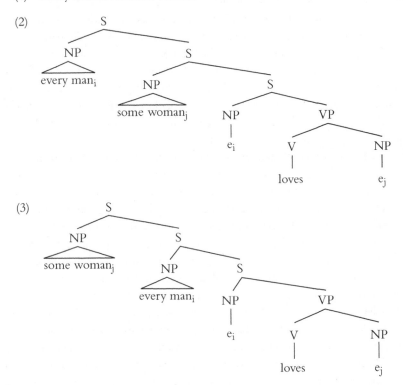

one might argue that the scope relations can be captured by a scope indexing method where the scope possibilities represented in (2) and (3) might better be captured as in (2′) and (3′), where the ordering of the indices on S indicates the relative scopes of the quantified noun phrases.[3]

[2] For example Reinhart (1983) and Häik (1984).

[3] I don't mean to suggest that this mechanism is explicitly endorsed by Williams. In point of fact, he remains neutral between such a proposal and one in which the scope orders corresponding to such a representation are "arbitrary": "Is the order of quantifiers in such a case ordered or free? If determined, we will want to attach significance to the order of i and j in S:i,j; if not, we won't" (1986, 267).

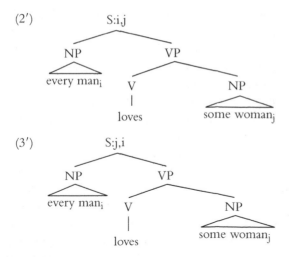

(2′)

(3′)

None of the authors cited here have advocated indexing proposals on grounds of simplicity, but one does hear arguments in the oral tradition that argue in this fashion. Perhaps there is some empirical way to distinguish these proposals (I have my doubts), but is there any clear sense in which the indexing proposal utilizes "less machinery" than the quantifier raising strategy? One can imagine arguments here. One might say that with the scope indexing strategy we can dispense with an entire level of representation. Or, one might argue that by dispensing with movement, we are making do with less onerous mechanisms. Or, one might argue that the second proposal allows us to carry on with "simpler" structures—ones without Chomsky-adjoined NPs. All such arguments are baseless.

While perhaps less toner is used by printers in putting (2′) and (3′) on paper, there is no basis for saying that the theory behind those structures is less complex than the theory which gave us (2) and (3). Arguably, we still need some "mechanism" which will tell us how to interpret an indexed structure, and arguably that mechanism amounts to new "machinery" in the semantics.

In each case there is a background theory that tells us how we are to interpret either the LF representations or the scope index representations, and that interpretive background theory is going to have a certain kind of complexity of its own—perhaps one that would swamp any considerations about the relative complexity of representations like (2) and (2′).

This is not to concede that (setting aside the interpretive background theory) (2′) is a simpler representation than (2). Even this claim can be challenged. Indeed, the two representations carry the same information, and appear to be notational variants of each other. Differences in notation can be significant, but it would take a very careful and intricate argument to show that given two apparent notational variants, one is simpler than the other, or that one involved more machinery than the other.

Just to be perfectly clear, I am not saying that a move to scope indexing forces us to introduce extra theoretical machinery. I'm saying that there is no answer to the question of which has the most machinery, since across theories there is no neutral way of defining theoretical machinery, or measuring its relative complexity.

The scope indexing case provided a concrete illustration of how difficult it is to make claims about machinery, but if we turn to a domain like mathematics we can make the same point at a more abstract level. Consider geometry. We might suppose that here at least, where everyone is restricted to the vocabulary of geometry, it should be easy enough to determine which of two theories is the simpler.

Prima facie, we might suppose that the simpler geometrical theory is the theory with the fewest axioms, but caution is necessary here. As Hempel (1966, 42) notes, there is no unambiguous way of counting axioms or basic concepts. For example, consider the statement that "for any two points there is a straight line containing them." Is this one axiom? As Hempel notes, one might think of it as a conjunction of two—that there is at least one such line, and that there is at most one such line. Similar considerations carry over to talk of basic concepts. In the absence of some neutral way of characterizing what is truly basic, there is no way to count the number of basic concepts in play.

Even if we *could* agree on what counts as a basic axiom or basic concept, we may find that the axiom system with fewer axioms is far from the simplest theory. For example, the system with the fewest axioms may lead to difficulty in theorem proving in the early stages, so the complexity of the computational task of theorem proving needs to be factored in as well if we are really interested in an overall measure of simplicity.

But we can't stop there. Even assuming that difficulty in theorem proving is not an issue, is a system with fewer axioms always the simplest? Not according to many measures of simplicity in the philosophy of science literature. Sober (1975), for example, has argued that everything depends on the "naturalness" of the axioms (basic elements of the theory). If we trade in five natural axioms for four unintuitive axioms then according to Sober we have achieved no great gain in simplicity. So, by some accounts, even if we have a definition of machinery and a way of quantifying amount of machinery, we do not have a simpler theory simply by having fewer theoretical elements.

The many perplexities involved in trying to define a formal notion of simplicity are catalogued in, among other places, Goodman (1972, section VII), Barker (1961), and Rosenkrantz (1977, ch. 5). Perhaps Kyburg (1964, 267–268) sums up the state of affairs best when he says:

The whole discussion of simplicity has been curiously inconclusive. Not only has there been no growing body of agreement concerning the measurement of simplicity, but there has been no agreement concerning . . . the precise role that simplicity should play in the acceptance of scientific hypotheses.

However, one might argue that there is still a clear case in which we can say that one theory has more machinery than another—the case where theory B has the components of A, but where theory B has additional components. In that case, one might think, Postal is clearly right in making the following claim (p. 137):

Given two distinct theories of the same domain, one may make a clear choice between them if certain logical relations hold between these theories. In particular, if the theoretical machinery of one theory is included in that of the second, but the second has, in addition, certain additional theoretical machinery, then, all other things being equal, the first, most conceptually restricted is to be chosen. That is, the conceptual elaboration of the second theory can only be justified on the basis of direct empirical arguments showing the need for this extension. In general, this support will take the form of evidence showing that certain facts in the domain cannot be explained using only the original apparatus provided by the first theory, but that the facts in question do receive a formulation in terms of the additional theoretical apparatus provided by the second.

But even this claim is false. To see this, consider the linguistic case that Postal has in mind. As we saw in Chapter 1, Postal argued that a particular general approach to linguistic theory (Generative Semantics) was simpler because it eliminated a class of nontransformational mapping rules. The contrast is thus between an organization of the grammar as in (4), similar to Standard Theory proposals like that of Katz and Fodor (1963), and (5), which is consistent with Generative Semantics theories advocated in Postal (1972).

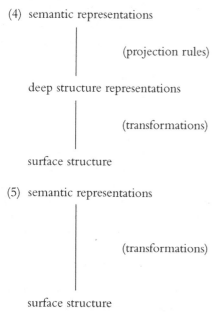

    (4) semantic representations

                                (projection rules)

      deep structure representations

                                (transformations)

      surface structure

    (5) semantic representations

                                (transformations)

      surface structure

According to Postal's reasoning, the theory that has fewer kinds of rules (in this case the theory diagrammed in (5), which has transformations only) is more "homogeneous" and hence is to be preferred unless there are *strong* empirical considerations favoring the Standard Theory alternative. In Postal's words:

What I wish to suggest briefly is that because of its *a priori* logical and conceptual properties, this theory of grammar . . . is the basic one which generative linguists should operate from as an investigatory framework, and it should be abandoned, if at all, only under the strongest pressures of empirical disconfirmation. (135)

But this is a mistake. Overlooked by Postal is the complexity of the additional transformations needed in (5), the utility of intermediate deep structure representations to theorists, and the methodological virtues of constraining the class of transformations. Is there some theory-neutral way to measure the relative complexity of the two approaches? As we have seen, the prospects are dim to non-existent.

On the other hand, I have hinted at the importance of representations and rules that are perspicuous to the theorist, suggesting that simplicity may have more to do with properties of the theorist than properties of the natural world. To some, this may be a counterintuitive way of thinking about simplicity, but I would suggest that it is in fact the most reasonable way to think about simplicity and is in fact the notion of simplicity that is at play in the more established sciences.

The view certainly has a long pedigree in the philosophy of science, dating at least to Peirce (1931–1958, 6:532), who held that we should "follow the rule that that one of all admissible hypotheses which seems simplest to the human mind ought to be taken up first." Peirce's idea here was that by first taking up hypotheses that are "simplest to the human mind," we achieve a kind of economy in the labor that we expend on our investigations. In Peirce's words "the simplest hypotheses are those of which the consequences are most readily deduced and compared with observation; so that, if they are wrong they can be eliminated at less expense than any others" (532).

Moreover, Peirce was convinced that it was this notion of simplicity (and not the logical notion of extra machinery) that Galileo had in mind when he advised us to always choose the simpler hypothesis.

That truly inspired prophet had said that, of two hypotheses, the *simpler* is to be preferred, but I was formerly one of those, who, in our dull self-conceit fancying ourselves more sly than he, twisted this maxim to mean the *logically* simpler, the one that adds least to what has been observed. . . . It was not until long experience forced me to realize that subsequent discoveries were every time showing I had been wrong, while those who had understood the maxim as Galileo had done early unlocked the secret, that the scales fell from my eyes and my mind awoke to the broad and flaming daylight that it is the simpler hypothesis in the sense of the more facile and *natural*, the one that instinct suggests, that must be preferred . . . I do not mean that logical simplicity is of no value at all, but only that its value is badly secondary to that of simplicity in the other sense. (6:477)

Indeed, when we look at other sciences, in nearly every case, the best theory is arguably not the one that reduces the number of components from four to three, but rather the theory that allows for the simplest calculations and greatest ease of use. This flies in the face of the standard stories we are told about the history of science. For example, it is usually supposed that when we talk about the superiority of the Copernican model of the solar system over the Ptolemaic system it is because of the relative simplicity of the

Copernican model, and it is further supposed that this is because simpler models are closer to the truth.

In point of fact however, the Copernican model probably triumphed because it was able to account for certain facts (known in Copernicus' time) that the Ptolemaic system could not handle. (See Rogers (1960, chs. 14, 16) for discussion of this point.) Furthermore, by the time the Copernican model was fully fleshed out, it had enough technical resources (from minor epicycles to eccentrics) so that it may well have matched the Ptolemaic theory on the amount of technical machinery. One might suppose that the Copernican theory was nevertheless still the more aesthetically elegant of the theories, and that this might amount to a kind of simplicity. Indeed, Copernicus himself seems to have thought this. The only problem is that there is no accounting for aesthetic preference (particularly if religion plays a role in our aesthetic theories), and some of the chief arguments against Copernicus included arguments that could only be characterized as aesthetic in character. What appears to have saved the Copernican theory was not its aesthetic qualities, but rather the fact that it helped to simplify astronomical calculations. Notoriously, when *De Revolutionibus* was published in Leipzig, Osiander inserted a preface that characterized the theory as merely a convenient tool for calculating, and not to be taken seriously as a cosmological theory. Obviously, this move was designed to deflect religious criticism, but the fact remains that the overarching value of the theory to astronomers of the day was not its elegant cosmology, but its utility as a tool in carrying out what had previously been impossibly complex astronomical calculations.

This way of viewing simplicity requires a shift in our thinking. It requires that we see simplicity criteria as having not so much to do with the natural properties of the world, as they have to do with the limits of us as investigators, and with the kinds of theories that simplify the arduous task of scientific theorizing for us. This is not to say that we cannot be scientific realists; we may very well suppose that our scientific theories approximate the actual structure of reality.[4] It is to say, however, that barring some argument that "reality" is simple, or eschews machinery, etc., we cannot suppose that there is a genuine notion of simplicity apart from the notion of "simple for us to use."[5]

In a certain sense, such a view is entirely natural. While we always seek the simplest theory, it is rare that we would suppose that our theory closes the book on a particular

---

[4] Of course this view is *consistent* with scientific anti-realism like that articulated in van Fraassen (1980). The point is that we are not forced to anti-realism.

[5] One way of knitting together a subjective notion of simplicity with a realist theory of the world has been offered up by Quine and Ullian (1970), who propose that there are evolutionary reasons for our having the subjective preferences that we do:

> Innate subjective standards of simplicity that make people prefer some hypotheses to others will have survival value insofar as they favor successful prediction. Those who predict best are likeliest to survive and reproduce their kind . . . and so their innate standards of simplicity are handed down. (47)

I have to confess that I find this a pretty implausible thesis. As Nozick (1983) has observed, while our simplicity judgments concerning hypotheses about midsize earth-bound objects may have stood the test of time, the same cannot be said of our simplicity judgments concerning theories of quantum mechanics and cosmology, or generative linguistics, for that matter.

domain of inquiry. To the contrary, we naturally suppose that complications will arise, and that the current theory shall have to be overthrown. Even if, for metaphysical reasons, we supposed that reality must be fundamentally simple, every science (with the possible exception of physics) is so far from closing the book on its domain it would be silly to think that simplicity (in the absolute sense) must govern our theories on the way to completion. Whitehead (1955, 163) underlined just such a point.

Nature appears as a complex system whose factors are dimly discerned by us. But, as I ask you, Is not this the very truth? Should we not distrust the jaunty assurance with which every age prides itself that it at last has hit upon the ultimate concepts in which all that happens can be formulated. The aim of science is to seek the simplest explanations of complex facts. We are apt to fall into the error of thinking that the facts are simple because simplicity is the goal of our quest. The guiding motto in the life of every natural philosopher should be, Seek simplicity and distrust it.

Let's suppose, however, that I am mistaken about most of the preceding discussion as it applies to the physical sciences. Let's suppose, that is, that there is a clear and serviceable notion of simplicity in some absolute sense (one independent of us as theorists). Does it follow that this notion of simplicity carries over to the other sciences (in particular linguistics)? Probably not.

Russell (1913; 1917, 204) noted that little follows from the fact that in some sciences, "simple laws have hitherto been found to hold." Not only are there no a priori grounds for supposing that the domains of other sciences are simple, but there are also no inductive grounds.

[I]t would be fallacious to argue inductively from the state of the advanced sciences to the future state of the others, for it may well be that the advanced sciences are simple because, hitherto, their subject-matter has obeyed simple and easily ascertainable laws, while the subject-matter of other sciences has not done so. (205)

Does this pose a problem for the minimalist program as discussed in section 1.4? Not necessarily. Apart from ease of use considerations (methodological minimalism), which don't seem to motivate the minimalist program in linguistics, we can distinguish two different notions of simplicity that are possible candidates for motivating the program. One is the abstract notion of simplicity I have been criticizing in this section. But another notion is one in which we want an account of the language faculty which reduces to low level biophysical processes. This is the notion of simplicity argued for by Sober (1975). Attempting to make the case for minimalism on grounds of abstract simplicity strikes me as misguided. Attempting to pursue the reductive strategy on the other hand seems like a plausible research program.

Setting aside notions of simplicity that are based in the preparation of science for reduction, what we expect of a linguistic theory is that it be perspicuous enough for us to know what is predicted, and that its notation be easy for us to use. In this sense, the simplicity criterion is not really an absolute criterion, but one that is relative to the investigators. For example, is it easier for linguists to posit a level of representation LF, or is it easier to utilize a mechanism like Cooper's (1983) quantifier storage mechanism (where the set-theoretic resources of the model theory can do the work of quantifier raising)?[6] Neither is simpler absolutely, but there is an issue about which is easier for the investigators to use, and which leads to further linguistic discoveries. For example, the question of relative simplicity of these theories might turn on the relative perspicuity of these theories when applied to the phenomenon of "inverse linking" that we discussed in section 1.1, and accounted for within a quantifier storage framework by Larson (1985). The answer is not really one to be given by pronouncement, but one that emerges as the field as a whole, over time, gravitates to one framework or the other. Indeed, it may be that different subfields of linguistics, with different interests and training, may see the simplicity of these proposals quite differently.

We can summarize the above considerations in the following way.

I. Simplicity is in the eye of the theorist

By this I don't mean that simplicity is determined by individual theorists, but rather that it is determined by a community of theorists with a shared set of interests and a shared technical background. To such a community, given two proposals with roughly the same empirical coverage and explanatory power, the simplest theory is that theory which they find the easiest to use for constructing and evaluating hypotheses.

Some provisos are necessary here. The point is not that the simpler theory will be recognized as such *immediately*. One has to allow time for the new theory to be understood. But the learning curve of the new theory should not be so steep as to swamp any advantages it might have once learned. Lindsay (1937, 166) saw this point in the course of his discussion of the "economy" notion of simplicity.

If, for example, a person familiar with classical mechanics can become equally well acquainted with another physical theory in a time of the same order of magnitude as that which he took to learn mechanics, he should consider this new theory as simple as mechanics, no matter how complicated it may seem at first examination to one unfamiliar with it. Human life is short and time is fleeting. In endeavoring to understand the world around us we must make the most of the brief span allotted. We must therefore build our theories in such a way that, with given intellectual background, the manipulation of these theories leads in minimum time to success in physical prediction.

II. Simplicity may vary from research community to research community

It may be that this sort of variation is temporary. Theorists utilizing different technical methods do communicate with one another after all, and after time research methods

---

[6] I should note that Cooper (1983) does not offer simplicity considerations on behalf of his theory—rather he appeals to processing considerations. There are, however, arguments in the oral tradition parallel to those raised in Postal (1972)—specifically arguments that a theory utilizing quantifier storage mechanisms is "simpler" because it avoids overt quantifier movement and the level of representation LF.

merge, or at least become more readily understood. But familiarity is not the only issue here. Different theorists have different interests and different philosophical assumptions resting at the base of their empirical theories. Until those interests and philosophical differences are resolved, their views of simplicity may well fail to merge.[7]

III. Simplicity will vary over time

The quote from Lindsay above suggested that some things may seem complex to us at first, although simple after a short while. This can happen for the field as a whole. So, theories that may seem complex at the outset, may turn out to be viewed as utterly simple as the field progresses. As Lindsay (167) notes, "we shall ultimately consider [theories] simple when we have grown sufficiently familiar with them to forget that they ever seemed difficult to understand."

This is not just a point about technical machinery, however. It is also an important point about how certain basic concepts are viewed. The Kepplerian theory of planetary motion, for example, was considered aesthetically inferior by some commentators, who could not make the conceptual leap from the idea of circular orbits to that of less perfect ellipses. Sometimes it just takes time to "wrap your mind" around an unfamiliar concept or piece of machinery. On the other hand, sometimes it takes forever.

IV. Barring bad advice, theorists will gravitate towards simplicity

This point is really the moral of this section. I have argued that the simplest theory is that which allows us to simplify our calculations and theorizing (given our current interests). Assuming that theorists are sensible, simplicity will take care of itself, as investigators will naturally gravitate to the notation and theoretical resources that are the easiest to use and which therefore more naturally serve their goals of understanding and explanation. Troubles only arise when, under the spell of bad philosophy of science, linguists suppose that they must adopt best theory criteria other than those that would otherwise naturally guide their investigations.

7.2 Formal Rigor

As I noted in section 1.3, in the 1980s it was argued that Government–Binding (GB) theory was defective because it was not presented in a fixed and rigorously worked out formalism. These criticisms were often supposed to show that alternative linguistic theories were superior to GB. Gazdar, Klein, Pullum, and Sag (1985), for example, argue that the formal rigor of Generalized Phrase Structure Grammar (GPSG) weighed in its favor. Likewise Bresnan and Kaplan (1982) argued that Lexical Functional

---

[7] A not so distant point was stressed by Quine (Quine and Ullian 1970), who argued that simplicity would vary with our conceptual schemes.

Grammar (LFG) is a better framework for theorizing because it is more formally constrained.

If our discussion of formal rigor is to be productive, we need to get clear on what formal rigor is. As we shall see, various writers have offered a number of claims about what counts as formal rigor, who does and doesn't respect the demands of formal rigor, and why formal rigor is valuable.

We can distinguish three uses of the phrase 'formal rigor'. I shall argue that the first two views of formal rigor will not do as characterizations of how linguistics ought to proceed, nor indeed of how the "hard sciences" in fact proceed. Rather, I shall contend, the third version will provide the most productive way for linguists to think about rigor.

version 1: formal rigor as recursive specifiability
version 2: formal rigor as entertaining and evaluating proposals within a predetermined mathematical language
version 3: formal rigor as a statement of the proposal (not necessarily mathematical) which is clear enough for current purposes to be understood, evaluated, and debated

version 1: formal rigor as recursive specifiability

This view of formal rigor is among those that are advocated by Gazdar, Klein, Pullum, and Sag. They make the following remarks.

There may not even be algorithmic ways of confirming the consequences of some theories of grammar, of course: if the theory allows grammars for non-recursive sets, then we run the risk that the claim that some string is not generated by some grammar cannot be verified in principle. Familiar statements of the type 'Thus our grammar excludes examples like (158)', in other words, may simply be untestable conjectures. (1985, 2)

Like Gazdar et al., Bresnan and Kaplan also think that it is important that the set of well-formed sentences generated by the theory be recursive.

The reliability constraint implies that the subset of data in the domain of the mapping for which there are well-formed grammatical relations is a recursive set (for the mapping must effectively compute whether an arbitrary string is grammatically well formed or not). (1982, xl)

In addition, Pullum (1989) has proposed that the following three conditions on formal theories of grammar be "non-negotiable."[8]

(I) The notion of 'structural representation' must be effective. That is, there must be an algorithm for determining whether some arbitrary string, graph, or diagram counts as a structural representation according to the theory.

---

[8] Pullum notes that the conditions are paraphrased from Robert Stoll (1961, ch. 3).

(II)   The notion of 'rule' (or 'principle' or 'law' or 'condition' or 'constraint' or 'filter' or whatever) must be effective. That is, there must be an algorithm for determining whether some arbitrary string, graph, or diagram is a rule (or 'principle' or 'law'...) according to the theory.

(III)   The notion 'generates' (or 'admits' or 'licenses' or whatever) must be effective. That is, there must be an algorithm for determining whether some arbitrary structural representation is generated (or admitted or licensed...) by a given set of rules (or 'principles' or 'laws'...).

Contrary to the above claims, the demand that there be an algorithm to determine the predictions of the theory is far too strong. There isn't even an effective procedure for deciding if an arbitrary formula of first order logic is a theorem (see Church 1936). Would we really say that we run the risk that an assertion like (6),

(6)   t is a theorem of first order logic

where t is some formula of first order logic is merely an "untestable conjecture" and "cannot be verified in principle" because there is no effective decision procedure for first order logic—because the theorems of first order logic do not constitute a recursive set? The mistake made by the above authors is their supposing that the only reliable procedures are recursive procedures. Even first order logic cannot satisfy such a stringent notion of reliability.

In point of fact, there has never been a science in which all the consequences of a theory could be effectively determined. While some philosophers have *advocated* views of science like the above (and have endorsed efforts like Woodger's (1937, 1939) attempt to axiomatize biology[9]), such views were never influential in the individual sciences and have not been taken seriously by philosophers since the days of logical positivism.

One might argue that while physics and other basic sciences do not construct theories with recursive sets of predictions, there is no reason why linguistics shouldn't so proceed. The argument might go as follows: In the early 1960s it was argued by folks like Putnam that the mind was a Turing machine. If their view was correct, then it follows that if we are interested in characterizing the ability of such a machine to parse the sentences of a language—or even accept those and only those strings that are sentences of the language—then it is crucial that the set of sentences be recursive.

Even if we accept such a view of the human mind—and few would today[10]—the conclusion that linguistic theory should be so constrained does not follow. One problem is that the Turing machine view of the mind, if true, at best tells us about some of the constraints that we should expect to be placed on a mature linguistic theory. But it tells us nothing about the kinds of constraints that ought to be placed on the theory *on the way* to maturity. The key is to see that the form of the theory must be such that it drives discovery rather than inhibits it.

---

[9] For criticism of Woodger's program, see Smart (1951).

[10] For criticism of Turing machine functionalism see Block (1978) and Putnam (1975b). Both articles appear in Beakley and Ludlow (1992).

Apart from this concern, there is also the question of whether the Turing machine view of the mind would put such severe constraints on linguistic theory. Imagine a language like that described by Chomsky (1980a, 127) in which well-formed sentences must satisfy a number-theoretic condition C, which may be of arbitrary complexity. Although the language may be non-recursive, it is entirely conceivable that there should be a Turing machine that has a decision procedure for recognizing well-formed sentences that is effective for sentences with lengths of (let's say) fewer than one million words, but is not effective for sentences of greater length. Such languages would be entirely compatible with the thesis that the mind is a Turing machine—at least it would satisfy the motivations for such a theory that were first suggested by Putnam and others.

A tactical retreat is possible here. One might propose that the idea is not to have *effective* procedures for checking the theorems of the theory, but nonetheless to still have mechanical procedures for doing so. Here a mechanical procedure would be one in which it is possible to automate the checking of theorems of the theory. The virtue of having a mechanical procedure would be that one could use the procedure to check theorems that might otherwise escape the scrutiny of investigators, thus providing more opportunities for testing and possibly falsifying the theory. In addition, the availability of such a mechanical procedure would ensure that claims about what counted as a theorem of a given theory might be proved, and not left to simple inspection.[11]

There is surely merit to the claim that having mechanical procedures can be very useful in certain circumstances. It is not immediately obvious, however, that such procedures are useful in *all* circumstances. Mechanical procedures are useful when it is difficult to see what the consequences of a theory might be, or when falsifying evidence is hard to come by. But is this really the state of affairs that we find in current linguistic theory? Is it really the case that we lack clear testable consequences of existing theories? It hardly seems so. Rather the situation is that we are hard pressed to come up with theories that comport well with the obvious consequences. And when theories are proposed which comport with existing data, or rather some fragment of them, it is seldom long before counterexamples are discovered. Matters would be different if we had competing theories that withstood the test of available evidence but for which predictions on a large class of data were unclear. But again, this does not seem to be the state of affairs in current linguistic theory.

version 2: formal rigor as entertaining and evaluating proposals within a predetermined mathematical language

Consider the following remarks from Gazdar et al.

---

[11] This possible position was drawn to my attention by Stuart Shieber and Fernando Pereira.

This approach to language is characterized by its goal of investigating natural language through the construction of fully explicit descriptions of particular languages and a formalized general framework for defining the space within which to locate such descriptions. (1985, 1)

We can find similar remarks from Kaplan and Bresnan (1982) within the LFG framework:

[T]his formalism, called *lexical-functional grammar* (LFG), has been developed to serve as a medium for expressing and explaining important generalizations about the syntax of human languages and thus to serve as a vehicle for independent linguistic research. Of equal significance, it is a restricted, mathematically tractable notation for which simple, psychologically plausible processing mechanisms can be defined. (173–174)

The question arises as to why providing formal frameworks like this is the way that linguistics, or any other science, ought to proceed. One might point to the rise of the Göttingen School at the turn of the century and argue that it is here that science took its mathematical turn, and that it is from this turn in science that linguists ought to take their cue. For surely, this thinking might go, it was the influence of Göttingen mathematicians such as Courant, Minkowski, Weyl, and Hilbert, on the young scientists of the day—Einstein, Heisenberg, Schrödinger and von Neumann—which ultimately led to the great advances in twentieth-century physics.

There are two problems with this argument. First, it is not clear that these physicists believed in Hilbert's program for axiomatizing physics. Second, it is not the case that these physicists tackled the problems of physics with rigorous formal models in hand. A good illustration of these points would be the application of matrices to quantum mechanics. The versions of matrix theory employed were not paradigms of formal integrity. Moreover, at the time they were applied to physics, matrices were poorly understood.

In 1925 Jordan and Born collaborated with Heisenberg on a paper applying matrix mechanics to Heisenberg's quantum-theoretical series. The very day that the paper was received by the *Zeitschrift für Physik*, Heisenberg wrote to Wolfgang Pauli and confessed deep reservations about the underpinnings of the theory.

I've taken a lot of trouble to make the work physical, and I'm relatively content with it. But I'm still pretty unhappy with the theory as a whole and I was delighted you were on my side about mathematics and physics. Here I'm in an environment that thinks and feels exactly the opposite way, and I don't know whether I'm just too stupid to understand the mathematics. Göttingen is divided into two camps: one, which speaks like Hilbert (and Weyl, in a letter to Jordan), of the great success that will follow the development of matrix calculations in physics; the other, which like Franck, maintains that the matrices will never be understood.[12]

---

[12] Letter to Wolfgang Pauli, Nov. 16, 1925. In A. Hermann, K. V. Meyenn, and V. F. Weisskopf (1979, vol. 1). Translated by Crease and Mann (1986, 52).

He later remarked that throughout his career he had used "dirty mathematics," arguing that when you "think of the experimental situation . . . you get closer to reality than by looking for rigorous methods" (1968, 39).

Even Weyl, who played a leading role in efforts to mathematize physics and whom Heisenberg cites as being in the formalization camp, came to reject the program.

[T]he maze of experimental facts which the physicist has to take into account is too manifold, their expansion too fast, and their aspect and relative weight too changeable for the axiomatic method to find a firm enough foothold, except in the thoroughly consolidated parts of our physical knowledge. Men like Einstein or Niels Bohr grope their way in the dark toward their conception of general relativity or atomic structure by another type of experience and imagination than those of the mathematician, although no doubt mathematics is an essential ingredient.[13]

Two morals can be drawn from the above examples. In the first place, mathematical frameworks, if available, need not be paradigms of formal integrity and do not guarantee clarity of exposition. Second, developing sciences will often expand too fast for the development of a mathematical framework to be possible.

One might argue that mathematical rigor of the type we have been discussing is at worst harmless, so we may as well adopt such rigor and in the process will avoid poorly stated proposals and the confusions that can arise from them. However, excessive attention to rigor is not necessarily harmless. It can, in certain cases, be quite harmful. Interestingly one of the best examples of this comes not from an empirical science but from mathematics itself, which is supposed to be the paradigm example of the value of rigor.

Soon after Newton published his *Quadrature of Curves*,[14] George Berkeley noted that the calculus involved the logical fallacy of shift in hypothesis.[15] In particular he noted that Newton had assumed in one argument both that o is nonvanishing and that it is zero. This problem exercised some, but in a number of cases, as noted by Eves and Newsom (1965), the problems with the logical integrity of the calculus were overlooked because applications of the calculus were successful.

It was natural that this wide and amazing applicability of [the calculus] should attract mathematical researchers of the day, and that papers should be turned out in great profusion with seemingly little concern regarding the very unsatisfactory foundations of the subject. It was much more exciting to apply the marvelous new tool than to examine its logical soundness, for, after all, the processes employed justified themselves to the researchers in view of the fact that they worked.

Although for almost a hundred years after the invention of the calculus by Newton and Leibniz little serious work was done to strengthen logically the underpinning of the rapidly growing superstructure of the calculus, it must not be supposed that there was no criticism of the

---

[13] Quoted in Reid (1986, 171).

[14] Reprinted in Newton (1964, 141–160).

[15] Berkeley's observation is found in "The Analyst: or a Discourse Addressed to an Infidel Mathematician," in Berkeley (1979, 65–102).

existing weak base. Long controversies were carried on by some mathematicians, and even the two founders themselves were unsatisfied with their accounts of the fundamental concepts of the subject. (198)

Now it might be argued that though there were problems in the foundations of the calculus, it was the drive to make the calculus rigorous that led to the great progress in the calculus. In fact, just the opposite is true. Phillip Kitcher (1981, 486–487) notes that Leibniz and his followers, by postponing "rigorization," were able to make far greater advances than the Newtonians—who were obsessed with making the calculus rigorous immediately. Leibniz's point throughout the debate was that the new theory was so revolutionary that the usual techniques for making the theory rigorous would be unsuccessful. None of this is to say that the Newtonians were irrational for pursuing the rigorization of the theory. But of course neither were the continental mathematicians, and they turned out to be correct. Again, from Kitcher:

Leibniz' successors produced so many apparently successful reasonings, which could not be readily reinterpreted using the methods favored by the eighteenth century Newtonians, that, by 1750, the Newtonian claim that all the unrigorous reasonings of the calculus could be reconstructed according to Newtonian proposals was no longer defensible. Similarly, the achievements of the Bernoulli, Euler, and other continental mathematicians, undercut the thesis that the question of rigorizing the calculus was an urgent one. (1981, 487)

The moral is that one often has a theory that is rigorous enough to allow use of the theory for problem solving. If one devotes energies to rigorization under these circumstances, then one neglects the application of the theory. Should we insist, for example, that generative linguists provide rigorous foundations for their new theories before they present them to us? Would this be the most productive use of time for theoretical linguists? Would it help in application of the framework to the class of problems currently of interest to linguists?

There is another way in which the second version of formal rigor can be counterproductive. We all know of cases in which formal mathematical machinery merely obscures the essential point, or where it merely gives the *air* of respectability to an otherwise bankrupt proposal. Einstein saw the distinction between mathematical formalization and clarity of exposition, and complained that "The people in Göttingen sometimes strike me, not as if they want to help one formulate something clearly, but as if they want only to show us physicists how much brighter they are than we." Formal machinery does not always obscure what is important, of course, but the point is that it is not of necessity harmless.

version 3:   formal rigor as a statement of the proposal (not necessarily mathematical) which is clear enough (for current purposes) to be understood, evaluated, and debated

Is there a place for formal rigor in linguistics? Surely there is. It is imperative, however, that we get clear on the kind of rigor that is valuable in science generally. The first thing to understand is that rigor should not be confused with the use of a mathematical language. Mathematical languages need not be rigorous, and rigorous theories need not be mathematical.

We should also see that what counts as rigorous is context dependent. Indeed, we might make a habit of never saying that a proposal is rigorous, but rather saying that it is "rigorous enough for our purposes." There are several cases in which this might be so.

A proposal may be introduced to solve a given problem A, and the proposal may be clear enough so that we can see whether it, in fact, solves the problem. But there may be unanticipated problems, B–D, which we cannot resolve until we clarify certain aspects of the proposal. Is the proposal rigorous? There is no harm in saying that it was rigorous enough at introduction, but that it stands in need of rigorization at a later time.

It might also be the case that although we were aware of problems B–D, they just didn't seem as important as A. That is, the demands of rigorization will depend upon our interests, and our interests may well change over time.

An analogy to the development of the calculus will be helpful here. Kitcher notes that the real impetus for change in the calculus came not in response to the problem of infinitesimals, but rather from worries about using infinite series representations of functions. According to Kitcher, Euler had noted that some substitutions of infinite series representations of functions could lead to troubles, but that one might avoid these troubles by judicious use of substitutions. Cauchy and Abel both found this strategy to be unacceptable. Cauchy went on to propose a way of rigorizing the use of infinite series that Euler had entertained and rejected a half century before. The interesting question, as Kitcher puts it, is "why was the problem of rigorizing the use of infinite series urgent for Cauchy (and Abel) but not for Euler, and why did Cauchy adopt and Euler reject the same proposed rigorization?"

The answer, according to Kitcher, is that Euler and Cauchy were interested in a different class of questions. Euler was interested in questions which concerned computing the sums of an infinite series and in many cases his only available method was by representing a convergent series as a difference of two divergent series. For Cauchy, on the other hand, important questions in the theory of real numbers could not be resolved until the infinite series techniques were rigorized (see Kitcher 1981, 489). The moral of this for the linguist is that the demands of formal rigor will change as the interests of the field change. Likewise, different linguistic research programs will have different interests, and perhaps, therefore, different needs for rigorization.

We should also see that rigorization can be *partial*. We need not, as some linguists suggest, have a rigorous universal framework for inquiry, but we may rather wish to rigorize linguistics piecemeal. There are two ways in which piecemeal rigorization might take place. First, the entire field might be rigorized in stages. Second, different parts of the field might be rigorized at different times.

Kitcher (1981, 484) offers an example of the first kind of rigorization when he suggests that we can retrospectively understand Cauchy's achievement "as one of partially rigorizing the calculus, and we can see Weierstrass' work as extending the partial rigorization begun by Cauchy."

One can also certainly imagine that different domains can be rigorized at different times. One might also expect different components of generative linguistics to be rigorized at different times. The demands for rigor will depend upon time, and will vary in different parts of the theory.

I have argued that what counts as formal rigor is not to be confused with having a mathematical language in which to state and debate various proposals, that what counts as formal rigor will depend upon our interests, and that rigorization is not global but can proceed piecemeal. Is this just to suggest that there are no standards for rigor? Absolutely not. It is, however, to suggest that those standards cannot be established in advance of scientific inquiry. New discoveries and research programs lead to new questions and problems, and the intricacy of those questions and problems will determine the degree and kind of rigor necessary for research to proceed.

7.3 Minimal Effort and Optimal Switching Points

In sections 7.1 and 7.2 we looked at two features of best theory criteria—formal rigor and simplicity. The approaches I suggested for these criteria had a kind of unifying theme: Make our lives as investigators as easy as possible. Or to put it more soberly: How can we achieve the most fruitful results for the least expenditure (expenditure understood to include intellectual labor)?

In the case of formal rigor, we want to deploy as much rigor as is necessary to resolve the questions that we are interested in. In the case of simplicity, we want the theory to be simpler because simpler theories (on the theory of simplicity that I advanced) are just theories that make it easier for us to conduct the business of science—in this case linguistics.

This point dovetails with earlier chapters in this book (particularly Chapters 2 and 5). In Chapter 2, for example, I argued that many of the theoretical choices we make (for example between derivational and representational constraint based approaches to grammar) do not entail different pictures of our basic cognitive architecture—like different computer languages, they are simply ways for us to understand what is going on at the hardware level. They don't describe different states of the circuits of the computer (or the micro-organization of the mind/brain).

If this is right, then the choices linguists make in theory construction should not be driven by assumptions about which approach is more faithful to lower level cognitive architecture, but rather should be driven by whatever makes it easier to construct theories that satisfy our explanatory goals. Now this might mean that derivational approaches are superior, but it would be a mistake to think this reflects something deeper than that derivational approaches make our jobs easier in the current state of the theory.

If we were really interested in investigating best theory criteria, then the idea would be to find criteria that best measured and predicted the amount of cognitive labor that would go into opposing theoretical approaches. We are now in the domain of social epistemology, but the kind of social epistemology that typically takes place in business schools today—it is about the theory of organizations that are trying to optimize for knowledge acquisition, where there are costs associated with knowledge acquisition. We want to quantify the costs, and try to expend our intellectual energy for optimum effect.

Just as in linguistics we have different tools for tackling problems, so too in the aircraft industry, integrated circuitry design, and automotive engine design there are different tools. Suppose, for example, one was interested in designing a new airplane and was looking for an airplane design with optimal aerodynamic properties. There are two ways we might approach this. One is by using computer simulation and the other is by prototyping (for example building a model and putting it in a wind tunnel). Which should we use? As Stefan Thomke at Harvard Business School (2001) observes, this would be the wrong question. The real question is what is the optimal time to switch from one method to another.

As it turns out, in initial phases of development, computer simulation is often fairly inexpensive. Prototyping, on the other hand, is substantially more expensive. But this is in the beginning. Product development typically runs through the following "developmental cycle."

(i) Design: One conceives of or designs an experiment.
(ii) Build: One builds the (physical or virtual) apparatus needed to conduct that experiment.
(iii) One runs the experiment.
(iv) One analyzes the result.
(v) Repeat.

In business, unlike in many academic contexts, it is possible to quantify the economic value of the information gained by the experiment. It is also possible to quantify the costs of conducting the experiments (including opportunity costs—that is, the cost of missing out on doing something else). Thomke defines the *efficiency of the experiment* as the economic value of information gained from experiment minus the costs of doing the experiment.

Returning to our developmental cycle, we find that in each iteration of the cycle the economic value of the experiment drops off slightly. This is because costs tend to increase on successive iterations of experiments, and because the knowledge gained in each iteration gets marginally smaller. For example, suppose one was doing computer simulations of the aerodynamic properties of an airplane design. A rough and ready simulation can be thrown together in a hurry and this might tell us if the design is plausible or a disaster, but subsequent iterations of the experiment (say to test fuel efficiencies at various altitudes) will require increasingly more sophisticated programming and thus more programmer hours. Plus, the bang for the buck is smaller because we are looking into finer questions that have less significant economic impact.

We can even draw a curve for this, moving downward and to the right, showing how the efficiency of the experiment decreases over each iteration. But of course a downward sloping curve does not mean we should abandon the method, because we need something to abandon it for. Sometimes this happens. Let's stay with our aircraft example to illustrate. Prototyping methods also generate a downward sloping curve, as their experimental efficiency decreases over time. Prototyping experiments are also relatively more expensive than computer simulations (it is more expensive to construct prototypes than write programs—at least initially). But in many cases the curve for prototyping does not drop as rapidly as for the computer simulation case; the efficiency of prototyping experiments does not degrade as rapidly. In the airline case we can imagine that successive changes to a model (once built) are not as expensive as providing subtle tweaks to the computer simulation of an aircraft and the flow of a turbulent fluid (air) across its surface.

If the curve for the efficiency of prototyping drops off more slowly than the efficiency curve for computer simulations, then the curves will intersect—computer simulation could be more efficient for the first n iterations but less efficient after that. The real game then is not to take sides as to which method is better, but rather figure out the best point at which to switch methods. Thomke calls this the *optimal switching point*.

Of course, the optimal switching point is itself dynamic. Developments like rapid-prototyping can push the entire prototyping curve upwards, so that it intersects the simulation curve sooner (after fewer iterations). As the business world has learned, we shouldn't be glued to methods, but we need to move to the best methods at the moment, and the best methods are the most efficient ones.

What does efficiency mean in a domain like linguistics where it is difficult to quantify the value of knowledge? Here we are in a very tricky area, since ultimately the value of the knowledge that the field generates is largely a function of the kinds of questions that we and our peers are interested in. One is reminded of the mathematician Erdös' habit of assigning monetary value to hard mathematical problems ("this is a $5 prize," "this is a $10 prize," etc.); it was his way of indicating which questions were more interesting and harder (and hence valuable to solve).

Obviously, different researchers may value discoveries differently, depending upon their goals. Some may be looking for results in linguistics that can aid in natural language processing. Others may be looking for results that help us to understand the nature of the language faculty and how it evolved. If that's how it is, then people will look at experimental efficiency in the linguistic context in very different ways; what is valuable to one linguist may be worthless to another.

For the moment let's just focus on the goal of understanding the nature of the language faculty—a goal that dominated most of my discussion of linguistics in Chapter 1. Even once we fix the goals, we still have a range of conflicting methodologies, and through the years we have witnessed plenty of pressure to change methods, from the Standard Theory of Chomsky (1965) to the Extended Standard Theory, to Government-Binding Theory, the Principles and Parameters Framework and the Minimalist Program. Each of these shifts was triggered by the perception of the field that the current framework had run its course and that a more efficient theoretical framework was now available (more efficient in the sense of getting closer to the goal of explaining the language faculty in the least expensive way possible).

These shifts are bound to be difficult. Some people train up on old methodologies and may not consider the cost of retooling to be worth it. There is, for sure, a steep learning curve with each theoretical shift. Is it worth it? Not to everyone. Some will not be technically agile enough to shift. Others may find that the results they prized are no longer the target of the new research paradigm.

The interesting thing about an academic field like linguistics is that there is no corporate research officer to decide when is the optimal time to switch methods. For the most part, academics are driven by their own abilities and interests. Some are gifted in technical methods; others are gifted in observing surprising new facts. Still others can see how changes to the theory can result in more explanatory approaches to the nature of language. My point in this chapter is that we should see this for what it is—each of us works with the methods that make our work as theorists easier, given our goals. It really accomplishes nothing to proclaim that an invented notion of simplicity or formal rigor is somehow necessary to do linguistics properly. What does make sense is for us to discover new ways to more efficiently tackle the problems that interest us, and convince those who share our interests that the new methods will help them too— that the learning curve will be worth it.

Appendix: Interview with Noam Chomsky

Chomsky on Chomsky, Language, Mind, and Freedom. The Stony Brook Interviews (organizer, Gary Mar)
INTERVIEW 4. Chomsky on the Mind. Interviewed by Peter Ludlow (transcript edited by Chomsky and Ludlow)

PETER LUDLOW: Noam Chomsky is the principal architect of generative linguistics and has been the driving force in recent evolutions of the theory, including in the development of the principles and parameters framework, which one commentator has described as, quote, "the first really novel approach to language in the last two and a half thousand years." Professor Chomsky has also been a key figure in development of the cognitive sciences generally. Indeed, the most important figure in the development according to Harvard's Howard Gardner [*The Mind's New Science*]. He is perhaps most famous for his writings and lectures on international politics and in media theory. It is less well known, however, that Professor Chomsky has been an important figure in Anglo-American philosophy over the last fifty years and that he has been a key interlocutor with all the leading philosophers of language and mind within that tradition. He's had lively exchanges with, for example, Willard Van Orman Quine, Hilary Putnam, Donald Davidson, Saul Kripke, John Searle, Michael Dummett, and now a new generation of philosophers. And I guess the first question has to be the following: Given everything that's on your plate, why do you bother with the philosophers?

NOAM CHOMSKY: Oh, that's the most fascinating topic of all. It's what I grew up with and still am obsessed with.

PL: Why do you think other linguists are not, or, in general other scientists don't seem to be as engaged with the philosophical community?

NC: Well, scientists tend, I think, to be involved in their own technical problems and often don't think much about what it's about. So, for many years, I've taught courses in these questions and would have students read, say, Quine's papers in which he argues that everything they are doing is complete folly. He gives arguments that you can't possibly do it this way. The students will read the papers, and say, "kind of interesting," and then go back to doing exactly the same work, even though they have just read that it is folly and can't be done and so on and so forth. And I think that is not unusual. If you read the scientific literature, there's a lot of expressed contempt for what philosophers have to say. So you'll read somebody working on the neurophysiology of consciousness—a hot topic—and there will be an obligatory first couple of paragraphs saying, "well, the philosophers have mucked this up for centuries, but now we'll show

how it's done," but with no engagement in the arguments that have been given or the thinking behind them.

PL: Does it trouble you that, say, most other linguists don't engage philosophers on these issues?

NC: It troubles me, not so much, I mean it's connected to a deeper problem. I think it should trouble us that we're not thinking about what we're up to, and those questions happen to be the domain of what philosophers pay attention to.

PL: Right. Let's turn to some of these philosophers and some of the things that they have said. And the first one I want to look at is the Harvard philosopher, Hilary Putnam. In the mid-seventies, he wrote a paper called "The Meaning of 'Meaning'," which is very influential, and I guess the key slogan that came out of that is that "meanings just ain't in the head." Agree? Disagree? Or is that just incoherent?

NC: It's incoherent without further explanation. First, you have to clarify what you are talking about. If by meanings, we have in mind what people have in mind when they are using the word in English, then, sure, they're not in the head. They're all over the place. Talk about the meaning of life, it's not in the head. If you have some more technical notion in mind, you got to explain what it is. If the technical . . . and there it's a matter of choice. You can define the technical notions so it's in the head or so that it's not in the head. When you define technical notions, you have a choice. The way it's done in the sciences, and the way it ought to be done, is you define a technical notion in the context of an explanatory theory. You don't just define a technical notion out in space. So, let's ask what's the explanatory theory in which we're going to give a technical notion, which will be pronounced *meaning* or pronounced some other way. And then we'll ask whether that theory is a sensible theory and does it place this technical concept in the head or not. But all that extra work hadn't been done.

PL: Why can't we say there's just a pre-theoretical notion of meaning and what we want to do is try and elucidate or precisify it in some way or other?

NC: Yeah, you could do that, but there's a million ways of doing it. So what about the meaning of life, for example? That's part of the pre-theoretical notion.

PL: Is it?

NC: Is it? Sure it is. I mean, I thought people talk about what's the meaning of life all the time.

PL: And you think that's the same notion of meaning as when you say what's the meaning of the word?

NC: No, there's thousands . . . it's a huge range of things. What did he mean by saying so and so usually has to do with what was his intention or something like that. So, part of the pre-theoretical meaning has to do with people's intentions. But that doesn't tell us what the meaning of a word is. In fact, when you talk about the meaning of a word, that's a rather English-specific locution. And we could focus on that if we like, and if you want, you can try to clarify it, but again to try and clarify and reshape a pre-theoretical notion makes sense within the framework of an effort to understand something, an explanatory account.

PL: Well, suppose we go with the following attempt to clarify, or at least introduction of a piece of technical terminology. Philosophers will talk about the content of a mental state or the content of some sort of expression. Is that helpful?

NC: No, because "content" is a technical notion. It's not being used in the sense of the ordinary concept, "content." It's typically used to refer to something out there. So, the content of our expression is not in the head by definition because we've defined it to be not in the head. Well, then the question is, well, does that have anything to do with our notions of... does that have anything to do with our understanding of the way language works and is used. OK, that's the question. You can certainly think it has very little to do with it.

PL: But, suppose we thought of the enterprise being sketched in the following way. There are two ways in which you might study primates, for example. You might study primate anatomy, in which case you're just concerned about bones and muscles and tendons and so forth. And then you might also study primate ecology, in which case you're studying the relation between the primate and its environment. And I take it that what these philosophers are talking about here when they talk about external content is that they're saying a part of talk about meaning has to be analyzed in terms of thinking about the human organism in relation to its environment, right? So . . .

NC: That's fine (by definition) if you want to study the relation between the human organism and its environment. That's fine. There's nothing wrong with studying the human organism in its environment. That's what sociologists are doing all the time. But if you want to do it seriously, you ask . . . first of all, let's go back to primates. When you study primates and their ecology, you don't just look at the anatomy of primates. You look at the physiology of primates, also what you might call mental processes of primates. The way they seem to be interpreting the world, the perceptual abilities of primates. In fact, what you try to do is exploit to the extent that you can what we know about an individual ape **or other animal**. You want to know what we understand about that ape, and that information we will bring to bear in the study of how the ape interacts with other apes and with the rest of the environment and so on. That's the way it's done with primates, or with ants, or any other organism, and I think that's the way it ought to be done with humans. So we should ask, OK, what do we understand about . . . the internal nature of the creature that's doing all these things, and to the extent that we understand something about that, we can ask sensible questions about how it interacts with the external world, with other people and so on and so forth.

PL: Do you think that could potentially inform the sort of internalist investigation as well?

NC: Sure, it can go the other way. I mean, there is no fixed order of inquiry. You can study the sociology of ape communities, and that'll tell you something, could tell you something important about the internal thinking processes of apes, or even their internal anatomy.

PL: And vice versa, presumably.

NC: Yeah, sure, science goes all ways.

PL: Here's another technical term that has been used: 'reference'. You consider that to be incoherent as well? Or...

NC: Well, until it's explained, it's incoherent. Once it's explained, then it becomes non-incoherent.

PL: Well, you see one thing that I've never quite understood is exactly what the problem is with reference because I can say look, OK, now I'm referring to this coffee cup.

NC: No, that's different. That's quite different. You're talking about an action of referring. That's a common sense notion. It's part of English and every language I know of. There's some way to talk about such actions, but what philosophers have introduced is a different notion, a notion that's supposed to hold between a linguistic entity and something in the world. Now, that's not referring. Referring is an act that people do. Philosophers pointed this out fifty years ago.

PL: Yeah, well, this is a point that goes back to Peter F. Strawson, Right?

NC: Yes. It's just a fact! And if you want to make up a technical term that you pronounce the same way, first of all, it's questionable that you should pronounce it the same way because it's misleading. But if you do, let's at least keep clear that it's a technical term, kind of like the way physicists use 'energy'. They don't mean it the way we do in ordinary language. They mean it the way they say they mean it. So let's take the technical term, 'refer,' or 'denote', or whatever you want to call it and tell us what it's supposed to... tell us what you mean by it and tell us what explanatory theory it enters into. So when a physicist defines 'energy', you're not interested in a definition. You're interested in the set of principles and assumptions and problems and so on within which that technical concept is introduced, and then you look and you see how good the theory is. Well, here you don't have any theory. And we don't even have an explanation about what the technical notion is, so it's impossible to talk about it.

PL: Yeah, I think it might be a mistake to think of it as a technical notion. I mean, I think it's just a sort of precisified way of describing certain core level facts, right?

NC: That's presumably the intention.

PL: So for example, I might say, well, once you understand that people refer to things and so forth, it's not a hard step to say, well, OK [...] certain names are canonically used to refer to certain things and certain individuals. So the name 'Noam Chomsky', I can ask the audience here what person in this room does that term refer to . . .

NC: Well, you could ask what do you use that term for when you refer to something in the world. That you can ask. When you ask what the term refers to, you are assuming that there is a relation between terms and things, and then have to explain what that relation is, what are the entities between which it holds, because that's a new concept. In this case, what do you mean by *person*. We don't have that concept of reference in ordinary language. In fact, I think it's leading us off into a wrong picture, as Wittgenstein would've put it. It's leading us to a picture of language, which is . . . we know what it's based on. I mean, it's based on Frege's theory of arithmetic, and that's just the wrong picture for language.

PL: OK, now I want to change directions briefly. We may actually end up being sucked back into this issue of reference. Donald Davidson in a paper called "A Nice Derangement of Epitaphs" said, or basically argued, that there is no such thing as language, and I've always sort of thought that you probably—you may not want to admit it—but on some level or another, you probably agree with that, right?

NC: No. In fact, I think he ended up contradicting himself. I think there's some discussion of it in here somewhere. If you look at the end of the paper, it turns out that he's saying that there isn't a notion of language in the technical sense, the technical sense of an internal generative procedure that relates sounds and meanings and so on. He actually argues there is no notion of language in another sense, the sense of some community property, or whatever. Well, OK, first of all I don't even think that's true. It's an informal notion, even if it may not have a scientifically usable sense. But I think the paper is just rifled with confusions that I've written about.

PL: So you think there are such things as languages?

NC: Yeah, yeah . . .

PL: In an informal sense?

NC: . . . like there's such things as the meaning of life. And I understand it when people ask what's the meaning of life. So yeah, there's such a thing as the meaning of life. There's such a thing as the financial crisis in Argentina, and there are all kinds of things in the world. But if you want to proceed to understand what you and I are doing, those notions just don't help. You've got to look at it differently, the way we look at other primates, in fact.

PL: Well, let me read a quote from something you wrote recently, OK. You say, "I doubt that people think that among the constituents of the world are entities that are simultaneously abstract and concrete like books and banks, or that have the amalgam of properties we discover when we explore the meanings of even the simplest words like river, person, city, etc."

NC: Yeah, that's an empirical question. It's a question of figuring out what a person's folk science is, how people think the world is actually constituted of entities, which is not, "do I talk about books?" Of course we talk about books, we talk about the meaning of life, and so on. But if you ask people, well, how do you think the world really works, that's a problem of ethno-science. Like you go to some other community and you try to figure out what's their idea about how the world works. Like maybe the classical Greeks thought that Apollo pulls the sun through the sky or something. That's their folk scientific picture of how the world works. That's a hard topic. You can't just do armchair philosophy about it. That's why ethno-scientists have to work. And when they work, what they find . . . I think if they worked on people like us instead of just talking about us while sitting in the common room, they would discover that our folk science, yours and mine, does not include entities that are simultaneously abstract and concrete and does not include entities like the meaning of life. That doesn't mean we can't talk about them. Sure, we talk about them all the time, but we don't—at least I don't—and I presume other people don't think of them as constituents of the way the world operates. We don't do that when we are talking to each other informally.

PL: Now, that sounds a little bit more moderate than what you've said elsewhere. Here's a passage from, I believe this is from *New Horizons*, where you say, "In the domain where questions of realism arise in a serious way, in the context of the search for laws of nature, objects are not conceived from the peculiar perspectives provided by the concepts of common sense."

NC: That's absolutely right. There are several different enterprises that you have to distinguish here. I don't think it's more or less moderate. It's about a different topic. When you're trying to understand something about the nature of the world, you and I—anybody—you start with some kind of what's called folk science. Almost every society we know has some picture of the way the world works which is more or less commonly shared. If you try to do this more reflectively and carefully and bringing in other criteria and probably bringing in other cognitive faculties—we don't know that for sure, but I suspect it—then it becomes the enterprise of science. Which is a different enterprise, and a peculiar one. It's not folk science. It's science. That works in other ways. This comment has to do with our culture in which the enterprise of science is understood . . .

PL: Right.

NC: . . . our intellectual culture, and in that, when we try to find out how the world works, we discard the concepts of common sense very quickly.

PL: But it sounds to me here like what you're saying is that the only things that are real, right, are the things that science tells us are real. So . . .

NC: Well . . .

PL: It sounds like what you're saying here is that, well, this table isn't real, but maybe quarks...

NC: 'Real' is an honorific term. You can use it any way you like. I mean, to say, if I say something is true, and then I add, well, it's the real truth, I'm not saying they are two different kinds of truths, the truth and the real truth. I'm just emphasizing what I said, and the term 'real' is basically used honorifically. So yeah, you can use it honorifically in various ways. If you're trying to find out the way the world works, to really understand it in the manner of the sciences, then we'd very quickly give up common-sense notions. If we're carrying out folk science, less reflectively, probably using different cognitive faculties, we also give up commonsense notions, but in different ways.

PL: Well, you can say a lot of them... I mean, claims about something being honorific, like 'real' being honorific. Some philosophers have argued that terms like 'rational' and 'moral' are honorific.

NC: Well, I don't quite agree with that. I think 'real' is quite different.

PL: But, what's the difference in these cases then?

NC: Because I think rationality is something that we can understand and morality is part of us, and we can try to figure out what it is. We can try to figure out what our moral faculties are. We understand something about what rational action is. But about reality, we have to ask what we are talking about.

PL: Right...

NC: But, if we're talking about reality in the enterprise of trying to discover the way the world works in a physics department or a linguistics department or whatever, commonsense notions are irrelevant. If we're trying to explore our intuitive under-standing of the way the world works, commonsense notions are relevant as an object of study. If you're using them in a more informal way, like what is the meaning of life, yeah, sure, OK.

PL: Well, look, there's a sort of space between ethno-science and science, right, commonsense and all of those. It's then explored by philosophers for 2,500 years, and it's called metaphysics, right?

NC: No, that's different.

PL: OK, but that is a question about what's real, right?

NC: Ethno-science is a branch of science.

PL: Right...

NC: Ethno-science is the branch of science that tries to figure out what people's beliefs are about the way the world works. Metaphysics is not that.

PL: I understand that.

NC: OK.

PL: But do you think metaphysics is impossible?

NC: No, science is metaphysics.

PL: OK, good.

NC: It's talking about what the world is made of.

PL: Alright. So then the question is why do you think that science gets to claim what's real? Now, let me give you an example. So, in *The Scientific Image*, Bas van Fraassen is a scientific anti-realist so he says the things posited by science, quarks, etc., are not real, but mid-size earth-bound objects are real. Now, you got the flipside of that.

NC: I don't have any side because I don't think the word 'real' is sensible enough to use informatively in this context, although we can say informally that they're all real in different senses. If you're trying to understand the way the world actually works, whether you're van Fraassen or you or me, we're going to go to the scientists because they try to tell us how the world really works. If we're interested in exploring people's commonsense beliefs, we'll go to the ethno-scientists and see what they discover.

PL: What if we're interested in something like whether there are events or whether there are properties or whether there are mereological sums or something?

NC: Well, let's take events, which play a prominent role in modern semantics. So, here you can ask a lot of different questions. For one thing, you can ask whether in, say, Davidsonian semantics, where there's a lot of... or anything that developed from an event based semantics, whether what are called events are internal to the mind or outside the head. I think they are internal to the mind.

PL: Right, but can't they be both?

NC: They could, but then we're asking another question. If we're asking, well, how do these things that are internal to the mind relate to something in the outside world, we'll say, OK, let's take a look at what you mean by an event. So, for example, is the American Revolution an event? Yeah, it was an important event in history. Does that event include the fact that the man who the indigenous population called the Town Destroyer took off a little time in the middle of the Revolution to destroy the Iroquois civilization? Is that part of the event called the American Revolution? Well, not when you study it in school. You want to find out about that event, you've got to—probably the Iroquois remember, the ones who are left—you've got to look at serious scholarly history. Then you find out that one part of what was going on in the event that we call the American Revolution was a side operation in [1779] to wipe out the Iroquois civilization so that the colonies could expand if they got rid of the British. Well, is that part of the event or isn't it? Well, here comes hard questions about what we're really going to call events in the outside world, and those questions don't have independent answers because they're highly dependent on our interests, our perspective, our goals; all kinds of factors. So, I don't think we're going to find external events in any sense worth pursuing for investigation for what the world is like.

PL: Why can't these external events just be complicated objects?

NC: They could be anything you like, but is the Town Destroyer's exploit part of the American Revolution or isn't it? That event? It's your choice, but that's my answer.

PL: Well, now it sounds like you're saying that, well, I have representations of events, right?

NC: No, I have representations.

PL: You have representations.

NC: I have representations, some of which we informally say are of events.

PL: Right, but now one might ask what on earth is a representation if it is not a representation *of* something.

NC: That's a mistake that comes from a philosophical tradition. The way the term 'represent' is used in the philosophical tradition, it's a relation between an internal object and an external object. It's not the way it's used either in ordinary speech or in the sciences. So, when a perceptual psychologist, say, talks about an internal representation of a cube or something, there doesn't have to be any cube there. They're talking about something that's going on in the head. In fact, what they may be studying, and usually are studying, is the relation between things like tachistoscopic presentations and internal events. There's no cube. But, nevertheless, they talk about it as an internal representation. The concept, internal representation... There's a long discussion of that in here. The concept, internal representation, is used in the sciences—and I think that's true in ordinary speech too—in ways which don't involve a relation between an internal thing and an external thing. That technical concept derives from a particular interpretation of the theory of ideas, which said, well, ideas represent something out there.

Incidentally, I should say that that's not the interpretation of the theory of ideas that **was** given by the people that used it. So let's take Hume for example. I quote him in there. He raises a serious empirical question. He's says it's about the nature of the terms he uses, "the identity that we ascribe to things," meaning how do we individuate things. And he asks the question, well, is this a peculiar nature common to the thing, or is it, what he calls "fictitious," a construction of the mind? And he says, "fictitious." There is no entity. There is no common nature. There is no nature common to the thing. There is a construction of the mind, which we use to talk about the world.

PL: But he's an idealist.

NC: No, not here. He's saying we interact with the world. He believes there is an external world out there. There's a coffee cup on the table, and so on. But he's talking about the individuation of things, how we organize things, how we construct our picture of the world, and that involves the way our minds work. And that doesn't mean the world isn't there. No. It's just what his predecessors called our "cognoscitive powers," which use the data of sense to construct an account of the world. And he's saying, well, you want to look at the identity of things, the identity that we ascribe to things, like what makes us call something a book or an event and so on. He's saying, well, it's fictitious in the sense that it's a construction of the mind based on the data of sense. That's not an idealist position. In fact, that's the position of modern science.

PL: . . . because people will call you a crypto-idealist.

NC: Well, then they're misunderstanding what idealism is.

PL: OK. Let me . . . There's an issue that I want to get to here, and this involves the thing we mentioned about representations and whether representation requires there being something that it is a representation of. Now, in a very important and somewhat influential book by Saul Kripke, there's a revival of the sort of Wittgensteinian argument about rule following. Let me just read the relevant passage here. So in that book, Kripke says, "If statements attributing rule following are neither to be regarded as stating facts nor to be thought of as explaining a behavior, it would seem that the use of the idea of rules and competence in linguistics needs serious reconsideration even if these notions are not rendered meaningless." I know that you've written on that in the *Knowledge of Language*.

NC: The crucial word is 'if'. In the sense in which the term 'rule' has been used for thousands of years, in fact, in the study of language, it is not the kind of rule he had in mind. So if you studied Latin let's say, or you studied it a thousand years ago; they would have a rule that would tell you when to use the ablative case or something. That's not a rule in Wittgenstein's sense. It's a description of a part of the language. So the questions about rule following just don't arise.

PL: But, we don't need to get hung up on rules and so forth.

NC: But that's what he's talking about.

PL: I understand that, but in a certain sense he's talking about any sort of computational state. So, take just a computer. Forget about human beings for a second.

NC: See, computers are a different story.

PL: OK.

NC: Let's take an insect. Why aren't these questions asked about insects? When you study insects, you attribute to them computational states. Is that a problem? I mean, is it not real? Like, if you say that an insect is determining the position of the sun as a function of the time of year and time of day and here's the computation it's using, why isn't that science?

PL: That would be, but the argument would be that the reason you can get away with that is because you're talking about—the representations that you're attributing to the insect—are externalistically anchored . . .

NC: No.

PL: . . . and that is you couldn't do it unless what you had is an embedded system.

NC: That's not true. You could do it in an experimental situation in which you have a light, and, in fact, if you knew how to do it, you could do it by stimulating the sensory organs of the insect. It would all be internal. There doesn't have to be a sun there. It's just that, yeah, you're talking about the way it happens actually in the real world, but you would say the same thing in an experimental setting where you don't have that external world . . .

PL: Well . . .

NC: . . . because you're talking about the internal computations of the insect on the occasion of sense. It doesn't matter what's out there.

PL: Notice the shift there though, because you went from saying you don't need the sun in the experimental setting to saying that you could run the experiment in a world that didn't have the sun, and that's a different story. Right?

NC: No, no, it's not a different story. The point is if you look at the insect scientists are studying, they are studying what seventeenth-century philosophers used to call the "constructions of the mind on the occasion of sense." Now, it happens that in the world that they're looking at, the occasions of sense happen to be related to the fact that there's something 93 million miles away, but the study could go on as if it's what Hilary called a brain-in-a-vat. The studies are internalist because we don't know anything else to study.

PL: But this is disputed, right? There is this dispute about David Marr. I mean, there are two stories for this. Tyler Burge and Martin Davies, for example, argue that Marr is an externalist of sorts . . .

NC: Yeah, but I think they are just misreading him. I mean, in fact, I happened to know Marr personally, but I'm sure if he was here he would say this. If you look at the informal exposition in Marr, in Marr's *Vision*, let's say. The book, *Vision*. If you look at the informal exposition, in order to motivate what he's doing, he says, well, imagine an elephant, or anything—like a stick figure—and we want to know how that thing out there is interpreted by the visual system as some three-dimensional object. However, if you look at the experimental procedures of Marr, they didn't have elephants out there. In fact, what they were using was tachistoscopic images. So, they were presenting dots on screens, and if they had known how to stimulate the optic nerve, they would've done that. When you go from the informal exposition to the actual science, you see that like everything else, it's a study of the internal nature of the beast. In fact, they would've loved to get to the point where they could tell you something about how you identify an elephant, but they never got anywhere near that. However, even if they did, it wouldn't matter whether the elephant is there or not, it wouldn't matter what's the occasion of sense. Again, the seventeenth-century formulation of this was, I think, quite appropriate. On the occasion of sense, the cognoscitive—sounds archaic— but the cognoscitive powers of the mind construct complicated internal structures, which have all sorts of properties, gestalt properties, what Hume later called the identity that we ascribe to things, and so on. And that looks correct, and that's the way modern science looks at it. The fact that the informal expositions talk about—sort of motivating what you're doing—talk about identifying objects on the outside, that's fine, but you have to know how to distinguish informal expositions from the actual scientific program. And if you look at the actual program, then you'll never look at the things outside, aside from tachistoscopic images because they are as close as you can get to the actual occasion of sense.

PL: It's time to move to our very eager studio audience here. So, let's turn to them.

Audience 1: Hi, how are you. You mentioned event semantics and how that's sort of been pulled into, or is a part of some linguistic research, and I'd like to ask a question about that and just hear more about it. The way Pietroski uses it in the article in the book that's sitting on your table. He will take a sentence . . .

PL: We've been referring to this book, and I should point out it's called *Chomsky and His Critics* which just came out from Blackwells.

A1: Right, and the article is by Paul Pietroski, I think. So, he'll take the sentence, 'John boiled the water'—I'm going to ignore the larger context—and then turn that into something that's like there was an event of which John was the agent and it was concerning a boiling and the theme was water—terminated in a boiling, excuse me— and the theme was water, something like that, right? And then Pietroski tries to fit that together with a syntactic account of how that formal representation can turn into the sentence that you have here. So, you see, you recognize in your reply that it's an open question whether the subject matter of this whole analysis is in the language faculty or in the cognitive . . .

NC: It's all in the cognitive system. It's all internal though. It's all syntax in the sense that it's involved with internal computations.

A1: Right. Fine. So, the question then is—and you say it's an empirical question whether it's in the language faculty or in the cognitive system. So, first of all, what would be some ways to determine empirically what that is and also what would it even mean for it to be . . . I have a trouble understanding what it would mean for it to be in the language faculty because then it seems that our language faculty has certain event metaphysics built into it.

NC: Not event metaphysics. It's a, well, first of all, there is no event metaphysics in the ordinary sense of event. Events are things out there. And all of this is formal manipulations inside. We're now asking the question what is the architecture of the mind, which is like asking what's the structure of the benzene molecule. You want to know the structure of the benzene molecule, you can't just think about it. You have to have some theory that tells you how you look at such questions. Well, the study of the architecture . . . I think there are real answers to the question of what is the architecture of the mind, but they're not going to be easy to find. You want to find out what the language faculty is, well you're going to . . . when you talk about any subsystem of an organism—say, the circulatory system, or the immune system, or the digestive system, or whatever it might be—you're kind of presupposing that it makes sense to look at a complex organism as if it has components, each component having kind of an integrated character with its own properties. It's worth studying in itself, but it's not separable. You can't cut the immune system out of the body, but you're saying, look, it has properties that you can study by themselves. You can learn things about them. But when you put the whole picture together, you hope you'll understand something about the organism. Well, same when you're studying the cognitive architecture, we want to see is there a component, call it the language faculty. We don't know in advance what it is. You have to discover and refine it and change it. Is there a component, which is critically involved in what you and I are doing in some fashion, which has some intrinsic properties? So, is it going to turn out, say, that it has particular interface conditions and some kind of internal recursive computational process? Well, if it does, then the more we understand about that and how it fits into the general cognitive architecture, the clearer these questions become about whether something is inside it or outside it, and those are very concrete questions. I mean, take, say, anaphora, what are called relations of intended referential dependency, OK. Are they inside the language faculty or outside? Well, that's a substantive issue. If you'd asked me ten years ago, I would've said inside. Now, I think there's evidence that they're outside, right on the edge. And the reason for that has to do with beliefs about how the language faculty works. So, if the language faculty does involve optimal computation that requires cyclic derivations, and if anaphora looks at global properties—condition C of the binding theory—well, it's outside. But that's a question that you can't ask in advance. You have to ask what does it seem these faculties are like. The more you learn about them, the more you can formulate these questions clearly, and that's the kind of question that comes up about the internal notion of event. Is it in the language faculty, the semantic component of the language faculty, or is it in some other faculty that's linked to it? And you can't, you just can't speculate about that. You have to learn about it.

A1: And I guess that's my question, I just, from ignorance, have a hard time imagining what kind of empirical evidence would count in adjudicating between those.

NC: If I'd known it, I would've said it. I mean, I think these are the kind of questions that can't be posed clearly until we learn more about the relevant context. What is the empirical evidence that bears on whether anaphora is on one or the other side of the border of the language faculty? Well, part of the empirical evidence—in my mind at least—turns on whether in fact there's a single cyclic derivational process that goes by, what I call phases, stepwise. That's an empirical question but all kinds of things bear on it coming from everywhere. And once that empirical question is sharpened, you can ask whether the global property of anaphora is inside or outside.

A1: Thank you.

NC: Actually, similar questions, I might say, arise on the phonetic side. So take, say, prosody. Prosody appears to have global properties, OK, so is it inside or outside the cyclic derivation, which is forming bigger and bigger units? Well, if the properties really are global, it's outside. But you can't answer that, and the kind of evidence that bears on it comes from everywhere. It might come from chemistry for all we know, when we try to figure out how these processes work.

A2: You've made clear that science plays a primary role in philosophy, and I was curious to know what role, if any, does philosophy play in science?

NC: Well, here I think it helps to look at the question in a little more historical depth. If you had asked Hume, "are you a scientist or a philosopher," he couldn't have answered because there was no distinction. If you had asked Kant, "are you a philosopher or a scientist," he couldn't have answered. In fact, until the latter part of the nineteenth, around the middle of the nineteenth century, there was no really clear distinction between science and philosophy. If you study in Oxford and Cambridge, it's the department of natural philosophy or moral philosophy because science was just one part of philosophy. They weren't distinct. By the latter part of the nineteenth century, they sort of became separated, and after that it's really a matter of choice. Disciplines don't exist in themselves. We construct them. So, I mean, deans have to have ways of organizing departments because it's too much trouble to have everybody do everything. But there's no boundary to what's in chemistry. There's no boundary to what's in philosophy. It just depends on what people choose to call themselves . . . what those who come out of this tradition want to study, and a lot of what they want to study is questions in the foundations of science or say the kind of things that van Fraassen is trying to clear up by using the results of science. These are all fine questions, and people tend to call them philosophy. You could call them—parts of them at least—you could call thoughtful science or reflective moral theory or you can call them anything you want. But there's a range of questions which have come to be in the domain of philosophy, and they can extend all over the place. I mean, there are people in philosophy departments that are working on the foundations of quantum theory and making contributions to it.

A3: Hello. I'd like to go back to insect navigation once more, and I take it that we explore insect navigation because we want to find out how insects navigate in their natural environment. And, you're right to point out that in an experiment, we can replace the sun by an artificial light and so on. But, it seems like we still, in the whole explanatory context, we cannot just do without the sun and the actual objects in the real world because otherwise an explanation of insect navigation becomes meaningless. And, so, it seems to me that we have to have the assumption that insects represent the actual sun and not just dots of light.

NC: We don't have to have that. Of course, you're interested in the outside world. But if you're taking a physics course here, they don't use videotapes of what's happening outside the windows because that's just useless. It doesn't let you figure out how the world is working. So you disregard that beyond the earliest stages of science. Yeah, in the earliest stages, you see apples falling from trees and that kind of thing. But as soon as you get anywhere, you start designing artificial situations called experiments in which you try to refine the evidence so that it will shed light on principles, which you believe will ultimately bear on what's going on outside the window. But that's not what you're looking at. When you're studying an organism, say, an ant, you don't necessarily start . . . yes, you start with noticing that the ant is figuring out where the sun is and has a very strange computation—we can't do it—as a function of the time of day and time of year. But as you go beyond, you ask, well, what are the actual computations going on inside. And if you get far enough, you would set up experimental situations in which you wouldn't bother with the sun. You'd figure out what those internal computations are. You'd then find that they interact with all kinds of other things. They are not done in isolation, and out of that, you expect you're going to shed some light on what's going on when the occasion of sense that the insect is operating on happens to be connected to an external object, like the one 93 million miles away. But that's just kind of like a consequence of the investigation of the ant.

PL: If I can follow up on this question. This seems to be inconsistent with what you say in your "Reply to Ludlow" [from *Chomsky and His Critics*] here where you're quoting Gallistel. So you say, "Gallistel (1990) argues that the representations play a key role in animal behavior and cognition. Here, representation is understood as an isomorphism, a one [to] one relation between mind/brain processes and an aspect of the environment to which these processes adapt the animal's behavior."

NC: It's not inconsistent. He's making an empirical claim. It's a very interesting one, in an introduction to a couple of volumes on animal representation, and his conclusion, which I quote there, is that for animals, there is in fact a one to one relation, an isomorphism, between an internal event and some property of the external world. Like . . . an odor is the example he uses. So the property of the external world is a particular odor, which is out there in the world all right. But you could, if you knew how to do it, you could just stimulate the sensory organs. And he says that's how animal representation works, with this one to one correlation between things that are outside the animal, though you're really studying them at the sensory boundary, and the internal representations. Well, if that's correct, that's an interesting fact about animals, and they are very different from humans in that case.

PL: So then maybe he's [Audience 3] right about that.

NC: Yeah, he [Audience 3] could be. Take the example I mentioned there. It's taken from him [Gallistel]. That an ant—some species of ants, at least—will identify a corpse of a conspecific on the basis of a particular odor. Of course, if you give the ant that odor, and there's no conspecific around, they'll do exactly the same thing. Because, according to this picture, he's saying, well, it's just triggered by the odor, which usually has to come from a conspecific. But if you can control the odors the way you can control lights, you could get the same behavior according to him, when there's no conspecific.

A3: Yeah, but just one more clarification question. It's seems to me that no scientist can claim he has explained any kind of animal behavior if what we take to be its natural environment doesn't play an essential role in this explanation. So, I think, if the relation between an ant and the sun, for example, doesn't show up in this theory, then we haven't really explained what we wanted to explain.

NC: Well, it depends on what you want to explain. As modern sciences have developed since Galileo, this is something of an innovation. They really are not trying to account for the phenomena of experience. I mean, indirectly, that's what motivates them. But what they're trying to do is discover the principles that enter into the way the world functions, and if you ask the guys in the physics department here, "can you explain this videotape of what's going [on] outside the window?" They won't even bother answering. They can't say anything about that. It's way too complicated, and way too many factors, and it's not even their topic. Their topic is to find out the principles of nature. Galileo had a lot of problems with this. You go back and look at the history. He had a lot of trouble convincing the funders, the rich aristocrats who were the funders in those days, convincing them that it's worth studying something as ridiculous as a ball rolling down a frictionless plane. First of all, there's no such thing. Who cares anyway, you know. It was a conceptual breakthrough to get to the point where you began to understand that the phenomena of the world are of interest for the sciences in so far as they provide evidence for the principles of nature. And as soon as you proceed very far, you find out that the ordinary phenomena of nature are useless for this purpose, and you do what are called experiments. And sometimes thought experiments. Like, you look back at Galileo, there's no reason to believe he ever dropped the balls from the top of the Tower of Pisa. If you look at the argument, he gives a purely conceptual argument, a convincing one, to show what is going to happen and it didn't matter if you observed it or not. In fact, you don't observe what he predicted in actually dropping balls from the Tower of Pisa. But his argument was convincing because of the logic of it, and that's true of a lot of his experiments if you read through them. Scholars have now determined he couldn't have carried out some of those experiments. There was no way for him to do it. Some of them he probably did. Some of them he was thinking about. But the point is almost none of them had to do with observations of a casual look at the world. The same with the theory of perception. Take an example of Descartes, which I'll adapt to this situation, but it's a Cartesian example. He said if I look out there [pointing to the audience], what I see is a lot of people sitting in a room. Well, Descartes points out literally that's not what's hitting your eye. What's hitting your eye is something that's coming from that guy's head and that guy's foot. But there's nothing about people sitting in a room. Nevertheless, what you see is people sitting in a room. And then he says, "how does this happen?" Then comes the whole story about **the mind's constructions** on the occasion of sense. The cognoscitive powers make these complicated constructions, which include imposing the structure of people sitting in a room on these fragmentary sensations that are coming to me. But, in perceptual psychology, as it proceeds, you don't study phenomena, like people sitting in a room. That's just way too complicated.

PL: But this isn't fair to the questioner though because he's not arguing against idealization. I mean, you can have a perfectly controlled experiment and still talk about ... For example, take an old sort of Skinner type experiment with a pigeon pressing a bar. You can describe that behavior as the pigeon going, moving it's claw or whatever, or you can describe it as bar-pressing behavior, right? Now, this is not ... If it's not an issue about idealization, the questioner could easily say. . . .

NC: No, no, but we're asking ... at least I understood him to be saying something different: if the scientist cannot give an account of my seeing people in a room, they're not giving an explanation. That's far too strong. I mean, the scientists are giving explanations even they can't get anywhere near describing real life situations, and in fact that's about all of modern science. The bar-pressing is an interesting case because Skinner did impose on it the interpretation, "bar-pressing," and that turns out to be wrong. It turns out with a closer look, that the pigeon pecking, which is what it was doing, actually incorporates different instinctive behaviors; the behavior of pecking for a seed and pecking for water turn out to be different instinctual behaviors, which happen to converge in this experiment. You just mislead yourself if you call them the same thing.

PL: Well, isn't that Skinner's mistake is that he was an internalist, and if he'd been an externalist, then he would see that pressing for a seed and pressing for water are different behaviors.

NC: It has nothing to do with externalism and internalism. I mean, the motivation for distinguishing seed pecking from water dipping comes from observing pigeons. But if you want to really carry it out further, you'll find out what's going on in the pigeon's head on the occasion of sense. And if you could carry out the programs far enough, you'd forget about the seed and the water. Just like David Marr does. He doesn't talk about external things because he's trying to really discover what the principles are. So it's not anything to do with internalism and externalism. What it has to do with is giving the right idealization or a wrong idealization, and we're always facing that. Every experiment involves all kinds of interpretation as to what you're going to think about this thing and that thing. As the sciences get more refined, you try very hard to—not to cut interpretation out because you can't—but at least be consciously aware of what you're putting in. So you can sort of compensate for it if it's the wrong thing to put in.

PL: OK. Next question.

Audience 4: Hi. I think I have a much less sophisticated question than the previous one. You've characterized I-language generally as an interface of sound and meaning and at the same time here you've also been very critical of the various senses of the term 'meaning' and 'reference.' So, I just wanted to ask you if you could clarify what do you mean by 'meaning.'

NC: Well, that's again like David Marr saying I'm trying to figure out how you see an elephant. We start with the intuitive notions of sound and meaning, whatever they are. You can go back to Aristotle and he describes language as a pairing of something like sound and meaning, saying it in Greek. And, yeah, that's what we start with. But as we proceed, we're going to have to refine both of these notions. So, sound, as it's used here, doesn't have to do with what you and I call sound in ordinary talk, and "meaning" will be something very special. So, like maybe it will be Davidsonian event semantics. OK, maybe it will be something built on that and maybe "sound" will be something built on my colleague Morris Halle's conception of instructions for articulatory gestures or it will be whatever it turns out to be as the sciences progress. And it will end up having some loose relation to what we call "sound" and "meaning." But, no more so than "energy" or "work" or "life" or any of the other informal concepts that are dropped in the sciences. Although they often keep the sounds when they talk about their new concepts. So that's to be answered, not to start with.

PL: OK. I guess that's it. Thanks a lot.

Bibliography

Absalom, M., and J. Hajek, 1997. "Raddoppiamento Sintattico: What Happens When the Theory is on Too Tight?" In P. M. Bertinetto et al. (eds.), *Certamen Phonologicum* II. Turin: Rosenberg and Sellier, 159–179.

Arpaly, N., 2003. *Unprincipled Virtue: An Inquiry into Moral Agency.* Cambridge: Cambridge University Press.

Assad F., and W. Cockburn, 1972. "Four-Year Study of WHO Virus Reports on Enterovirus other than Poliovirus." *Bulletin of the World Health Organization* 46: 329–336.

Bach, E., 1970. "Problominalization." *Linguistic Inquiry* 1: 121–122.

Baker, M., 2001. *The Atoms of Language.* New York: Basic Books.

Baker, M., 2003. "Linguistic Differences and Language Design." *Trends in Cognitive Science* 7: 349–353.

Barker, S., 1961. "On Simplicity in Empirical Hypotheses." *Philosophy of Science* 28: 162–171.

Barwise, J., 1989. *The Situation in Logic.* Stanford: CSLI Publications.

Barwise, J., and J. Perry, 1983. *Situation Semantics.* Cambridge, MA: MIT Press.

Beakley, B., and P. Ludlow (eds.), 1992. *Philosophy of Mind: Classical Problems / Contemporary Issues.* Cambridge, MA: MIT Press.

Berkeley, G., 1979. *The Works of George Berkeley*, A. A. Luce and T. E. Jessop (eds.). Nendeln: Kraus Reprint.

Bever, T., 1970. "The Cognitive Basis for Linguistic Structures." In J. Hayes (ed.), *Cognition and the Development of Language.* New York: John Wiley and Sons.

Bever, T., 1972. "The Limits of Intuition." *Foundations of Language* 8: 411–412.

Biermann, A., 1997. *Great Ideas in Computer Science.* Cambridge, MA: MIT Press.

Blackburn, S., 1984. *Spreading the Word.* Oxford: Oxford University Press.

Blackburn, S., 1988. "Attitudes and Contents." *Ethics* 98: 501–517.

Block, N., 1978. "Troubles with Functionalism." In C. W. Savage (ed.), *Perception and Cognition: Issues in the Foundations of Psychology.* Minnesota Studies in the Philosophy of Science, 9. Minneapolis: University of Minnesota Press, 261–325. Reprinted with major revisions in Beakley and Ludlow (1992).

Bloomfield, L., 1933. *Language.* New York: Holt, Rinehart, and Winston.

Bloomfield, L., 1939. *Linguistic Aspects of Science. International Encyclopedia of Unified Science,* vol. 1, #4. Chicago: University of Chicago Press.

Bogen, J., and J. Woodward, 1988. "Saving the Phenomena." *Philosophical Review* 97: 3–25.

Boghossian, P., 1992a. "Externalism and Inference." *Philosophical Issues* 2: 11–28.

Boghossian, P., 1992b. "Reply to Schiffer." *Philosophical Issues* 2: 39–42.

Bontly, T., 1998. "Individualism and the Nature of Syntactic States." *The British Journal for the Philosophy of Science* 49: 557–574.

Bouton, L., 1970. "Antecedent-Contained Proforms." *Proceedings of CLS* 6: 154–167.

Bresnan, J., and R. Kaplan, 1982. "Introduction: Grammars as Mental Representations of Language." In J. Bresnan (ed.), *The Mental Representation of Grammatical Relations*. Cambridge, MA: MIT Press, xvii–lii.

Brown, J., 2009. "From Semantics to Metaphysics." Ph.D. dissertation, Dept. of Philosophy, University of Michigan.

Buffon, C., 1750. *Histoire naturelle des minéraux*, vol. 1. Paris.

Burge, T., 1979. "Individualism and the Mental." In P. A. French, T. E. Euhling, and H. K. Wettstein (eds.), *Midwest Studies in Philosophy 4: Studies in Epistemology*. Minneapolis: University of Minnesota Press, 73–121.

Burge, T., 1986. "Individualism and Psychology." *Philosophical Review* 95: 3–45.

Carlson, G., and F. J. Pelletier, 2002. "The Average American has 2.3 Children." *Journal of Semantics* 19: 73–104.

Chalmers, D., 1996. "Does a Rock Implement Every Finite-State Automaton?" *Synthese* 108: 310–333.

Chomsky, N., 1957. *Syntactic Structures*. The Hague: Mouton.

Chomsky, N., 1962. "The Logical Basis of Linguistic Theory." *Proceedings of the 9th International Congress of Linguistics*. The Hague: Mouton.

Chomsky, N., 1965. *Aspects of the Theory of Syntax*. Cambridge, MA: MIT Press.

Chomsky, N., 1969. "Quine's Empirical Assumptions." In D. Davidson and J. Hintikka (eds.), *Words and Objections: Essays on the Work of W.V. Quine*. Dordrecht: D. Reidel.

Chomsky, N., 1970. "Remarks on Nominalization." In R. Jacobs and P. Rosenbaum (eds.), *English Transformational Grammar*. Waltham: Ginn, 184–221.

Chomsky, N., 1973. "Conditions on Transformation." In S. Anderson and P. Kiparsky (eds.), *A Festschrift for Morris Halle*. New York: Holt, Rinehart, and Winston, 232–286. Reprinted in Chomsky (1977).

Chomsky, N., 1975a. *The Logical Structure of Linguistic Theory*. Chicago: University of Chicago Press. (Originally appeared in unpublished manuscript form in 1955.)

Chomsky, N., 1975b. *Reflections on Language*. New York: Pantheon.

Chomsky, N., 1976. "Conditions on Rules of Grammar." *Linguistic Analysis* 2, 303–351. Reprinted in Chomsky (1977).

Chomsky, N., 1977. *Essays on Form and Interpretation*. Amsterdam: Elsevier North-Holland.

Chomsky, N., 1980a. *Rules and Representations*. New York: Columbia University Press.

Chomsky, N., 1980b. "On Binding." *Linguistic Inquiry* 11: 1–46.

Chomsky, N., 1981. *Lectures on Government and Binding*. Dordrecht: Foris Publications.

Chomsky, N., 1982a. *Some Concepts and Consequences of the Theory of Government and Binding*. Cambridge, MA: MIT Press.

Chomsky, N., 1982b. *The Generative Enterprise: A Discussion with Riny Huybregts and Henk van Riemsdijk*. Dordrecht: Foris.

Chomsky, N., 1986. *Knowledge of Language*. New York: Praeger.

Chomsky, N., 1993. "Explaining Language Use." *Philosophical Topics* 20: 205–231.

Chomsky, N., 1994a. "Noam Chomsky." In S. Guttenplan (ed.), *A Companion to the Philosophy of Mind*. Oxford: Blackwell, 153–167.

Chomsky, N., 1994b. "Naturalism and Dualism in the Study of Language and Mind." *International Journal of Philosophical Studies* 2: 181–209.

Chomsky, N., 1995a. *The Minimalist Program*. Cambridge, MA: MIT Press.

Chomsky, N., 1995b. "Language and Nature." *Mind* 104: 1–61.

Chomsky, N., 2000a. *New Horizons in the Study of Language and Mind.* Cambridge: Cambridge University Press.

Chomsky, N., 2000b. "Minimalist Inquiries: The Framework." In R. Martin, D. Michaels, and J. Uriagereka (eds.), *Step by Step: Essays in Honor of Howard Lasnik.* Cambridge, MA: MIT Press, 89–155.

Chomsky, N., 2001a. "Derivation by Phase." In M. Kenstowicz (ed.), *Ken Hale: A Life in Language.* Cambridge, MA: MIT Press, 1–52.

Chomsky, N., 2001b. "Beyond Explanatory Adequacy." Manuscript, Dept. of Linguistics and Philosophy, MIT.

Chomsky, N., 2003a. "Reply to Ludlow." In N. Hornstein and L. Antony (eds.), *Chomsky and His Critics.* Oxford: Blackwell, 287–295.

Chomsky, N., 2003b. "Reply to Horwich." In N. Hornstein and L. Anthony (eds.), *Chomsky and His Critics.* Oxford: Blackwell, 295–304.

Chomsky, N., and M. Halle, 1968. *The Sound Pattern of English.* New York: Harper and Row.

Chomsky, N., and H. Lasnik, 1993. "The Theory of Principles and Parameters." In J. Jacobs, A. von Stechow, W. Sternefeld, and T. Vennemann (eds.), *Syntax: An International Handbook of Contemporary Research.* Berlin: Walter de Gruyter. Reprinted as chapter 1 of Chomsky (1995a).

Church, A., 1936. "A Note on the Entscheidungsproblem." *Journal of Symbolic Logic* 1: 40–41, 101–102.

Clark, A., and D. Chalmers, 1998. "The Extended Mind." *Analysis* 58: 7–19.

Collins, C., 2002. "Eliminating Labels." In Epstein and Seeley (2002), 42–61.

Collins, H., 1981. "'Son of seven sexes', The Social Destruction of a Physical Phenomenon." *Social Studies of Science* 11: 33–62.

Cooper, R., 1979. "The Interpretation of Pronouns." In F. Heny and H. S. Schnelle (eds.), *Syntax and Semantics 10.* New York: Academic Press, 61–92.

Cooper, R., 1982. "Binding in Wholewheat* Syntax (*unenriched with inaudibilia)." In P. Jacobson and G. Pullum (eds.), *The Nature of Syntactic Representation.* Dordrecht: D. Reidel, 59–77.

Cooper, R., 1983. *Quantification and Syntactic Theory.* Dordrecht: D. Reidel.

Crease, R., and C. Mann, 1986. *The Second Creation: Makers of the Revolution in 20th Century Physics.* New York: Macmillan.

Cudia, D., 1988. "The Information in the Genetic Code." Abstract, *Journal of Symbolic Logic* 53: 1291–1292.

Culbertson, J., and S. Gross, forthcoming. "Are Linguists Better Subjects?" *British Journal of Philosophy of Science.*

Darwin, F., and A. Seward (eds.), 1903. *More Letters of Charles Darwin: A Record of His Work in a Series of Hitherto Unpublished Letters.* London: John Murray.

Davidson, D., 1967. "Truth and Meaning." *Synthese* 17: 304–323. Reprinted in *Inquiries Into Truth & Interpretation.* Oxford: Oxford University Press, 1984.

Davidson, D., 1987. "Knowing One's Own Mind." *Proceedings of the American Philosophical Association* 60: 441–458.

den Dikken, M., R. Larson, and P. Ludlow, 1996. "Intensional Transitive Verbs." *Rivista di Linguistica* 8: 331–348. Abridged version reprinted in P. Ludlow (ed.), *Readings in the Philosophy of Language,* Cambridge, MA: MIT Press, 1997, 1041–1053.

de Villiers, J., 2007. "The Interface of Language and Theory of Mind. " *Lingua* 117: 1858–1878.

Devitt, M., 2006. *Ignorance of Language*. Oxford: Oxford University Press.

Dummett, M., 1973. *Frege: Philosophy of Language*. Cambridge, MA: Harvard University Press.

Egan, F., 1992. "Individualism, Computation, and Perceptual *Content*." *Mind* 101: 443–459.

Emerton, N., 1984. *The Scientific Reinterpretation of Form*. Ithaca: Cornell University Press.

Emonds, J., 1970. *Root and Structure-Preserving Transformations*. Bloomington: University of Indiana Linguistics Club.

Epstein, S., and D. Seely (eds.), 2002. *Derivation and Explanation in the Minimalist Program*. Oxford: Blackwell.

Epstein, S. and D. Seely, 2006. *Derivations in Minimalism*. Cambridge: Cambridge University Press.

Evans, G., 1975. "Identity and Predication." *Journal of Philosophy* 72: 343–363.

Evans, G., 1977. "Pronouns, Quantifiers, and Relative Clauses (I)." *Canadian Journal of Philosophy* 7: 467–536.

Evans, G., 1981. "Semantic Theory and Tacit Knowledge." In S. Holtzman and C. Leich (eds.), *Wittgenstein: To Follow a Rule*. London: Routledge and Kegan Paul.

Evans, G., 1982. *The Varieties of Reference*. Oxford: Oxford University Press.

Eves, H., and C. Newsom, 1965. *An Introduction to the Foundations and Fundamental Concepts of Mathematics*. New York: Holt, Rinehart, and Winston.

Fiengo, R., 1977. "On Trace Theory." *Linguistic Inquiry* 8: 35–61.

Fodor, J., 1970. "Three Reasons for Not Deriving 'Kill' from 'Cause to Die'." *Linguistic Inquiry* 1: 429–438.

Fodor, J., 1975. *The Language of Thought*. New York: Crowell.

Fodor, J., 1981. "Introduction: Some Notes on What Linguistics is Talking About." In N. Block (ed.), *Readings in the Philosophy of Psychology*, vol. 2. Cambridge, MA: Harvard University Press.

Fodor, J., 1984. "Observation Reconsidered." *Philosophy of Science* 51: 23–42.

Fodor, J. D., and I. Sag, 1982. "Referential and Quantificational Indefinites." *Linguistics and Philosophy* 5: 355–398.

Gallistel, C. R., 1990. "Introduction." In C. R. Gallistel (ed.), *Animal Cognition, Cognition* 37: 1–2.

Gans, C., 1985. "Vertebrate Morphology: Tale of a Phoenix." *American Zoology* 25: 689–694.

Gazdar, G., E. Klein, G. Pullum, and I. Sag, 1985. *Generalized Phrase Structure Grammar*. Cambridge, MA: Harvard University Press.

Geach, P., 1958. "Imperative and Deontic Logic." *Analysis* 18: 49–56.

Geach, P., 1960. "Ascriptivism." *Philosophical Review* 69: 221–225.

Geach, P., 1965. "Assertion." *Philosophical Review* 74: 449–465.

Gear, J., 1981. "Non-polio Causes of Polio-Like Paralytic Syndromes." *Review of Infectious Diseases* 6: 5379–5384.

George, A., 1989. "How Not to Become Confused About Linguistics." In A. George (ed.), *Reflections on Chomsky*. Oxford: Blackwell, 90–110.

Gerstein, M. et al., 2007. "What is a Gene, Post-ENCODE? History and Updated Definition." *Genome Research* 17: 669–681.

Gethin, A., 1990. *Antilinguistics: A Critical Assessment of Modern Linguistic Theory and Practice*. Oxford: Intellect.

Gibbard, A., 1990. *Wise Choices, Apt Feelings*. Cambridge, MA: Harvard University Press.

Gibbard, A., 2003. *Thinking How to Live*. Cambridge, MA: Harvard University Press.

Gooding, D. 1990. *Experiment and the Making of Meaning*. Dordrecht: Kluwer Academic.

Goodman, N., 1955. *Fact, Fiction, & Forecast*. Cambridge, MA: Harvard University Press.

Goodman, N., 1972. *Problems and Projects*. Indianapolis: Bobbs-Merrill.

Gould, S. J., and R. Lewontin, 1979. "The Spandrels of San Marco and the Panglossian Program: A Critique of the Adaptionist Programme." *Proceedings of the Royal Society of London* 205: 281–288.

Grandy, R., 1981. "Some Thoughts on Data and Theory in Linguistics." In P. Asquith and R. Giere (eds.), *PSA 1980: Proceedings of the 1980 Biennial Meeting of the Philosophy of Science Association. Volume 2: Symposia*. East Lansing: Philosophy of Science Association.

Graves, C., J. Katz, Y. Nishiyama, S. Soames, R. Stecker, and P. Tovey, 1973. "Tacit Knowledge." *Journal of Philosophy* 70: 318–330.

Haegeman, L., and J. Guéron, 1999. *English Grammar: A Generative Perspective*. Oxford: Blackwell.

Häik, I., 1984. "Indirect Binding." *Linguistic Inquiry* 15: 185–224.

Halle, M., 1961. "On the Role of Simplicity in Linguistic Description." *Proceedings of Symposia in Applied Mathematics* 12: 89–94.

Hanson, N. R., 1958. *Patterns of Discovery*. Cambridge: Cambridge University Press.

Harman, G. (ed.), 1974. *On Noam Chomsky: Critical Essays*. New York: Doubleday Anchor.

Harris, R., 1993. *The Linguistics Wars*. Oxford: Oxford University Press.

Hatt, R. T., 1932. "Vertebral Columns of Ricochetal Rodents." *Bulletin of the American Museum of Natural History* 63: 599–738.

Hauser, M. D., N. Chomsky, and W. T. Fitch, 2002. "The Faculty of Language: What Is It, Who Has It, and How Did It Evolve?" *Science* 298: 1569–1579.

Heim, I., 1990. "E-Type Pronouns and Donkey Anaphora." *Linguistics and Philosophy* 13: 137–178.

Heim, I., and A. Kratzer, 1998. *Semantics in Generative Grammar*. Oxford: Blackwell.

Heisenberg, W., 1925. "Letter to Wolfgang Pauli, Nov. 16, 1925." In A. Hermann, K. V. Meyenn, and V. F. Weisskopf (eds.), *Wolfgang Pauli, Wissenschaftlicher, Briefwechsel mit Bohr, Einstein, Heisenberg, u.a.*, 1979 (vol. 1), 1985 (vol. 2). New York: Springer-Verlag.

Heisenberg, W., 1968. "Theory, Criticism, and Philosophy," in *From a Life of Physics: Evening Lectures at the International Centre for Theoretical Physics*, Trieste, Italy, Supplement to the IAEA Bulletin, Vienna: International Atomic Energy Agency, 31–48.

Hempel, C., 1966. *Philosophy of Natural Science*. Englewood Cliffs: Prentice-Hall.

Higginbotham, J., 1980. "Pronouns and Bound Variables." *Linguistic Inquiry* 11: 679–708.

Higginbotham, J., 1983. "Is Grammar Psychological?" In L. Cauman, I. Levi, C. Parsons, and R. Schwartz (eds.), *How Many Questions: Essays in Honor of Sydney Morgenbesser*. Indianapolis: Hackett.

Higginbotham, J., 1985. "On Semantics." *Linguistic Inquiry* 16: 547–594.

Higginbotham, J., 1990. "Contexts, Models, and Meanings: A Note on the Data of Semantics." In R. Kempson (ed.), *Mental Representations: The Interface Between Language and Reality*. Cambridge: Cambridge University Press.

Hill, A. (ed.), 1958. *Proceedings of the Third Texas Conference on Problems of Linguistic Analysis in English*. Austin: University of Texas Press.

Hill, A., 1961. "Grammaticality." *Word* 17: 1–10.

Hornsby, J., 1977. "Singular Terms in Contexts of Propositional Attitude." *Mind* 86: 31–48.

Hornstein, N., 1984. *Logic as Grammar*. Cambridge, MA: MIT Press.

Hornstein, N., 1995. *Logical Form: From GB to Minimalism*. Oxford: Blackwell.

Hornstein, N., and J. Uriagereka, 2002. "Reprojections." In Epstein and Seely (2002), 106–128.

Horwich, P., 1998. *Meaning*. Oxford: Oxford University Press.

Horwich, P., 2003. "Meaning and its Place in the Language Faculty." In N. Hornstein and L. Anthony (eds.), *Chomsky and His Critics*. Oxford: Blackwell, 162–178.

Horwich, P., 2005. *Reflections on Meaning*. Oxford: Oxford University Press.

Householder, F., 1965. "On Some Recent Claims in Phonological Theory." *Journal of Linguistics* 1: 13–34.

Huang, J., 1982. "Logical Relations in Chinese and the Theory of Grammar." Ph.D. dissertation, MIT, Dept. of Linguistics.

Huxley, J., 1926. *Birds and the Territorial System*. London: Chatto & Windus.

Hyams, N., 1986. *Language Acquisition and the Theory of Parameters*. Dordrecht: D. Reidel.

Jackendoff, R., 1972. *Semantic Interpretation in Generative Grammar*. Cambridge, MA: MIT Press.

Jackendoff, R., 1977. *X-Bar Syntax*. Cambridge, MA: MIT Press.

Jackendoff, R., 1983. *Semantics and Cognition*. Cambridge, MA: MIT Press.

Jacobson, P., 1999. "Towards a Variable-Free Semantics." *Linguistics and Philosophy* 22: 117–184.

Jeng, M., 2006. "A Selected History of Expectation Bias in Physics." *American Journal of Physics* 74: 578–583.

Johnson, M., 1991. "Deductive Parsing: The Use of Knowledge of Language." In B. Berwick, S. Abney, and C. Tenny (eds.), *Principle Based Parsing: Computation and Psycholinguistics*. Dordrecht: Kluwer, 39–64.

Kamp, H., and U. Reyle, 1993. *From Discourse to Logic*. Dordrecht: Kluwer Academic.

Kaplan, D., 2001. "The Meaning of Ouch and Oops (Explorations in the Theory of *Meaning as Use*)." Draft #3, ms., UCLA.

Kaplan, R., and J. Bresnan, 1982. "Lexical-Functional Grammar: A Formal System for Grammatical Representation." In Bresnan (ed.), *The Mental Representation of Grammatical Relations*. Cambridge, MA: MIT Press, 173–281.

Kapranov P., J. Drenkow, J. Cheng, J. Long, G. Helt, S. Dike, and T. Gingeras, 2005. "Examples of the Complex Architecture of the Human Transcriptome Revealed by RACE and High-Density Tiling Arrays." *Genome Research* 15 (7): 987–997.

Katz, J., 1981. *Language and Other Abstract Objects*. Totowa, NJ: Rowman and Littlefield.

Katz, J. (ed.), 1985. *The Philosophy of Linguistics*. Oxford: Oxford University Press.

Katz, J., and J. Fodor, 1963. "The Structure of a Semantic Theory," *Language* 39: 170–210.

Katz, J., and P. Postal, 1964. *An Integrated Theory of Linguistic Description*. Cambridge, MA: MIT Press.

Kayne, R., 2002. "Pronouns and Their Antedents." In Epstein and Seely (2002), 133–158.

Kitcher, P., 1981. "Mathematical Rigor—Who Needs It?" *Nous* 15: 469–494.

Korsgaard, C., 1996. *The Sources of Normativity*. Cambridge: Cambridge University Press.

Krazter, A., and I. Heim, 1998. *Semantics in Generative Grammar*. Oxford: Blackwell.

Kripke, S., 1980. *Naming and Necessity*. Cambridge, MA: Harvard University Press.

Kripke, S., 1982. *Wittgenstein on Rules and Private Language*. Cambridge, MA: Harvard University Press.

Kuhn, T., 1970. *The Structure of Scientific Revolutions*, 2nd ed. Chicago: University of Chicago Press.

Kyburg, H., 1964. "Recent Work in Inductive Logic." *American Philosophical Quarterly* 1: 249–287.

Lakoff, G., 1973. "Fuzzy Grammar and the Performance/Competence Terminology Game." *Papers from the 9th Regional Meeting of the Chicago Linguistics Society*. University of Chicago, 271–291.

Lakoff, G., and J. Ross, 1976. "Is Deep Structure Necessary?" In J. McCawley (ed.), *Syntax and Semantics*, vol. 7. New York: Academic Press, 159–164.

Lakoff, R., 1968. *Abstract Syntax and Latin Complementation*. Cambridge, MA: MIT Press.

Larson, M., R. Doran, Y. McNabb, R. Baker, M. Berends, A. Djalali, and G. Ward, 2008. "Distinguishing the SAID from the IMPLICATED Using a Novel Experimental Paradigm." Manuscript, University of Chicago and Northwestern University.

Larson, R., 1985. "Quantifying into NP." Manuscript, Available online at http://semlab5.sbs.sunysb.edu/~rlarson/qnp.pdf.

Larson, R., 1987. "'Missing Prepositions' and the Analysis of English Free Relative Clauses." *Linguistic Inquiry* 16: 239–266.

Larson, R., M. den Dikken, and P. Ludlow, 1997. "Intensional Transitive Verbs and Abstract Clausal Complementation." Manuscript, SUNY Stony Brook, and Frei Universiteit Amsterdam. Available online at http://semlab5.sbs.sunysb.edu/~rlarson/itv.pdf.

Larson, R., and G. Segal, 1995. *Knowledge of Meaning: Semantic Value and Logical Form*. Cambridge, MA: MIT Press.

Lévi-Strauss, C., 1953. "Remarks." In S. Tax et al. (eds.), *An Appraisal of Anthropology Today*. Chicago: University of Chicago Press, 349–352.

Lewis, D., 1972. "General Semantics." In D. Davidson and G. Harman (eds.), *Semantics of Natural Language*. Dordrecht: D. Reidel, 169–218.

Lieber, R., 1980. "On the Organization of the Lexicon." Ph.D. dissertation, Dept. of Linguistics, MIT.

Lightfoot, D., 1993. *How to Set Parameters*. Cambridge, MA: MIT Press.

Lindsay, R. B., 1937. "The Meaning of Simplicity in Physics." *Philosophy of Science* 4: 151–167.

Loporcaro, M., 1989. "History and Geography of Raddoppiamento Sintattico: Remarks on the Evolution of a Phonological Rule." In P. M. Bertinetto and M. Loporcaro (eds.), *Certamen Phonologicum: Papers from the 1987 Cortona Phonology Meeting*. Turin: Rosenberg and Sellier, 341–387.

Ludlow, P., 1982. "Substitutional Quantification and the Problem of Expression Types." *Logique et Analyse* 100: 415–424.

Ludlow, P., 1985. "The Syntax and Semantics of Referential Attitude Reports." Ph.D. dissertation, Philosophy, Columbia University.

Ludlow, P., 1992. "Formal Rigor and Linguistic Theory." *Natural Language and Linguistic Theory* 10: 335–344.

Ludlow, P., 1994. "Conditionals, Events, and Unbound Pronouns." *Lingua e Stile* 19: 3–20.

Ludlow, P, 1995. "The Logical Form of Determiners." *Journal of Philosophical Logic* 24: 47–69.

Ludlow, P., 1999. *Semantics, Tense, and Time: an Essay in the Metaphysics of Natural Language*. Cambridge, MA: MIT Press.

Ludlow, P., 2002a. "Externalism, Logical Form, and Linguistic Intentions." In A. Barber (ed.), *The Epistemology of Language*. Oxford: Oxford University Press, 132–168.

Ludlow, P., 2002b. "LF and Natural Logic." In G. Preyer (ed.), *Logical Form, Language and Ontology: On Contemporary Developments in the Philosophy of Language and Linguistics*. Oxford: Oxford University Press.

Ludlow, P., 2003. "Referential Semantics for I-Languages?" In N. Hornstein and L. Antony (eds.), *Chomsky and His Critics*. Oxford: Blackwell, 140–161.

Ludlow, P., and N. Martin (eds.), 1998. *Externalism and Self-Knowledge*. Stanford: CSLI Publications. Distributed by Cambridge University Press.

Ludlow, P., and S. Neale, 1991. "Indefinite Descriptions: In Defense of Russell." *Linguistics and Philosophy* 14: 171–202.

Lycan, W., forthcoming. "Epistemology and the Role of Intuitions." In S. Bernecker (ed.), *Routledge Companion to Epistemology*. London: Routledge.

Mach, E., 1960. *The Science of Mechanics*, 6th ed. Chicago: Open Court.

Maclay, H., and M. Sleator, 1960. "Responses to Language: Judgments of Grammaticalness." *International Journal of American Linguistics* 26: 275–282.

McCawley, J., 1968. "The Role of Semantics in Grammar." In E. Bach and R. Harms (eds.), *Universals in Linguistic Theory*. New York: Holt, Rinehart, and Winston, 125–170.

McCawley, J. 1985. "Review of *Linguistic Theory in America* (New York: Academic Press, 1980), by Frederick J. Newmeyer." *Linguistics* 18: 911–930.

McLaughlin, B., and M. Tye, 1999. "Externalism, Twin-Earth, and Self-Knowledge." In C. Macdonald, B. Smith, and C. Wright (eds.), *Knowing Our Minds: Essays on Self-Knowledge*. Oxford: Oxford University Press.

Manning, C., and H. Schütze, 1999. *Foundations of Statistical Natural Language Processing*. Cambridge, MA: MIT Press.

Marcus, M., 1986. *A Theory of Syntactic Recognition for Natural Language*. Cambridge, MA: MIT Press.

May, R., 1977. "The Grammar of Quantification." Ph.D. dissertation, Department of Linguistics, MIT.

May, R., 1985. *Logical Form: Its Structure and Derivation*. Cambridge, MA: MIT Press.

Mayr, E., 1993. *One Long Argument: Charles Darwin and the Evolution of Modern Evolutionary Thought*. Cambridge, MA: Harvard University Press.

Montague, R., 1970. "English as a Formal Language." in Montague (1974), 188–221.

Montague, R.,1974. *Formal Philosophy*, Richmond Thomason, ed. New Haven: Yale University Press.

Morgan, J., 1969. "On the Treatment of Presupposition in Transformational Linguistics." *Papers from the 5th Regional Meeting of the Chicago Linguistics Society*. University of Chicago, 167–177.

Neale, S., 1990. *Descriptions*. Cambridge, MA: MIT Press.

Neale, S., 1993. "Term Limits." *Philosophical Perspectives 7: Logic and Language*. Atascadero: Ridgeview Publishing, 89–123.

Newmeyer, F., 1986. *Linguistic Theory in America*, 2nd ed. San Diego: Academic Press.

Newton, I., 1964. *The Mathematical Works of Isaac Newton*, D. Whitesid (ed.), vol.1. New York: Johnson Reprint.

Nozick, R., 1983. "Simplicity as Fall-Out." In L. Cauman, I. Levi, and C. Parsons (eds.), *How Many Questions: Essays in Honor of Sydney Morgenbesser*. Indianapolis: Hackett, 105–119.

Parret, H., 1974. *Discussing Language: Interviews with [Various Linguists]*. The Hague: Mouton.

Parsons, C., 1983. *Mathematics in Philosophy: Selected Essays*. Ithaca: Cornell University Press, 142–172.

Parsons, T., 1978. "Pronouns as Paraphrases." Manuscript, University of Massachusettes at Amherst.

Parsons, T., 1980. *Nonexistent Objects*. New Haven: Yale University Press.

Peirce, C. S., 1931–1958. *Collected Papers of Charles Sanders Peirce*, C. Hartshorne, P. Weiss, and A. Burks (eds.), 8 vols. Cambridge, MA: Harvard University Press.

Polanyi, M., 1974. *Personal Knowledge*. Chicago: University of Chicago Press.

Popper, K., 1969. *The Logic of Scientific Discovery*. London: Routledge and Kegan Paul.

Postal, P., 1970. "On Coreferential Complement Subject Deletion." *Linguistic Inquiry* 1: 439–500.

Postal, P., 1971. *Cross-Over Phenomena*. New York: Holt, Rinehart, and Winston.

Postal, P., 1972. "The Best Theory." In S. Peters (ed.), *Goals of Linguistic Theory*. Englewood Cliffs: Prentice-Hall, 131–179.

Postal, P., 1976. "Linguistic Anarchy Notes." In J. McCawley (ed.), *Syntax and Semantics 7: Notes from the Linguistic Underground*. New York: Academic Press.

Prinz, J., 2007. *The Emotional Construction of Morals*. Oxford: Oxford University Press.

Prior, A., 1961. "The Runabout Inference Ticket." *Analysis* 21: 38–39.

Pullum, G., 1989. "Topic . . . Comment: Formal Linguistics Meets the Boojum." *Natural Language and Linguistic Theory* 7: 137–143.

Putnam, H., 1975a. "The Meaning of 'Meaning'." In K. Gunderson (ed.), *Language, Mind and Knowledge*, Minnesota Studies in the Philosophy of Science, 7. Minneapolis: University of Minnesota Press.

Putnam, H., 1975b. "Philosophy and Our Mental Life." In *Mind, Language, and Reality: Philosophical Papers Vol. 2*, Cambridge: Cambridge University Press, 291–303.

Putnam, H., 1988. *Representation and Reality*. Cambridge, MA: MIT Press.

Quetelet, A., 1835. *Sur l'homme et le développement de ses facultés, ou Essai de physique social*. Paris: Bachelier.

Quetelet, A., 1842. *A Treatise on Man and the Development of his Faculties*. Edinburgh: Chambers. (Translation of Quetelet 1835.)

Quine, W. V. O., 1960a. *Word and Object*. Cambridge, MA: MIT Press.

Quine, W. V. O., 1960b. "Variables Explained Away." *Proceedings of the American Philosophical Society* 104: 343–347.

Quine, W. V. O., 1963. "On Simple Theories of a Complex World." *Synthese* 150: 103–106.

Quine, W. V. O., 1970. "Methodological Reflections on Current Linguistic Theory." *Synthese* 21: 386–398.

Quine, W. V. O., 1972. "Meaning and Translation." In Harold Morick (ed.), *Challenges to Empiricism*. New York: Wadsworth, 70–95.

Quine, W. V. O., 1987. "Indeterminacy of Translation Again." *Journal of Philosophy* 84: 5–10.

Quine, W. V. O., and J. Ullian, 1970. *The Web of Belief*. New York: Random House.

Railton, P., 2006. "Normative Guidance." In R. Schaefer-Landau (ed.), *Oxford Studies in Metaethics*, vol. 1. Oxford: Oxford University Press, 3–34.

Reid, C., 1986. *Hilbert–Courant*. New York: Springer-Verlag.

Reinhart, T., 1976. "The Syntactic Domain of Anaphora." Ph.D. dissertation, Department of Linguistics, MIT.

Reinhart, T., 1983. "Coreference and Bound Anaphora: A Restatement of the Anaphora Questions." *Linguistics and Philosophy* 6: 47–88.

Rey, G., 2007. "Externalism and Inexistence in Early Content." In R. Schantz (ed.), *Prospects for Meaning.* New York: de Gruyter.

Rizzi, L., 1982. *Issues in Italian Syntax.* Dordrecht: Foris.

Roberts, I., 1985. "The Representation of Implicit and Dethematized Subjects." Ph.D. dissertation, Department of Linguistics, USC.

Roeper, T., 2005. *The Prism of Language: How Child Language Illuminates Humanism.* Cambridge, MA: MIT Press.

Roeper, T., and W. Snyder, 2005. "Language Learnability and the Forms of Recursion." In A.-M. Di Sciullo (ed.), *UG and External Systems: Language, Brain, and Computation.* Amsterdam: John Benjamins.

Rogers, E., 1960. *Physics for the Inquiring Mind.* Princeton: Princeton University Press.

Rosen, G., 1998. "Blackburn's *Essays in Quasi-Realism.*" *Noûs* 32: 386–405.

Rosenkrantz, R., 1977. *Inference, Method and Decision: Towards a Bayesian Philosophy of Science.* Dordrecht: D. Reidel.

Ross, D., 1939. *Foundations of Ethics.* Oxford: Oxford University Press.

Ross, J., 1967. "Constraints on Variables in Syntax." Ph.D. Dissertation, Department of Linguistics, MIT.

Ross, J., 1969. "Auxiliaries as Main Verbs." *Studies in Philosophical Linguistics* 1: 77–102.

Ross, J., 1970. "On Declarative Sentences." In R. Jacobs and P. Rosenbaum (eds.), *Readings in English Transformational Grammar.* Waltham: Ginn, 222–272.

Ross, J., 1974. "Excerpts from 'Constraints on Variables in Syntax'." In G. Harman (ed.), *On Noam Chomsky: Critical Essays.* New York: Doubleday Anchor.

Rouveret, A., and J.-R. Vergnaud, 1980. "Specifying Reference to the Subject: French Causatives and Conditions on Representation." *Linguistic Inquiry* 11: 97–202.

Russell, B., 1905. "On Denoting." *Mind* 14: 479–493.

Russell, B., 1910–1911. "Knowledge by Acquaintance and Knowledge by Description." *Proceedings of the Aristotelean Society* 11: 108–128. Reprinted in Russell (1917).

Russell, B., 1913. "On the Notion of Cause." *Proceedings of the Aristotelean Society* 13: 1–26. Reprinted in Russell (1917).

Russell, B., 1917. *Mysticism and Logic.* London: George Allen and Unwin.

Russell, B., 1919. *Introduction to Mathematical Philosophy.* London: George Allen and Unwin.

Russell, B., 1985. *The Philosophy of Logical Atomism.* Chicago: Open Court.

Sabin A., 1981. "Paralytic Poliomyelitis: Old Dogmas and New Perspectives." *Review of Infectious Diseases* 3: 343–364.

Sadock, J., 1969. "Hypersentences." *Papers in Linguistics* 1: 283–370.

Sadock, J., 1970. "Whimperatives." In J. Sadock and A. Vanek (eds.), *Studies Presented to Robert B. Lees by His Students.* Edmonton: Linguistics Research, 223–238.

Sag, I., 1976. "A Note on Verb Phrase Deletion." *Linguistic Inquiry* 7: 664–671.

Sampson, G., 1975. *The Form of Language.* London: Weidenfeld and Nicolson.

Schiffer, S., 1992b. "Boghossian on Externalism and Inference." *Philosophical Issues* 2: 29–37.

Schroeder, M., 2008. *Being For: Evaluating the Semantic Program of Expressivism.* Oxford: Oxford University Press.

Schütze, C., 1996. *The Empirical Basis of Linguistics: Grammaticality Judgments and Linguistic Methodology.* Chicago: University of Chicago Press.

Searle, J., 1958. "Proper Names." *Mind* 67: 166–173.

Searle, J., 1962. "Meaning and Speech Acts." *Philosophical Review* 71: 423–432.

Searle, J., 1969. *Speech Acts: An Essay in the Philosophy of Language*. Cambridge: Cambridge University Press.

Searle, J., 1980. "Minds, Brains, and Programs." *Behavioral and Brain Sciences* 3: 417–457.

Searle, J., 1990. "Is the Brain a Digital Computer?" *Proceedings and Addresses of the American Philosophical Association* 64: 21–37.

Sellars, W., 1949. "Acquaintance and Description Again." *Journal of Philosophy* 46: 496–504.

Sennert, Daniel, 1650. *Tractatus de consensu et dissensu Galenicorum et Peripateticorum cum Chymicis, Opera omnia*, vol. 3. Lyons.

Shieber, S., 1985. "Evidence Against the Context-Freeness of Natural Language." *Linguistics and Philosophy* 8: 333–344.

Smart, J. J. C., 1951. "Theory Construction." *Philosophy and Phenomenology Research* 11, 457–473.

Smith, N., 2000. "Foreword." In Chomsky (2000a).

Soames, S., 1998a. "Skepticism about Meaning: Indeterminacy, Normativity, and the Rule-Following Paradox." In A. Kazmi (ed.), *Meaning and Reference*, Canadian Journal of Philosophy, Supplementary Volume 23. Calgary: University of Calgary Press, 211–250.

Soames, S., 1998b. "The Modal Argument: Wide Scope and Rigidified Descriptions." *Nous* 32: 1–22.

Sober, E., 1975. *Simplicity*. Oxford: Oxford University Press.

Spencer, N. J., 1973. "Differences between Linguists and Nonlinguists in Intuitions of Grammaticality-Acceptability." *Journal of Psycholinguistic Research* 2: 83–98.

Spilianakis C., M. Lalioti, T. Town, G. Lee, and R. Flavel, 2005. "Interchromosomal Associations between Alternatively Expressed Loci." *Nature* 435 (7042): 637–645.

Stabler, E., 1992. *The Logical Approach to Syntax: Foundations, Specifications, and Implementations of Theories of Government and Binding*. Cambridge, MA: MIT Press.

Stanley, J., 2001. "Hermeneutic Fictionalism." In H. Wettstein and P. French (eds.), *Midwest Studies in Philosophy 25: Figurative Language*. Oxford: Blackwell, 36–71.

Stanley, J., and C. Kennedy, forthcoming. "On 'Average'." *Mind*.

Stevenson, C., 1944. *Ethics and Language*. New Haven: Yale University Press.

Stich., S., 1971. "What Every Speaker Knows." *Philosophical Review* 80: 476–496.

Stich, S., 1972. "Grammar, Psychology, and Indeterminacy." *Journal of Philosophy* 69: 799–818.

Stigler, S., 1986. *The History of Statistics: The Measurement of Uncertainty before 1900*. Cambridge, MA: Harvard University Press.

Stoll, R., 1961. *Sets, Logic, and Axiomatic Theories*. San Francisco: W. H. Freeman.

Szabó, Z., 1999. "Expressions and Their Representations." *Philosophical Quarterly* 49: 145–163.

Thomke, S., 2001. "The Impact of Technology on Knowledge Creation: A Study of Experimentation in Integrated Circuit Design." In I. Nonaka and T. Nishiguchi (eds.), *Knowledge Emergence: Social, Technical, and Evolutionary Dimensions of Knowledge Creation*. Oxford: Oxford University Press, 76–92.

Thompson, D., 1966. *On Growth and Form*, Abridged Edition. Cambridge: Cambridge University Press.

Tichner, E. B., 1912. "Prolegomena to a Theory of Introspection." *American Journal of Psychology* 23: 427–448.

Unwin, N., 1999. "*Quasi*-Realism, Negation and the Frege–Geach Problem." *Philosophical Quarterly* 49: 337–352.

Unwin, N., 2001. "Norms and Negation: A Problem for Gibbard's Logic." *Philosophical Quarterly* 51: 60–75.

Van Deemter, K., and S. Peters (eds.), 1996. *Semantic Ambiguity and Underspecification*. Stanford: CSLI Lecture Notes.

van Fraassen, B., 1970. *An Introduction to the Philosophy of Time and Space*. New York: Random House.

van Fraasen, B., 1980. *The Scientific Image*. Oxford: Oxford University Press.

Venter, C., 2008. "Bigger, Faster, Better." In *Seedmagazine.com*, posted Nov. 20, 2008. http://seedmagazine.com/stateofscience/sos_feature_venter_p2.html.

Venter, C., et al., 2004. "Environmental Genome Shotgun Sequencing of the Sargasso Sea." *Science* 304 (5667): 66–74.

Wasow, T., 1972. "Anaphoric Relations in English." Ph.D. Dissertation, Department of Linguistics, MIT.

Watson, J. L., 1913. "Psychology as the Behaviorist Views It." *Psychological Review* 20: 158–177.

Webster, D., and M. Webster, 1971. "Adaptive Value of Hearing and Vision in Kangaroo Rat Predator Avoidance." *Brain, Behavior and Evolution* 4: 310–322.

Webster, D., and M. Webster, 1988. "Hypotheses Derived from Morphological Data: When and How They Are Useful." *American Zoologist* 28: 231–236.

Wexler, K., and P. Culicover, 1980. *Formal Principles of Language Acquisition*. Cambridge, MA: MIT Press.

Whitehead, W. N., 1955. *The Concept of Nature*. Cambridge: Cambridge University Press.

Williams, E., 1981. "On the Notions 'Lexically Related' and 'Head of a Word'." *Linguistic Enquiry* 12: 245–274.

Williams, E., 1986. "A Reassignment of the Function of LF." *Linguistic Inquiry* 17: 265–299.

Williamson, T., 2004. "Philosophical 'Intuitions' and Scepticism about Judgement." *Dialectica* 58: 109–153.

Wilson, R., 1994. "Wide Computationalism." *Mind* 103: 351–372.

Wittgenstein, L., 1956. *Remarks on the Foundations of Mathematics*. Trans. G. E. M. Anscombe. Cambridge, MA: MIT Press.

Wittgenstein, L., 1958. *Philosophical Investigations*. Trans. G. E. M. Anscombe. New York: Macmillan.

Woodger, J., 1937. *The Axiomatic Method in Biology*. Cambridge: Cambridge University Press.

Woodger, J., 1939. *The Technique of Theory Construction*, International Encyclopedia of Unified Science, vol. 2, no. 5. Chicago: University of Chicago Press.

Wright, C., 2001. *Rails to Infinity: Essays on Themes from Wittgenstein's Philosophical Investivations*. Cambridge, MA: Harvard University Press.

Zalta, E., 1983. *Abstract Objects: An Introduction to Axiomatic Metaphysics*. Dordrecht: D. Reidel.

Zalta, E., 1988. *Intensional Logic and the Metaphysics of Intensionality*. Cambridge, MA: MIT Press.

Zwart, J.-W., 2002. "Issues Relating to a Derivational Theory of Binding." In Epstein and Seely (2002), 269–294.

Index of Names

Index of Terms